Instructor's Manual
Volume I

to accompany

Strategic Management
Concepts and Cases

Thirteenth Edition

Arthur A. Thompson, Jr.
University of Alabama

A. J. Strickland III
University of Alabama

 **McGraw-Hill Irwin**

Boston   Burr Ridge, IL   Dubuque, IA   Madison, WI   New York   San Francisco   St. Louis
Bangkok   Bogotá   Caracas   Kuala Lumpur   Lisbon   London   Madrid   Mexico City
Milan   Montreal   New Delhi   Santiago   Seoul   Singapore   Sydney   Taipei   Toronto

McGraw-Hill Higher Education

A Division of The **McGraw-Hill** *Companies*

Instructor's Manual Volume I to accompany
STRATEGIC MANAGEMENT: CONCEPTS AND CASES
Arthur A. Thompson, Jr. and A. J. Strickland III

1 2 3 4 5 6 7 8 9 0 BKM/BKM 0 9 8 7 6 5 4 3 2

ISBN 0-07-249857-9

www.mhhe.com

TABLE OF CONTENTS

Section 1   Ideas for Using the Thirteenth Edition 1

Section 2   Test Bank.. 57

Chapter 1   The Strategic Management Process: An Overview....................................... 59

Chapter 2   Establishing Company Direction: Developing a Strategic Vision,
Setting Objectives, and Crafting a Strategy 78

Chapter 3   Industry and Competitive Analysis 101

Chapter 4   Evaluating Company Resources and Competitive Capabilities 131

Chapter 5   Strategy and Competitive Advantage 154

Chapter 6   Strategies for Competing in Globalizing Markets....................................... 184

Chapter 7   New Business Models and Strategies for the Internet Economy................ 207

Chapter 8   Tailoring Strategy to Fit Specific Industry and Company Situations......... 222

Chapter 9   Strategy and Competitive Advantage in Diversified Companies............... 237

Chapter 10   Evaluating the Strategies of Diversified Companies.................................... 258

Chapter 11   Building Resource Strengths and Organizational Capabilities................... 276

Chapter 12   Managing the Internal Organization to Promote Better
Strategy Execution 295

Chapter 13   Corporate Culture and Leadership—Keys to Effective
Strategy Execution 309

section | two 2

Test Bank

Chapter 1: The Strategic Management Process: An Overview

Multiple Choice Questions

Strategy, Business Models, and the Signs of Good Management

1. A company's strategy concerns
   A) its market focus.
   B) how it plans to make money.
   C) the game plan management is using to stake out a market position, conduct operations, attract and please customers, compete successfully, and achieve organizational objectives.
   D) the long-term direction that management has chosen to pursue.
   E) whether it is employing an aggressive offense to gain market share or a conservative defense to protect its market position.

   Answer: C   Difficulty: Medium

2. The game plan a company's management is using to stake out a market position, conduct operations, attract and please customers, compete successfully, and achieve organizational objectives is referred to as its
   A) strategy.
   B) business model.
   C) strategic vision.
   D) long-term business mission.
   E) strategic objective.

   Answer: A   Difficulty: Easy

3. A company's business model
   A) concerns the game plan a company's management is using to stake out a market position, conduct operations, attract and please customers, compete successfully, and achieve organizational objectives.
   B) deals with the revenue-cost-profit economics of its strategy—management's plan for making money in a particular line of business.
   C) concerns what combination of competitive moves it plans to make to outmaneuver its rivals.
   D) deals with how it can simultaneously maximize profits and operate in a socially responsible manner that keeps its prices as low as possible.
   E) concerns how to balance strategic objectives against financial objectives.

   Answer: B   Difficulty: Easy

4. A company's business model
   A) concerns whether management's strategy will permit the achievement of the company's strategic objectives.
   B) deals with the whether there is a close fit between the company's business mission and strategy.
   C) deals with whether the revenues and costs flowing from the company's strategy demonstrate that the business is viable from the standpoint of generating acceptable profits.
   D) concerns how a company plans to achieve high gross profit margins.
   E) concerns how to achieve the strategic vision in the shortest period of time.

   Answer: C   Difficulty: Medium

5. Management's plan for making money in a particular line of business and the revenue-cost-profit economics of the company's strategy is
   A) called a company's strategy.
   B) referred to as a company's primary strategic objective.
   C) referred to as a company's primary financial objective.
   D) a company's foremost business mission and business priority.
   E) referred to as a company's business model.

   Answer: E   Difficulty: Easy

6. The difference between a company's strategy and a company's business model is that
   A) a company's strategy is the plan for achieving strategic objectives while its business model is the plan for achieving financial objectives.
   B) the strategy concerns how to compete successfully and the business model concerns how to operate efficiently.
   C) a company's strategy is management's game plan for realizing the strategic vision whereas a company's business model is the game plan for accomplishing the business mission.
   D) strategy relates to a company's competitive moves and business approaches while the term business model relates to whether the revenues and costs flowing from the strategy demonstrate that the business is viable from a profit perspective.
   E) a company's strategy concerns how to please customers while its business model concerns how to satisfy employees and shareholders.

   Answer: D   Difficulty: Hard

7. Crafting, implementing, and executing strategy are top priority management tasks because
   A) without a strategy, managers have no prescription for doing business and no roadmap for building competitive advantage.
   B) there is a compelling need to proactively shape how the company's business will be conducted.
   C) it is management's responsibility to exert strategic leadership and commit the enterprise to going about its business in some particular fashion.
   D) absence of a conscious strategy and competent efforts to implement it are surefire tickets to organizational drift, competitive mediocrity, and lackluster performance.
   E) All of these.

   Answer: E   Difficulty: Medium

8. Good strategy combined with good strategy execution
   A) offers a surefire guarantee for avoiding periods of weak financial performance.
   B) are the two best signs that a company is a true industry leader.
   C) are more important management functions than forming a strategic vision and setting objectives.
   D) are the most trustworthy signs of good management.
   E) signal that a company has a superior business model.

   Answer: D   Difficulty: Easy

Crafting a Strategy

33. The task of crafting a strategy is principally concerned with
    A) how fast to try to accomplish the company's mission.
    B) determining how the organization can be more results-oriented and cost-efficient.
    C) keeping the organization free of debt and in strong financial shape.
    D) developing actions and business approaches that commit an organization to specific products, markets, competitive approaches, and ways of operating and that are calculated to improve the organization's performance and business position.
    E) how fast to try to increase the company's profits and return on investment.

    Answer: D   Difficulty: Medium

34. A company's actual strategy is
    A) mostly hidden to outside view and is known only to top-level managers.
    B) typically planned well in advance and usually deviates little from the planned set of actions and business approaches because of the risks of making on-the-spot changes.
    C) best delegated to the company's board of directors because of their fiduciary responsibility, their ultimate responsibility for the company's well-being, and their strong business expertise.
    D) partly planned and partly reactive to changing circumstances.
    E) partly a function of the strategic vision, partly a function of the target strategic and financial objectives, partly a function of market opportunities, and partly a function of the strategies being used by rival companies (particularly those that are in the ranks of the industry leaders).

    Answer: D   Difficulty: Medium

35. Crafting strategy is an exercise in entrepreneurship because
    A) industry leadership is predicated on company managers being good "strategic thinkers."
    B) good strategies require managers to be risk-averse and wary of deviating far from tried-and-true business approaches—especially when the future is uncertain.
    C) a company has to steer its business and its strategy in whatever new directions are dictated by changing buyer preferences, the latest actions of rivals, new technologies, the emergence of new market opportunities, and other newly-appearing market conditions.
    D) it is usually essential to seek out new strategic alliances and partnerships when external conditions are changing at a fairly rapid pace.
    E) strategic objectives take precedence over financial objectives.

    Answer: C   Difficulty: Medium

36. Crafting a strategy
    A) needs to be tackled before financial and strategic objectives are established.
    B) is primarily an entrepreneurial activity that calls for risk-taking, keen observation of customer needs and expectations, an eye for spotting good market opportunities, strong awareness of market conditions, and business creativity.
    C) is mainly an exercise that should be dictated by internal considerations, what is comfortable in terms of risk, and what is acceptable in terms of capital requirements.
    D) usually requires more inside-out strategic thinking and analysis than outside-in thinking and analysis.
    E) is mainly an exercise in planning and good strategic analysis.

    Answer: B Difficulty: Medium

37. Managers develop strategies to
    A) proactively shape how an organization conducts its business.
    B) indicate clearly to shareholders and to employees which target objectives are top priority.
    C) have a roadmap to manage to manage by and a framework for weaving the actions initiated by departments, managers, and employees across the company into a coordinated, company-wide game plan.
    D) provide a yardstick for measuring how fast the organization is progressing toward the achievement of long-term objectives.
    E) Both A and C.

    Answer: E Difficulty: Medium

Why Strategy Evolves

38. An organization's strategy evolves over time as a consequence of
    A) the need to keep strategy matched to changing market conditions and changing customer needs and expectations.
    B) efforts to fine-tune and improve one or more pieces of the strategy.
    C) new managerial priorities and changing managerial judgments about what the best future course for the company is.
    D) the need to respond to the actions and competitive moves of rival firms.
    E) All of these.

    Answer: E Difficulty: Easy

39. The "hows" of strategy are always evolving because of
    A) a need to respond to new developments in the external environment.
    B) the proactive efforts of managers to pursue new windows of opportunity.
    C) the budding of fresh ideas about how to make the strategy work better.
    D) a need to respond and react to the new moves of competitors.
    E) All of these.

    Answer: E Difficulty: Easy

40. Which one of the following does <u>not</u> really explain why a company's strategy tends to evolve over time?
    A) The need to prepare for the expected market and competitive conditions that tomorrow will bring.
    B) The appearance of new market opportunities.
    C) The budding of fresh ideas about how to fine-tune and modify the present strategy so as to bolster the organization's long-term competitive position.
    D) The need to cover rising costs by charging a higher price.
    E) The need to respond to technological breakthroughs or to counter the freshly initiated moves and actions of rival firms.

    Answer: D   Difficulty: Easy

Strategy and Strategic Plans

41. A strategic plan consists of
    A) an organization's objectives and its strategy for achieving them.
    B) an organization's vision of where it is headed, near-term and long-term objectives, and strategy.
    C) an organization's strategy and management's specific, detailed plans for implementing it.
    D) the freshly-conceived business moves and approaches managers are planning to institute in the near future.
    E) the actions an organization intends to take in the upcoming months and years to compete successfully.

    Answer: B   Difficulty: Medium

42. Strategic plans
    A) are nearly always written out in detail and circulated among organizational members as a way of communicating where the organization is headed.
    B) are generally developed once a year.
    C) ought to be modified whenever it makes sense for a company to alter its strategic course, its objectives or its strategy and certainly whenever unfolding events dictate.
    D) are being changed less frequently today than at any time in the last three decades.
    E) All of these but D.

    Answer: C   Difficulty: Medium

43. The task of reviewing and revising a company's strategic plan
    A) should be undertaken when profitability targets are reached.
    B) should be initiated as soon as a company achieves both its profit and market share objectives.
    C) is best done after the strategy is fully implemented and enough time has passed to decide if it is working.
    D) is an ongoing exercise that calls for making changes whenever they are needed.
    E) should be undertaken at least once every five years, and annual reviews are highly recommended.

    Answer: D   Difficulty: Medium

Implementing Strategy

44. Putting the chosen strategy into place and trying to make it work
    A) is primarily a task for senior executives; most other managers have very little role in the implementation process.
    B) is much easier and less time-consuming than crafting strategy.
    C) involves more emphasis on objective-setting than does the task of crafting strategy.
    D) primarily involves creating internal policies and procedures that make it easier for the organization to achieve its strategic objectives.
    E) None of these.

    Answer: E   Difficulty: Medium

45. The challenge of implementing and executing the chosen strategy in competent fashion is
    A) to create a strong "fit" between the way things are done internally and what it will take for the strategy to succeed.
    B) to get employees to set objectives in their areas of responsibility that are consistent with the company's overall financial and strategic objectives.
    C) to complete implementation tasks quickly enough to reap maximum profits.
    D) to periodically validate the strategy with the findings of customer satisfaction surveys.
    E) to do an effective job of administration and of supervising day-to-day operations.

    Answer: A   Difficulty: Medium

46. Which of the following is not among the principal managerial tasks associated with implementing and executing strategy?
    A) Building an organization capable of carrying out the strategy successfully
    B) Creating a company culture and work environment that is conducive to successful strategy implementation and execution
    C) Surveying employees on how they think organizational effectiveness can be enhanced and how their job satisfaction can be improved
    D) Exerting the internal leadership needed to drive implementation forward and to improve how the strategy is being carried out
    E) Tying the reward structure to the achievement of the targeted results

    Answer: C   Difficulty: Medium

47. The job of implementing and executing strategy involves
    A) deciding what strategic and financial objectives to pursue first.
    B) meeting with all organizational members to explain why the organization needs to change direction and become more cost efficient and more customer-oriented.
    C) choosing what kind of corporate culture to create as a replacement for the existing culture.
    D) managers at all levels, from headquarters on down to each operating department, deciding how they will answer the question, "What has to be done in my area to implement and execute my piece of the overall strategic plan and how can I best get it done?"
    E) All of these.

    Answer: D   Difficulty: Medium

Evaluating Performance, Monitoring New Developments, and Initiating Corrective Adjustments

48. Management is obligated to evaluate the organization's performance and progress in order to
    A) recast its strategic vision for the organization and/or reshape the organization's mission whenever unfolding events and circumstances make it wise to do so.
    B) make whatever adjustments in objectives, strategy, and approaches to strategy execution seem called for in light of unfolding events and circumstances.
    C) provide accurate reports to the company's board of directors and to keep shareholders well informed about changing market conditions and customer expectations.
    D) track whether the company's business model is well matched to customer needs and expectations.
    E) Both A and B.

    Answer: E Difficulty: Easy

Characteristics of the Strategic Management Process

49. Which of the following is not a basic characteristic of the five task process of managing strategy?
    A) The process is continuous and ongoing, not a one-time exercise or a start-stop event.
    B) The five tasks of strategic management are not done in planned, systematic fashion in isolation from everything else that managers do.
    C) Strategy management makes irregular demands on a manager's time, taking up big chunks of time some months and little time in other months.
    D) Each strategic decision tends to be made with a well-developed information base and only after careful strategic analysis and planning.
    E) The most time-consuming part of strategic management involves trying to get the best strategy-supportive performance out of every individual and trying to perfect and refine the strategy and how it is being executed.

    Answer: D Difficulty: Medium

Who Performs the Five Tasks of Strategic Management?

50. Strategy-making is
    A) primarily an individual responsibility rather than a group task.
    B) increasingly more of a group task (that involves, to some degree, all managers) as opposed to being a function of a few high-level executives.
    C) first and foremost the function of a company's strategic planning staff.
    D) first and foremost the function and responsibility of a company's board of directors.
    E) first and foremost the function and responsibility of a company's chief executive officer.

    Answer: B Difficulty: Medium

51. Managerial jobs with strategy-making responsibility
    A) are found only at the vice-president level and above in most companies.
    B) are more common in profit-seeking organizations than in not-for-profit organizations.
    C) are relatively rare because most strategy-making is done by the members of a company's board of directors.
    D) seldom exist within a functional department (e.g., marketing and sales) or in an operating unit (a plant or a district office) because these levels of the organization structure are well below the level where strategic decisions are typically made.
    E) extend throughout the managerial ranks and exist in every part of a company—business units, operating divisions, functional departments, manufacturing plants, and sales districts.

    Answer: E Difficulty: Medium

52. A company's board of directors is usually involved in
    A) crafting the major elements of a company's strategy.
    B) doing the analysis to confirm that major strategic moves under consideration are likely to produce attractive levels of profitability and will benefit shareholders.
    C) ensuring that new strategy proposals can be defended as superior to alternatives.
    D) evaluating the caliber of senior managers' strategy-making and strategy-implementing skills.
    E) Both C and D.

    Answer: E Difficulty: Medium

53. The task of crafting a company's strategy is best done by
    A) the company's board of directors.
    B) the chief executive officer.
    C) the company's strategic planning staff.
    D) the board of directors, the CEO, and the strategic planning staff, all working as a cooperative team.
    E) None of these.

    Answer: E Difficulty: Medium

54. Which one of the following does not accurately characterize the tasks of crafting and implementing strategy?
    A) Aspects of crafting and implementing strategy touch virtually every managerial job in one way or another, at one time or another.
    B) A company's board of directors usually delegates the tasks of crafting and implementing strategy to the CEO and to senior managers.
    C) The tasks of crafting and implementing strategy exist in non-profit organizations as well as in profit-seeking enterprises.
    D) The tasks of crafting and implementing strategy should not be the function of the company's board of directors.
    E) The tasks of crafting and implementing strategy are not the sole province of a company's CEO and other senior executives.

    Answer: B Difficulty: Easy

How Strategies Get Crafted

55. The process by which strategies get crafted
    A) nearly always involves broad participation among many organizational members and strong reliance on the "delegate-it-to-others" approach, such that the CEO has little of his or her own imprint on the overall strategy.
    B) is best carried out with a chief architect approach where the chief executive officer acts as a strategy commander and makes all the big strategic decisions.
    C) is more difficult when the corporate intrapreneuring approach to strategy-making is utilized because of the tendency of aggressive intrapreneurs to be so dogmatic about what is best for the organization as a whole.
    D) becomes much easier if corporate and business strategies are formulated using the collaborative or team approach.
    E) None of these.

    Answer: E   Difficulty: Medium

56. Which of the following represents the best way to manage the process of crafting a company's strategy?
    A) The chief architect approach
    B) The delegation approach
    C) The collaborative or team approach
    D) The corporate intrapreneuring approach
    E) None of these.

    Answer: E   Difficulty: Medium

57. The chief weakness of the delegation approach to crafting strategy is
    A) that the caliber of the strategy depends on how many managers really get involved in putting the strategy together.
    B) the potential lack of adequate top-down direction and strong strategic leadership.
    C) whether lower-level managers will buy in to the strategy and be strongly committed to implementing it.
    D) that too many people will get involved in shaping the strategy and no real consensus will emerge.
    E) that the strategy which emerges tends to be too political, too participatory, and too much of a compromise.

    Answer: B   Difficulty: Hard

58. The primary weakness of the chief architect approach to crafting strategy is that
    A) lower-level managers will not support the strategy.
    B) top-down strategy-making is inferior to bottom-up strategy-making.
    C) the caliber of the strategy depends so heavily on the strategy-making skills of the individual functioning as strategy commander.
    D) the strategy which emerges tends to be narrowly-focused, too autocratic, and too dogmatic.
    E) the strategy which emerges tends to lack entrepreneurial vision, be too heavily focused on internal considerations, and involve too little compromise.

    Answer: C   Difficulty: Medium

The Role of the Board of Directors

59. The role of a company's board of directors in the strategic management process is to
    A) play a heavy role in forming the strategy and directly supervise senior executives in implementing and executing the strategy.
    B) hire the chief executive officer and require the CEO to function as chief strategy architect.
    C) critically appraise and ultimately approve strategic action plans and to evaluate the strategic leadership skills of the CEO and others in line to succeed the incumbent CEO.
    D) work with the CEO, senior executives, and the strategic planning staff to develop a strategic plan for the company and then charge the CEO and senior executives with implementing and executing the strategic plan as rapidly and competently as possible.
    E) None of these.

    Answer: C   Difficulty: Medium

60. The role of a company's board of directors in the strategic management process is to
    A) critique the company's strategic plan, offer suggestions for improvement, and then supervise the efforts of the company's senior executives in implementing and executing the agreed upon strategic plan.
    B) take the lead in formulating the company's strategic plan but then delegate the task of implementing and executing the strategic plan to the company's CEO and other senior executives.
    C) come up with compelling strategy proposals of their own to debate against those put forward by management.
    D) work cooperatively with the CEO, other senior executives, and the company's strategic planning staff to see that all five tasks comprising the strategic management process are done competently.
    E) critically appraise and ultimately approve strategic action plans and to evaluate the caliber of senior executives' strategy-making and strategy-implementing skills.

    Answer: E   Difficulty: Medium

Benefits of Strategic Thinking and Planning

61. First-rate strategic thinking and conscious strategy management has the benefit of
    A) making managers and organizational members more alert to the winds of change, new opportunities, and threatening developments.
    B) creating a more proactive management posture.
    C) helping to unify the numerous strategy-related decisions by managers all across the organization.
    D) providing better guidance to the entire organization on "what it is we are trying to do and to achieve."
    E) All of these.

    Answer: E   Difficulty: Easy

62. Which of the following is not one of the advantages of first-rate strategic thinking and strong top management commitment to the strategic management process?
   A) The guidance provided to all managers in clarifying just "what it is we are trying to do and to achieve"
   B) Making managers more alert to changing external conditions and what needs to be done to respond to new opportunities and threatening developments
   C) Providing managers with a rationale for evaluating competing budget requests and helping them steer resources into strategy-supportive, results-producing areas
   D) Getting most all organizational members to enthusiastically participate in the process of deciding "where we are headed and how will we get there"
   E) Helping to foster a more proactive management posture

Answer: D   Difficulty: Medium

Short Answer Questions

63. What are the five tasks of strategic management and what does each one involve?

   Difficulty: Medium

64. Who is responsible for doing the five tasks of strategic management?

   Difficulty: Easy

65. What is the role of a company's CEO in the strategic management process?

   Difficulty: Easy

66. What is the role of a company's board of directors in the strategic management process?

   Difficulty: Easy

67. Why is it appropriate to argue that good strategy-making and good strategy-implementing are valid signs of good management?

   Difficulty: Medium

68. Why does crafting strategy have a strongly entrepreneurial character?

   Difficulty: Medium

69. What are the kinds of things to look for in identifying the components of an organization's strategy?

Difficulty: Medium

70. An organization's strategic plan consists of the actions which management plans to take in the near future. True or false. Explain and justify your answer.

Difficulty: Medium

71. Why is the task of strategizing an ongoing exercise rather than a one-time exercise?

Difficulty: Medium

72. Define and briefly explain what is meant by each of the following terms:
    a.) business model
    b.) strategic vision
    c.) strategic objective
    d.) strategy
    e.) strategic plan
    f.) strategy implementation
    g.) stretch objectives

Difficulty: Medium

73. Is it more accurate to think of strategy as being "crafted" or "planned?" Why?

Difficulty: Medium

74. Why does it make sense for all managers to be personally involved in the strategy-making and strategy-implementing process?

Difficulty: Medium

75. Explain the difference between a company's business model and a company's strategy.

Difficulty: Easy

76. Why does an organization need both financial and strategic objectives?

Difficulty: Medium

44. Organizations need strategies
    A) to avoid criticism that management does not have an official strategic plan.
    B) to avoid being at a competitive disadvantage.
    C) for the company as a whole, for each business the company is in, and for each functional piece of each business.
    D) to avoid losing money, being without a proven business model, and impairing shareholder wealth.
    E) All of these.

Answer: C Difficulty: Hard

The Levels of Strategy and the Strategy Pyramid

45. In a diversified company, the strategy pyramid consists of
    A) corporate strategy and a group of business strategies (one for each line of business the corporation has diversified into).
    B) corporate strategy, business strategy, managerial strategy, and operating strategy.
    C) business strategies, functional strategies, and operating strategies.
    D) corporate strategy, business strategies, functional strategies, and operating strategies.
    E) diversification strategy, line of business strategies, and operating strategies.

Answer: D Difficulty: Medium

46. In a single-business company, the strategy pyramid consists of
    A) business strategy and functional strategies.
    B) business strategy, functional strategies, and operating strategies.
    C) business strategy and operating strategy.
    D) managerial strategy, business strategy, functional strategies, and operating strategies.
    E) corporate strategy, functional strategies, and operating strategies.

Answer: B Difficulty: Medium

Corporate Strategy

47. Corporate-level strategy for a diversified or multi-business enterprise concerns
    A) how to compete and how to create a competitive advantage in each specific line-of-business the total enterprise is in.
    B) making moves to establish positions in different businesses and initiating actions to boost the combined performance of the group of businesses the company has diversified into.
    C) how best to allocate resources across the functional areas of each line of business the company is in.
    D) what the strategic intent for each business unit should be.
    E) how functional strategies should be aligned with business strategies in each of the various lines of business the company is in.

Answer: B Difficulty: Hard

48. Which of the following is <u>not</u> a characteristic to look for in identifying the corporate strategy of a diversified enterprise?
    A) Actions to divest weak or unattractive business units
    B) Efforts to build competitive advantage by capturing valuable cross-business strategic fits
    C) The attempts of a specific business unit to appeal to particular customer groups and to satisfy particular customer needs
    D) Whether the businesses the company has diversified into are related, unrelated, or a mixture of both
    E) Moves to add new businesses and build positions in attractive industries via merger, acquisition, internal start-up, or alliances

    Answer: C   Difficulty: Medium

49. Corporate strategy
    A) refers to the strategic action plan for a large corporation whereas business strategy refers to the strategic action plan for a small family-owned business.
    B) is the overall managerial game plan for a diversified company.
    C) concerns how a diversified company's various functional strategies will be coordinated and united.
    D) is crafted via a bottom-up approach that represents the consensus of many managers in the organization.
    E) consists of a diversification strategy, a collection of business strategies, and strategies for forming alliances.

    Answer: B   Difficulty: Medium

50. In diversified firms, the task of crafting a corporate strategy
    A) is chiefly an exercise in deciding how to build and manage a portfolio of businesses.
    B) entails the challenge of how to get sustained high performance out of a multi-industry mix of business activities.
    C) involves reviewing and approving the strategy-related proposals/actions of business-level managers.
    D) includes coordinating the strategies and related activities of subsidiary business units.
    E) All of these.

    Answer: E   Difficulty: Medium

51. The "wheel" of factors and considerations that help identify a diversified or multi-business firm's corporate strategy include:
    A) the firm's competitive approach to pricing, product differentiation, and customer service.
    B) whether the firm's product line is broad or narrow in comparison with the product lines of rival firms.
    C) the technological proficiencies and labor skill requirements characterizing each of the firm's businesses.
    D) whether diversification is based narrowly in a few industries or broadly in many industries.
    E) the functional and operating strategies employed in each of the diversified company's businesses.

    Answer: D   Difficulty: Medium

52. The "wheel" of factors and considerations in identifying corporate strategy include
    A) moves being made to deal with changing industry conditions and other emerging developments in the external environment.
    B) the company's approach to allocating investment capital and resources across its business lineup.
    C) moves to divest weak or unattractive businesses.
    D) moves to strengthen positions in existing businesses and to build new positions in attractive new industries.
    E) All of these except A.

    Answer: E   Difficulty: Hard

Business Strategy

53. Business strategy is concerned with
    A) the actions and approaches crafted by management to produce successful performance in one specific line of business.
    B) forming responses to changing industry and competitive conditions, shifting buyer preferences and expectations, and other new developments.
    C) crafting competitive moves and business approaches that can lead to sustainable competitive advantage.
    D) uniting and coordinating functional area strategic initiatives.
    E) All of these.

    Answer: E   Difficulty: Easy

54. What separates a powerful business strategy from a weak one is the strategist's ability to
    A) choose when and how to diversify.
    B) be clever at unifying functional strategies.
    C) forge a series of moves, both internally and in the marketplace, that are capable of producing sustainable competitive advantage.
    D) steer resources into the most attractive business units.
    E) marshall superior financial resources.

    Answer: C   Difficulty: Medium

55. The task of crafting a strategy for a particular business involves:
    A) forming responses to changes underway in the external environment.
    B) initiating moves and approaches to secure a sustainable competitive advantage.
    C) uniting the strategic initiatives of functional departments.
    D) building competitively valuable resources and capabilities.
    E) All of these.

    Answer: E   Difficulty: Easy

56. Business strategy, as distinct from corporate strategy, involves
   A) forging an action plan for successfully competing in a given industry.
   B) deciding what the appropriate mission statements should be for each functional area and operating department.
   C) what kind of strategic fit to have between different functional and operating departments.
   D) the ways to coordinate the competitive approaches of related business units.
   E) All of these.

   Answer: A   Difficulty: Medium

57. One of the facets of crafting a business strategy that yields sustainable competitive advantage is
   A) deciding what product/service attributes the company is best equipped to offer customers.
   B) deciding what basic approaches to take in each key functional area of the business.
   C) developing skills, know-how, resource strengths, and competitive capabilities that rivals don't have and cannot readily match.
   D) identifying all of the business's strategic issues and operating problems.
   E) expanding the company's geographic coverage to as wide a portion of the market arena as possible.

   Answer: C   Difficulty: Hard

58. Which one of the following is not really pertinent to identifying the strategy for a single business?
   A) The firm's key functional strategies and efforts to build competitively valuable resource strengths and competitive capabilities
   B) The scope of geographic coverage
   C) Planned, proactive efforts to outcompete rivals
   D) What top management is doing to tie the firm's diversification efforts to a theme that creates a strong business identity
   E) The moves being made to respond and react to changing industry conditions and other emerging developments in the external environment

   Answer: D   Difficulty: Hard

59. What separates a powerful business strategy from a weak one is
   A) whether it employs more offensive moves than defensive moves.
   B) how well functional strategies are united.
   C) the strategist's success in forging a series of moves and approaches capable of producing sustainable competitive advantage.
   D) the number of distinctive competencies the strategy is based on.
   E) the number of collaborative partnerships and strategic alliances included as part of the strategy.

   Answer: C   Difficulty: Hard

Functional Strategy

60. Functional strategies
    A) add relevant detail to the overall business strategy by setting forth the actions, approaches, and practices to be employed in managing a particular functional activity or business process or key department within a business.
    B) address the specific strategic issues and problems a business confronts.
    C) are normally crafted by the executive in charge of the overall business.
    D) describe the mission and strategic intent of each key functional piece of the business.
    E) are concerned with how to unify the firm's skills, competencies, and resource strengths.

    Answer: A Difficulty: Medium

61. Functional strategies
    A) deal mainly with how to build a distinctive competence in each functional part of the business.
    B) add detail to business strategy and govern how the principal subordinate activities within a business will be managed.
    C) set forth how many and what kind of competitive capabilities the business will develop in pursuing the targeted competitive advantage.
    D) are usually initially forged by teams of functional area experts who then submit their functional strategy recommendations directly to the board of directors for review and approval.
    E) indicate the kind of expertise and resource support which one business function will provide to sister functions.

    Answer: B Difficulty: Medium

62. The chief role of functional strategies is to
    A) integrate the various operating-level strategies across the whole company into a unified whole.
    B) define the mission and strategic intent of each functional area.
    C) help specify the needed kinds of distinctive competencies and resource strengths.
    D) support the overall business strategy.
    E) create strategic fit among the enterprise's different core competencies and resource strengths.

    Answer: D Difficulty: Easy

Operating Strategy

63. Operating strategies concern
    A) the game plans for managing key operating units within a business (plants, sales districts, distribution centers) and for performing strategically significant operating tasks (maintenance, shipping, inventory control, purchasing, advertising) so as to support functional strategies and the overall business strategy.
    B) the specific plans for building core competencies and resource strengths in each major operating unit.
    C) what the firm's operating departments plan to do to actually create the targeted competitive advantage.
    D) the plans managers have for creating strategic fit across all of the various operating departments.
    E) the mission and strategic intent of each operating unit.

    Answer: A Difficulty: Medium

Uniting the Strategy-Making Effort

64. Management's direction-setting, strategy-making effort is not complete until
    A) the separate layers of missions, objectives, and strategies devised by different managers at different organizational levels are tightly linked and unified into a coherent, supporting pattern.
    B) the mission and strategic intent of each functional area and each operating unit are agreed to by the whole management team.
    C) the needed kinds of distinctive competencies and resource strengths are fully developed and integrated.
    D) the corporate strategy, all of the business strategies, all of the functional strategies, and all of the operating strategies exhibit a common strategic intent.
    E) there's strong strategic fit among the enterprise's different skills, competencies, and resource strengths.

    Answer: A   Difficulty: Medium

65. The task of uniting a company's strategy-making effort entails
    A) harmonizing and fitting the missions, objectives, and strategies of all the various organizational units into a coherent supportive pattern.
    B) a collaborative effort among different organizational units to achieve cross-unit coordination.
    C) strong top-down leadership.
    D) broad participation of managers at different organizational levels and in different organizational units.
    E) All of these.

    Answer: E   Difficulty: Easy

Factors that Shape a Company's Strategy

66. Which of the following is not a chief factor affecting the choice of a company's strategy?
    A) Societal, political, regulatory and community citizenship considerations
    B) Competitive conditions and overall industry attractiveness
    C) How many strategic options a company has
    D) Company resource strengths, resource weaknesses, core competencies, and competitive capabilities
    E) The personal ambitions, business philosophies, and ethical principles of key executives

    Answer: C   Difficulty: Medium

67. Factors that typically shape a company's choice of strategy include
    A) competitive conditions and overall industry attractiveness.
    B) company opportunities and threats.
    C) company resource strengths, resource weaknesses, core competencies, and competitive capabilities.
    D) the influence of shared values and company culture.
    E) All of these.

    Answer: E   Difficulty: Easy

68. What an enterprise can and cannot do strategy-wise is always constrained by
    A) what is legal.
    B) what does and does not comply with government policies and regulatory requirements.
    C) what is in accord with societal expectations and the standards of good community citizenship.
    D) pressures from special interest groups, the glare of investigative reporting, and the stigma of negative public opinion.
    E) All of these put boundaries on a company's choice of strategy.

    Answer: E   Difficulty: Easy

69. An organization's resources, competencies, and competitive capabilities are important strategy-making considerations because
    A) it is foolish to pursue a strategic plan that cannot be executed with the resources, competitive assets, and capabilities a company can assemble.
    B) they may provide valuable strengths in pursuing and capitalizing on a particular opportunity.
    C) they may be sufficiently strong to yield a competitive edge in the enterprise's target market.
    D) they may well have potential for being a cornerstone of strategy.
    E) All of these.

    Answer: E   Difficulty: Easy

Strategy and Ethics

70. A company's strategy can be considered "ethical"
    A) as long as all pieces of the strategy are within the bounds of what is legal and conform to all government regulations.
    B) if managers weigh strategic decisions from the viewpoint of what is best for stockholders, employees, and customers.
    C) if the company's products or services meet legitimate customer needs and if the company's profits are not obscenely high.
    D) provided the actions the company takes to implement and execute the strategy can pass both the duty test and the public interest test.
    E) if all the elements of its strategy can pass the test of moral scrutiny.

    Answer: E   Difficulty: Hard

71. A company's strategy can be considered "ethical"
    A) provided all of the strategy elements are legal and conform to all regulatory requirements.
    B) so long as managers weigh strategic decisions from the viewpoint of what is best for shareholders, employees, suppliers, customers, the communities in which it has operations, and society at large.
    C) if the company's actions can pass the duty test, the stakeholder consideration test, the test of being legal, and the public interest test.
    D) if all the elements of its strategy can pass the test of moral scrutiny.
    E) provided it meets both the duty test and the social responsibility test.

    Answer: D   Difficulty: Hard

72. Every business has an ethical duty to its
    A) shareholders and employees.
    B) employees, shareholders, and the communities in which it operates.
    C) suppliers, customers, shareholders, and employees.
    D) shareholders, employees, suppliers, customers, the communities in which it has operations, and society at large—essentially all of its stakeholders or constituencies.
    E) shareholders, employees, customers, and the community at large.

    Answer: D Difficulty: Medium

73. Whether a company's strategy is "ethical"
    A) is secondary to whether the strategy is profitable.
    B) hinges upon whether the elements comprising the strategy are both legal and in the best interests of the company's customers.
    C) hinges upon whether any aspect of the strategy can be considered disadvantageous to the best interests of customers, shareholders, or employees.
    D) depends on whether the strategy is considered by government officials to be in the public interest.
    E) None of the above is appropriate for judging whether a company's strategy is ethical.

    Answer: D Difficulty: Medium

74. If beer brewer decided not to run promotional ads in college newspapers as a matter of corporate policy, it could be said that this move represented an ethically responsible action aimed at the following organizational constituency:
    A) Shareholders
    B) Employees
    C) Suppliers
    D) Customers (especially those of college age)
    E) Beer distributors

    Answer: D Difficulty: Easy

Tests of a Winning Strategy

75. To gauge how good a strategy is, analysts should use
    A) the strategic fit test, the social responsibility test, and the completeness test.
    B) the integrated test, the competitive strength test, and the strategic fit test
    C) the goodness of fit test, the competitive advantage test, and the performance test.
    D) the social responsibility test, the strategic intent test, and the competitive strength test.
    E) the opportunity-threat test, the ethical standards test, and the completeness test.

    Answer: C Difficulty: Medium

76. A winning strategy is one that
    A) builds strategic fit, is socially responsible, and maximizes shareholder wealth.
    B) is highly profitable and boosts the company's market share.
    C) results in a company becoming the dominant industry leader.
    D) fits the company's internal and external situation, builds competitive advantage, and boosts company performance.
    E) can pass the ethical standards test, the strategic intent test, and the profitability test.

    Answer: D   Difficulty: Medium

77. A winning strategy is one that
    A) maximizes shareholder wealth in the shortest period of time.
    B) is ethical, highly profitable, and customer-driven.
    C) fits the company's internal and external situation, builds competitive advantage, and boosts company performance.
    D) achieves the company's objectives.
    E) can builds shareholder value and also can pass the completeness test and the customer satisfaction test.

    Answer: C   Difficulty: Medium

Short Answer Questions

78. What is the difference between a mission statement and a strategic vision?

    Difficulty: Medium

79. What are the risks and pitfalls of defining a company's business in broad terms?

    Difficulty: Medium

80. What managerial purpose does the establishment of long-term objectives have?

    Difficulty: Easy

81. What is the managerial value of a well-conceived, well-said strategic vision?

    Difficulty: Medium

82. What is meant by stretch objectives? How important is it that companies establish stretch objectives?

    Difficulty: Medium

83. What are the qualities of a "well-stated" objective? Give an example of a well-stated objective.

Difficulty: Medium

84. Explain the difference between strategic objectives and financial objectives. Which is more important? Why?

Difficulty: Medium

85. Discuss the meaning and areas of focus for each of the following levels of strategy:
a.) corporate strategy
b.) business strategy
c.) functional area strategy
d.) operating strategy

Difficulty: Hard

86. What is the difference between corporate strategy and business strategy?

Difficulty: Medium

87. How can one identify the corporate strategy of a diversified company?

Difficulty: Medium

88. Discuss what is involved in crafting corporate strategy.

Difficulty: Hard

89. Discuss what is involved in crafting business strategy.

Difficulty: Hard

90. What are the principal elements that help identify what a company's business strategy is?

Difficulty: Hard

91. Explain why a company's strategy is really a collection of strategies.

Difficulty: Hard

92. What is the "strategy pyramid" for a diversified company? How does it differ from the strategy pyramid for a single business company?

    Difficulty: Medium

93. Discuss what is involved in crafting functional strategies.

    Difficulty: Medium

94. Why is sustainable competitive advantage so important to a winning business strategy?

    Difficulty: Medium

95. Discuss how the strategy-making effort is coordinated.

    Difficulty: Medium

96. Identify and briefly discuss the relevance of each of the six broad factors that shape strategy.

    Difficulty: Hard

97. What determines whether a company's strategy is "ethical"?

    Difficulty: Hard

98. What are the criteria for determining whether a company has a winning strategy?

    Difficulty: Medium

99. A company's strategy is really a collection of layered strategies. True or false. Discuss and explain.

    Difficulty: Easy

100. Discuss how business philosophies, values, and ethical considerations enter into strategy-making.

    Difficulty: Medium

101. What is the difference between a strategic objective and a financial objective? Give three examples of each type of objectives to illustrate the difference.

Difficulty: Hard

102. How can one tell an "ethical" strategy from an "unethical" strategy?

Difficulty: Medium

103. How can one tell a winning strategy from a strategy that is mediocre or a loser?

Difficulty: Medium

104. Explain why it is important for a company's strategy to be well-matched to its resource strengths, competencies, and competitive capabilities.

Difficulty: Medium

Chapter 3: Industry and Competitive Analysis

Multiple Choice Questions

A Company's Macro-environment and the Importance of Good Situation Analysis

1. A company's "macro-environment" refers to
    A) the immediate industry and competitive conditions with which it must contend.
    B) the global economic and competitive situation in which the company does business.
    C) all the relevant forces and factors outside a company's boundaries—the economy at large, population demographics, societal values and lifestyles, technological factors, governmental legislation and regulation, and the industry and competitive environment in which it operates.
    D) the nature of the competitive rivalry that exists between a company and its competitors.
    E) the dominant economic and business characteristics of a company's industry.

    Answer: C   Difficulty: Medium

2. The primary purpose of assessing a company's external environment and internal circumstances is to
    A) draw out those features in a company's internal/external environment which are shaping the competitive threats and business risks with which it must contend over the next few years.
    B) help managers be responsive to industry and competitive conditions.
    C) decide how best to undermine the competitive positions of rival firms.
    D) determine whether the company's objectives are sufficiently challenging.
    E) help managers craft a strategy that is well-matched to its situation.

    Answer: E   Difficulty: Hard

3. Which one of the following is not part of a company's macroenvironment?
    A) Conditions in the economy at large
    B) Population demographics and societal values and lifestyles
    C) Technological factors and governmental regulations and legislation
    D) Factors relating to competitive rivalry, a company's suppliers and customers, and competition from substitute products
    E) A company's resource strengths and weaknesses, competencies, and competitive capabilities

    Answer: E   Difficulty: Easy

4. The foremost reason for accurately diagnosing a company's internal and external situation is to
    A) identify the industry's dominant economic characteristics.
    B) evaluate forces in motion in the company's macroenvironment that are likely to alter buyer preferences and expectations.
    C) draw management's attention to those features in a company's internal/external environment that ought to drive managerial choices about the company's long-term direction, objectives, and strategy.
    D) assess the strength of each one of the five competitive forces.
    E) decide whether conditions in the company's macroenvironment will improve or deteriorate over the next few years.

    Answer: C   Difficulty: Medium

Methods of Industry and Competitive Analysis

5. Which of the following is <u>not</u> a major question to ask in thinking strategically about industry and competitive conditions in a given industry?
   A) What factors are driving change in industry and what impact will they have on the industry's competitive structure and business environment?
   B) Which rivals will likely make what competitive moves next?
   C) What are the key factors for competitive success in this industry?
   D) Is the industry attractive and what are the prospects for above-average profitability?
   E) Which companies have the best strategies and the best track records for earnings growth and return on shareholder investment?

   Answer: E   Difficulty: Medium

6. Which one of the following is <u>not</u> one of the analytical steps in industry and competitive analysis?
   A) Pinpointing key success factors
   B) Evaluating the strength of competitive forces
   C) Identifying and assessing driving forces
   D) Deciding what strategy best fits the situation
   E) Trying to predict which rivals will likely make what competitive moves next

   Answer: D   Difficulty: Easy

7. Industry and competitive analysis probes such considerations as
   A) the drivers of change in the industry's competitive structure and business environment.
   B) the dominant economic characteristics of the industry.
   C) the nature and strength of competitive forces.
   D) key factors influencing competitive success.
   E) All of the above.

   Answer: E   Difficulty: Easy

An Industry's Dominant Economic Characteristics

8. Which of the following is <u>not</u> a factor to consider in identifying an industry's dominant economic features?
   A) Market size and growth rate
   B) The extent of backward and forward integration and the types of distribution channels employed
   C) Whether the products or services of rival firms are strongly differentiated, weakly differentiated, or essentially identical
   D) How strong driving forces and competitive forces are
   E) The pace of technological change, scale economies and experience curve effects, and capital requirements

   Answer: D   Difficulty: Easy

9. Which of the following is <u>not</u> a relevant consideration in examining the dominant economic characteristics of an industry?
   A) Market size, market growth rate, and where the industry is in the growth cycle
   B) The extent to which economies of scale, learning curve effects, and experience curve effects are present
   C) How many strategic groups the industry has and which ones are most profitable and least profitable
   D) The number and sizes of buyers, the types of distribution channels used to reach consumers, and capital requirements
   E) The prevalence of backward and forward integration and the pace of technological change

   Answer: C Difficulty: Medium

10. An industry's market growth rate is strategically important because
    A) large, high-profit markets often draw the interest of big corporations looking to acquire companies with long-established positions in major industries.
    B) fast growth typically breeds new entry and growth slow-downs typically spawn increased rivalry and a shake-out of weak competitors.
    C) low-growth, low-profit industries usually have high barriers to entry and minimal scale economies and experience curve effects.
    D) it dictates whether entry barriers will be high and whether forward vertical integration into a variety of distribution channels will be an attractive strategy.
    E) the faster the growth rate, the stronger the experience curve effect and the more likely that a strategy aimed at being the industry's low-cost producer will be the winning strategy.

    Answer: B Difficulty: Hard

11. The strategic importance of rapid product innovation is that
    A) it shortens product life cycles and it increases business risk because of opportunities for companies to leapfrog rivals by introducing newer and better products.
    B) it raises the likelihood that a firm's investment in process technology and production facilities/equipment will be rapidly obsoleted by strong experience curve effects.
    C) it almost guarantees that the industry will be fiercely competitive.
    D) it creates a very high barrier to entry and also makes forward or backward vertical integration very difficult.
    E) it increases the number of distribution channels that a company must use to reach consumers, as well as increasing advertising and R&D costs.

    Answer: A Difficulty: Hard

12. Whether an industry has big economies of scale is strategically important because
    A) scale economies give rise to big learning and experience curve effects and push industry prices and profit margins down.
    B) big scale economies lower entry barriers and make an industry fiercely price competitive.
    C) big scale economies increase the volume and market share needed to be cost competitive.
    D) they often work against rapid product innovation and tend to give fully integrated firms a major cost advantage over partially and nonintegrated firms.
    E) big scale economies make backward vertical integration virtually essential if a firm is to remain cost competitive.

    Answer: C Difficulty: Hard

Experience Curve Effects

13. The stronger the experience curve effect is in an industry
    A) the more that market share is a function of profitability.
    B) the more that a firm's unit costs will go down as its cumulative production volume and production experience go up.
    C) the more likely that experienced producers of a product will have higher degrees of consumer loyalty than will new entrants to the market.
    D) the lower a firm's annual cost increases will be and the bigger the scale economies it can achieve.
    E) the more that older, established firms will have higher profit margins as compared to relative newcomers to the industry.

    Answer: B   Difficulty: Medium

14. The experience curve has to do with the fact that
    A) new entrants into an industry are less able to achieve cost reductions than are companies which have been in the industry for a number of years and which therefore have an experienced work force.
    B) a firm's unit costs decline over time.
    C) as a firm's cumulative volume of production builds up, the resulting knowledge and experience often lead to the discovery of additional ways to improve efficiency and save on unit costs.
    D) the bigger a firm's market share, the lower is its cost of capital.
    E) a company's unit costs are inversely related to the length of time that its senior mangers have worked in the industry and built up their base of experience and know-how.

    Answer: C   Difficulty: Medium

15. A strong experience curve effect in an industry
    A) allows a firm to use its experience to out-innovate rivals and build a competitive advantage based on rapid introduction of new products.
    B) is what causes older, well-established firms to have a cost advantage over industry newcomers.
    C) tends to result in higher prices for the industry's product and reduce competitive pressures in the industry.
    D) allows a firm to realize cost-savings as production experience with a new technology accumulates and as its volume of output grows.
    E) lowers entry barriers and tends to increase competitive pressures in the industry.

    Answer: D   Difficulty: Medium

The Five Competitive Forces

16. The forces of competition in an industry are a function of
    A) the competitive pressures among rival firms that result from their jockeying for better market position and their maneuvers to gain a competitive edge.
    B) the availability of substitute products that are competitively priced.
    C) the threat of potential entry into the marketplace.
    D) the bargaining power of suppliers and customers.
    E) All of these.

    Answer: E   Difficulty: Easy

17. The nature and strength of competition and competitive forces are generally a joint product of
    A) the pressures induced by the strategic moves and countermoves of rival firms.
    B) the threat of entry from new firms.
    C) the price and availability of substitute products.
    D) the bargaining power and economic leverage of customers and suppliers.
    E) All of these.

    Answer: E   Difficulty: Easy

18. Which of the following is not one of the five competitive forces?
    A) The strength of industry driving forces
    B) The bargaining power and economic leverage of suppliers
    C) The threat of potential entry
    D) Competition from substitute products
    E) The bargaining power and economic leverage of customers

    Answer: A   Difficulty: Easy

19. The most powerful of the five competitive forces is usually
    A) the market attempts of companies in other industries to win customers over to their own substitute products.
    B) the rivalry and jockeying for position among competing sellers in an industry.
    C) the benefits that emerge from close collaboration with suppliers and the competitive pressures that such collaboration creates.
    D) the potential entry of new competitors.
    E) the bargaining power and leverage that large customers are able to exercise.

    Answer: B   Difficulty: Easy

20. Typically, the weakest of the five competitive forces in an industry is/are:
    A) the threat posed by potential new entrants.
    B) the bargaining power and leverage that suppliers are able to exercise.
    C) competitive pressures from substitute products.
    D) the pressures that emerge from close collaboration with influential customers.
    E) None of the above is typically weakest.

    Answer: E Difficulty: Medium

21. A competitive environment where there is weak to moderate rivalry among sellers, high entry barriers, weak competition from substitute products, and little bargaining leverage on the part of both suppliers and customers
    A) can be said to lack powerful driving forces.
    B) gives an industry competitor the best potential for building sustainable competitive advantage over rival firms.
    C) seldom is very attractive for earning above-average profits.
    D) is competitively attractive from the standpoint of earning above-average and perhaps even superior profits.
    E) The information provided is insufficient to draw a valid conclusion about any of the above.

    Answer: D Difficulty: Medium

22. A competitive environment where there is weak rivalry among sellers, high entry barriers, weak competition from substitute products, and little bargaining leverage on the part of both suppliers and customers is
    A) competitively unattractive from the standpoint of earning superior profits.
    B) offers little ability to build a sustainable competitive advantage.
    C) competitively attractive for earning above-average profits.
    D) offers only moderate prospects for making a reasonable profit.
    E) The information provided is insufficient to draw a conclusion.

    Answer: C Difficulty: Medium

Rivarly Among Sellers

23. A firm's competitive strategy concerns
    A) management's plan for competing successfully and strengthening the firm's market position.
    B) how to build sustainable competitive advantage.
    C) how to jockey for better market position and try to outmaneuver rivals.
    D) how to defend against competitive pressures.
    E) All of these.

    Answer: E Difficulty: Easy

24. The essence of a firm's competitive strategy is
    A) how to defend against each driving force.
    B) whether to go on the offensive or, instead, to craft a defensive strategy.
    C) how to respond to changing industry conditions.
    D) how best to gain a competitive edge over rivals and to build defenses against the five competitive forces.
    E) which strategic group to attack first.

    Answer: D Difficulty: Medium

25. Factors that cause the rivalry among competing sellers to be less intense include
    A) low buyer switching costs.
    B) rapid growth in the demand for the product.
    C) high costs of exiting the market as compared to the costs of entering the market.
    D) a set of competitors that are quite diverse in terms of their strategies, resources, countries of origin, and internal corporate culture.
    E) conditions where it is customary for rivals to collaborate closely with both their suppliers and their customers.

    Answer: B Difficulty: Medium

26. The rivalry among competing sellers tends to be less intense when
    A) buyer switching costs are low.
    B) they are not particularly aggressive or active in employing the various weapons of competition (a lower price, frequent introductions of new features or new models, new advertising campaigns, new customer service features, and so on) to try to jockey for better position and take market share away from rivals.
    C) the costs of exiting the market are higher than the costs of new entry.
    D) competitors are quite diverse in terms of their strategies, resources, countries of origin, and internal corporate culture.
    E) All of these tend to weaken competitive rivalry.

    Answer: B Difficulty: Medium

27. Rivalry among competing sellers is typically stronger when
    A) when their products/services are strongly differentiated.
    B) the industry is composed of a relatively large number of competitors that are fairly equal in size and competitive capability.
    C) it is relatively easy and inexpensive for existing competitors to exit the industry.
    D) the products/services of rivals are strongly differentiated and customers have high switching costs.
    E) it is customary for rivals to collaborate closely with both their suppliers and their customers.

    Answer: B Difficulty: Medium

28. The rivalry among competing firms tends to be weaker
    A) when demand for the product is growing rapidly.
    B) when products/services are weakly differentiated such that customers have low switching costs.
    C) when they are tempted to use price cuts or other marketing tactics to boost unit volume instead of advancing the technology and making new-generation products having better quality and more performance features.
    D) when rival firms all belong to the same strategic group and also have comparable priorities, resources, and corporate cultures.
    E) the greater the number of firms in the industry and the more equal their market shares.

    Answer: A Difficulty: Hard

29. The competitive force of rival firms' strategies
    A) is a strong factor in competition analysis because every firm in an industry has incentive to employ a competitive strategy that it believes will ensure its survival and yield a sustainable competitive edge.
    B) is typically a weaker competitive force than is the threat of entry of new rivals.
    C) emerges from the use of fresh offensive strategies but not from the use of defensive strategies.
    D) is stronger when firms strive to be low-cost producers than when they use differentiation and focus strategies.
    E) is weaker when more firms are using defensive strategies than are using offensive strategies.

    Answer: A Difficulty: Medium

30. Which of the following is not among the factors that affect whether competitive rivalry among participating firms is strong, moderate, or weak?
    A) Whether more firms are using offensive strategies than are using defensive strategies or vice versa
    B) Whether demand for the industry's product is growing rapidly or slowly
    C) How vigorously rivals employ such tactics as lowering prices, introducing new products with snazzier features, increasing promotion and advertising, and other similar maneuvers calculated to gain a competitive edge
    D) Whether the products of rival sellers are strongly or weakly differentiated
    E) Whether buyer costs to switch to competing brands are relatively high or relatively low

    Answer: A Difficulty: Hard

31. In analyzing the strength of competition among rival firms, an important consideration is
    A) the potential for entry of new competitors.
    B) the frequency and aggressiveness with which rivals maneuver to try to gain a competitive edge and increase their market share.
    C) the number of firms pursuing differentiation strategies versus the number pursuing low-cost leadership strategies and focus strategies.
    D) the extent to which some rivals have more than two competitively valuable competencies or capabilities.
    E) whether the industry is characterized by a strong experience curve and whether the industry is composed of many or few strategic groups.

    Answer: B Difficulty: Medium

32. The "best" strategy for one firm in maneuvering for competitive advantage over its rivals depends in part on
    A) what strategies its rivals are employing.
    B) the resources that rivals are willing and able to put behind their strategic efforts.
    C) the industry's overall attractiveness and the prospects for above-average profitability.
    D) the impact of the driving forces that are at work and the what the industry's key success factors are.
    E) Both A and B.

    Answer: E   Difficulty: Medium

33. The intensity of rivalry among competing sellers is a function of
    A) whether the industry's driving forces are strong and whether being the low-cost producer is a key success factor.
    B) whether there is a high degree of seller-supplier collaboration.
    C) whether barriers to entry are high.
    D) how vigorously rivals employ such tactics as lowering prices, introducing new products with snazzier features, increasing promotion and advertising, and other similar maneuvers calculated to gain a competitive edge.
    E) whether most firms are trying to differentiate their products or are content to market imitative products.

    Answer: D   Difficulty: Medium

34. Rivalry among competing sellers tends to be stronger when
    A) several competitors are under pressure to improve their market share or profitability and launch fresh strategic initiatives to attract more buyers and bolster their business position.
    B) weaker competitors are exiting the business.
    C) competitors are very unequal in size and capability, such that small competitors must really scramble to even survive.
    D) the products of rival sellers are strongly differentiated.
    E) companies compete more on the basis of price than on the basis of product innovation, new product features, and product performance.

    Answer: A   Difficulty: Medium

35. Rivalry among competing sellers tends to be stronger when
    A) one or more competitors is dissatisfied with its market position and makes moves to bolster its standing.
    B) strong companies outside the industry acquire weak firms in the industry and launch aggressive moves to transform their newly-acquired competitors into stronger market contenders.
    C) competitors are more equal in size and capability.
    D) there is strong mutual interdependence among rivals such that whenever one firm makes a strategic move, its rivals often retaliate with offensive or defensive countermoves.
    E) All of these.

    Answer: E   Difficulty: Easy

36. The rivalry among competing sellers is an ever-changing dynamic because
    A) there is strong mutual interdependence among rivals such that whenever one firm makes a strategic move, its rivals often retaliate with offensive or defensive countermoves.
    B) in most industries the success of any one firm's strategy hinges on what strategies its rivals employ and one or another rival is always fine-tuning or overhauling its strategy.
    C) the relative emphasis that rival companies put on price, quality, performance features, customer service, advertising, and so on shifts as they try different tactics to catch buyers' attention.
    D) every competitor is challenged to craft (and re-craft as needed) a strategy that offers good prospects of improving its position and, ideally, producing a sustainable competitive advantage.
    E) All of these help explain why competitive rivalry is dynamic.

    Answer: E Difficulty: Medium

37. The competitive contests between rival sellers in different industries assume different intensities because
    A) the mix of rivals' competitive strategies varies from industry to industry.
    B) the mix and combination of rivals' resource strengths and capabilities vary from industry to industry.
    C) in different industries rivals place different emphasis on price, quality, product innovation, customer service, advertising, and so on and try different combinations of tactics to catch buyers' attention.
    D) the frequency and mix of fresh offensive and defensive maneuvers varies from industry to industry.
    E) All of these.

    Answer: E Difficulty: Easy

The Competitive Threat of New Entrants

38. Potential new entrants are more likely to be deterred from actually entering an industry when
    A) incumbent firms have previously been aggressive in defending their market positions against entry.
    B) incumbent firms are broadly diversified.
    C) buyer demand for the product is not particularly price sensitive and the industry already contains a dozen or more rivals.
    D) the relative cost positions of incumbent firms are about the same, such that no one incumbent has a meaningful cost advantage.
    E) buyer switching costs are moderately low because of strong product differentiation among incumbent firms.

    Answer: A Difficulty: Hard

39. The seriousness of the competitive threat of entry is greater when
    A) incumbent firms have do not have deep financial pockets or particularly strong competitive capabilities.
    B) incumbent firms are earning above-average profits and a number of outsiders have the expertise and resources to hurdle whatever entry barriers exist.
    C) the industry's capital requirements are low and incumbent firms do not enjoy sizable economies of scale.
    D) buyers have low switching costs.
    E) All of these conditions heighten the probability of fresh entry.

    Answer: E Difficulty: Easy

40. The competitive threat that outsiders will enter a market is stronger when
    A) the products of rival firms are weakly differentiated, buyers have no strong preferences for the brands of existing producers, and buyers exhibit low brand loyalties.
    B) incumbents are not inclined to fight vigorously to prevent a newcomer from gaining a market foothold.
    C) a newcomer can expect to earn attractive profits.
    D) there are interested entry candidates with sufficient expertise and resources to hurdle prevailing entry barriers.
    E) All of these.

    Answer: E   Difficulty: Easy

41. The competitive threat of entry of new firms is stronger when
    A) buyers of the industry's products like to experiment with buying different brands of the industry's product.
    B) the products of rival firms are weakly differentiated, buyers have no strong preferences for the brands of existing producers, and buyers exhibit low brand loyalties.
    C) incumbent firms have little ability to leverage distributors, dealers, and/or retailers to retain their business.
    D) incumbent firms have little way to retaliate directly against new entrants are likely to be very aggressive in defending their market positions.
    E) All of these make the threat of fresh entry more likely.

    Answer: E   Difficulty: Medium

42. The competitive threat of entry of new firms is weaker when
    A) buyers of the industry's products like to experiment with buying different brands of the industry's product.
    B) the products of rival firms are weakly differentiated, buyers have no strong preferences for the brands of existing producers, and buyers exhibit low brand loyalties.
    C) incumbent firms have little ability to leverage distributors, dealers, and/or retailers to retain their business.
    D) incumbent firms are likely to be very aggressive in defending their market positions.
    E) there are more than ten firms already in the industry.

    Answer: D   Difficulty: Medium

43. A potential entrant is likely to have second thoughts about actually attempting entry when
    A) incumbent firms are willing and able to cut prices to preserve their market shares.
    B) retailers are skeptical about giving a newcomer's products ample display and shelf space.
    C) market demand for the industry's product(s) is expanding slowly.
    D) it is hard for newcomers to gain access to needed technology and specialized know-how.
    E) All of these.

    Answer: E   Difficulty: Easy

44. Which of the following is generally not considered as a barrier to entry?
    A) Economies of scale and strong experience curve effects
    B) Capital requirements, regulatory policies, and tariffs
    C) Strong buyer preferences for and loyalty to existing brands
    D) Rapid market growth
    E) Difficulties in gaining access to technological know-how

    Answer: D Difficulty: Medium

45. The best test of whether potential entry is a strong or weak competitive force is
    A) to determine how loyal buyers are to existing brands.
    B) to consider whether the industry's driving forces make it harder or easier for new entrants to be successful.
    C) to determine how closely the strategies of industry rivals match the industry's key success factors.
    D) to see whether there are any vacant spaces on the industry's strategic group map.
    E) None of these is the best test.

    Answer: E Difficulty: Hard

The Competitive Threat Posed by Substitute Products

46. Just how strong the competitive pressures are from substitute products depends on
    A) the speed with which industry demand is growing, whether buyer switching costs are high or low, and whether product innovation is something that buyers value highly.
    B) whether attractively priced substitutes are readily available and the ease with which buyers can switch to substitutes.
    C) whether buyers are loyal to their present brand, the extent of strategic alliances in the industry, and whether the available substitutes are strongly or weakly differentiated.
    D) whether buyers believe that the available substitutes have attractive attributes, whether the producers of substitutes have ample budgets for new product R&D, and whether buyers purchase substitute products frequently or infrequently.
    E) the speed with which buyer needs and expectations are changing and whether the producers of substitutes have the product innovation skills to keep up with such changes.

    Answer: B Difficulty: Hard

47. The competitive force of substitute products tends to be stronger in a given market when
    A) the costs to buyers of switching over to the substitutes are low.
    B) buyers view substitutes as likely to be in short supply from time to time.
    C) the quality and performance of the substitutes is well above what buyers need to meet their requirements.
    D) buyers have high psychic costs in severing existing brand relationships and establishing new ones.
    E) when demand for the industry's product is not very price sensitive.

    Answer: A Difficulty: Medium

48. The competitive force of substitute products tends to be stronger in a given market when
   A) the costs to buyers of switching over to the substitutes are low.
   B) buyers view substitutes as unlikely to be in short supply from time to time.
   C) the quality and performance of the substitutes is well matched to what buyers need to meet their requirements.
   D) buyers have low brand loyalty and do not experience high psychic costs in severing existing brand relationships and establishing new ones.
   E) All of these factors tend to enhance the competitive pressures from substitute products.

   Answer: E Difficulty: Easy

49. The competitive force of substitute products is weaker when
   A) buyers incur high costs in switching to substitutes.
   B) the buyers of the industry's products are few in number and they have substantial amounts of leverage with sellers.
   C) rival sellers are locked in an intense competitive struggle to achieve product differentiation.
   D) barriers to entering the industry are high.
   E) the producers of substitute products are all pursuing strategies to strongly differentiate their products on the basis of quality and product performance.

   Answer: A Difficulty: Medium

50. Which of the following is the best example of a substitute product that poses a strong competitive force?
   A) Grated cheese as a substitute for sliced cheese
   B) Wireless phones as a substitute for wired telephones.
   C) Coca-Cola as a substitute for Pepsi.
   D) Snowmobiles as a substitute for ice skates.
   E) Surfing the Internet as a substitute for going to the movie.

   Answer: B Difficulty: Medium

Supplier-Seller Collaboration and Bargaining

51. Whether supplier-seller relationships in an industry represent a strong or weak source of competitive pressure is a function of
   A) whether the profits of suppliers are relatively high or low.
   B) the number of suppliers and the number of sellers.
   C) how aggressively rival sellers are maneuvering to form strategic alliances with each of the industry's major suppliers.
   D) whether suppliers can exercise sufficient bargaining power to influence the terms and conditions of supply in their favor and the extent of seller-supplier collaboration in the industry.
   E) whether the prices of the items being furnished by the suppliers are rising or falling.

   Answer: D Difficulty: Medium

52. The economic leverage and bargaining power of suppliers is greater when
    A) there are no good substitutes for the items being furnished by the suppliers and the number of suppliers is relatively small.
    B) the costs of switching from one supplier to another are low.
    C) the buying firms purchase in large quantities and thus are important customers of the suppliers.
    D) there is extensive seller-supplier collaboration.
    E) the supplier industry is composed of a large number of relatively small suppliers.

    Answer: A   Difficulty: Medium

53. The strength of suppliers as a strong competitive force is diminished when
    A) buying firms pose a credible threat of backward integration into the suppliers' business.
    B) the cost of switching from one supplier to another is low.
    C) the buying firms purchase in large quantities and thus are important customers of the suppliers.
    D) buying firms can readily switch to substitute inputs provided by alternative suppliers.
    E) All of these.

    Answer: E   Difficulty: Easy

54. Supplier bargaining power is less likely to be a source of strong competitive pressure when
    A) buying firms collaborate closely with their key suppliers to achieve mutual benefits.
    B) the cost of switching from one supplier to another is high.
    C) the suppliers furnish a critical part or component.
    D) buying firms are looking for suppliers with good just-in-time supply capabilities.
    E) suppliers are few in number and are relatively profitable.

    Answer: A   Difficulty: Medium

55. The competitive influence that a group of suppliers can have on an industry is mainly a function of
    A) whether competitively-priced substitutes for the item they are supplying are readily available.
    B) how significant the cost of the item they supply is to the buyer.
    C) the sensitivity of buyers to suppliers' prices.
    D) whether technological change in the suppliers' business is rapid or slow.
    E) Both A and B.

    Answer: E   Difficulty: Hard

56. Effective supply chain partnerships on the part of one or more industry rivals
    A) generally have little competitive impact and are seldom a source of significant competitive pressure on other rivals.
    B) are unlikely to be a source of significant competitive pressure unless the costs of the items furnished by supply chain partners amount to 50% or more of total cost.
    C) can sometimes become a major source of competitive pressure for other rivals.
    D) usually produce significant competitive pressures when technological change in the suppliers' business is rapid and when the item being supplied is pretty much a commodity.
    E) generally results in substantially increased bargaining power on the part of those suppliers having strong alliances with industry competitors.

    Answer: C Difficulty: Hard

57. Industry rivals are often motivated to enter into strategic partnerships with key suppliers in order to
    A) promote just-in-time deliveries and lower inventory and logistics costs.
    B) speed the availability of next-generation parts and components.
    C) enhance the quality of parts and components being supplied and reduce defects.
    D) help reduce suppliers' costs and thereby pave the way for lower prices on the items supplied.
    E) All of these.

    Answer: E Difficulty: Medium

Buyer-Seller Collaboration and Bargaining

58. Whether buyer-seller relationships in an industry represent a strong or weak source of competitive pressure is a function of
    A) the speed with which overall buyer demand is growing and with which buyers' needs and expectations are changing.
    B) the extent to which buyers can exercise enough bargaining power to influence the terms and conditions of sale in their favor and whether the extent of collaboration between certain sellers and certain buyers in the industry places rivals lacking such collaborative arrangements at a competitive disadvantage.
    C) how many buyers purchase all of their requirements from a single seller versus how many purchase from several sellers.
    D) whether the number of buyers is greater than the number of sellers or vice versa.
    E) the extent to which the prices of the items being furnished by rival sellers are rising or falling.

    Answer: B Difficulty: Medium

59. Whether buyer-seller relationships in an industry represent a strong or weak source of competitive pressure is a function of whether
    A) all buyers possess an equal degree of bargaining power and leverage.
    B) the number of buyers engaged in collaborative partnerships with sellers is greater than the number of sellers.
    C) all rival sellers have entered into strategic alliances with the most prestigious and important buyers of the industry's product.
    D) the overall quality of the items being furnished by rival sellers is rising or falling.
    E) buyers can exercise enough bargaining power to influence the terms and conditions of sale in their favor and the extent of seller-buyer collaboration in the industry.

    Answer: E Difficulty: Medium

60. Collaborative relationships between particular sellers and buyers in an industry can represent a source of competitive pressure when
    A) virtually all buyers are without any real degree of bargaining power and leverage.
    B) the number of sellers engaged in collaborative partnerships with buyers is greater than the number of buyers.
    C) one or more rival sellers form mutually advantageous partnerships with important or prestigious buyers such that rivals lacking such partnerships are placed at a competitive disadvantage.
    D) sellers are racing to add the latest and greatest performance features so as to attract the patronage of important or prestigious buyers.
    E) buyers pose a real threat of integrating backward into the business of sellers.

    Answer: C Difficulty: Medium

61. The bargaining power of an industry's customers tends to be weaker when
    A) customers' purchases are a large percentage of the selling industry's total sales.
    B) there are relatively few customers and each tends to purchase in large quantities.
    C) the buyer group consists a few large buyers and the seller group consists of numerous small firms.
    D) buyers purchase the item frequently and the number of sellers is substantially large (more than a dozen).
    E) the costs incurred by buyers in switching to competing brands are relatively high.

    Answer: E Difficulty: Medium

62. The bargaining power of an industry's customers tends to be greater when
    A) customers' purchases are a small percentage of the selling industry's total sales.
    B) there are relatively few customers and each tends to purchase in large quantities.
    C) the industry is composed of a few, large sellers and the customer group consists of numerous, small firms.
    D) the number of rival sellers is substantially large (more than a dozen).
    E) the costs incurred by buyers in switching to competing brands or to substitute products are relatively high.

    Answer: B Difficulty: Medium

63. Customers are seldom in position to exert strong leverage and bargaining power over a group of sellers when
    A) their costs to switch to competing brands or to substitute products are relatively high.
    B) the product/service being bought saves the customer a lot of money.
    C) they purchase the item infrequently.
    D) the customer population is large and each buyer tends to purchase in relatively small quantities.
    E) All of the above

    Answer: E Difficulty: Easy

64. The economic leverage and bargaining power of customers tends to be relatively weaker when .
    A) customer purchases are a sizable percentage of the selling industry's total sales.
    B) customer switching costs are relatively high.
    C) the industry's product carries a relatively high price tag and buyers are quite price sensitive.
    D) customers follow the practice of purchasing from several sellers instead of one.
    E) demand for the product is growing slowly and sellers have excess production capacity.

    Answer: B Difficulty: Hard

65. In which of the following circumstances is the economic leverage and bargaining power of customers not relatively strong?
    A) When buyer demand is growing rapidly and the industry product is in short supply
    B) When customers are relatively well informed about sellers' products, prices, and costs
    C) When buyers pose a major threat to integrate backward into the product market of sellers
    D) When sellers' products are weakly differentiated, making easy for buyers to switch to competing brands
    E) When buyers have considerable discretion over whether and when they purchase the product

    Answer: A Difficulty: Medium

66. Which of the following factors is not a relevant consideration in judging whether the economic leverage and bargaining power of customers is relatively strong or relatively weak?
    A) Whether certain customers offer sellers important market exposure or prestige
    B) Whether customers are relatively well informed about sellers' products, prices, and costs
    C) Whether buyer needs and expectations are changing rapidly or slowly
    D) Whether sellers' products are highly differentiated, making it troublesome or costly for buyers to switch to competing brands or to substitute products
    E) Whether sellers pose little threat of forward integration into the product market of their customers and whether buyers pose a major threat to integrate backward into the product market of sellers

    Answer: C Difficulty: Easy

67. Which of the following factors is a relevant consideration in judging whether seller-buyer relationships are an important source of competitive pressure in an industry?
A) Whether winning the business of certain customers offers sellers important market exposure or prestige
B) The extent and importance of collaborative partnerships and alliances between particular sellers and buyers
C) Whether buyers pose a major threat to integrate backward into the product market of sellers
D) Whether sellers' products are weakly differentiated, making it easy for buyers to switch to competing brands
E) All of the above

Answer: E   Difficulty: Easy

68. Which of the following factors is not a relevant consideration in judging whether seller-buyer relationships are an important source of competitive pressure in an industry?
A) Whether winning the business of certain customers offers sellers important market exposure or prestige
B) Whether the number of buyers exceeds the number of sellers
C) Whether buyers pose a major threat to integrate backward into the product market of sellers
D) Whether sellers' products are weakly differentiated, making it easy for buyers to switch to competing brands
E) Whether collaborative partnerships and alliances between particular sellers and buyers put rivals lacking such collaborative relationships at a competitive disadvantage

Answer: B   Difficulty: Medium

Driving Forces Analysis

69. The "driving forces" in an industry
A) are usually the result of either changing technology or growing experience curve effects.
B) usually are associated with growing competitive pressures, the outbreak of price-cutting, and mounting competition from substitute products.
C) are major underlying causes of changing industry and competitive conditions and have a big influence on what kinds of changes will take place in the industry structure and competitive environment.
D) appear when an industry begins to mature but are seldom present during industry takeoff and rapid growth.
E) are almost always triggered by shifting buyer needs and expectations or by changes in entry barriers.

Answer: C   Difficulty: Easy

70. Industry conditions change
A) because of changing prices, changing customer needs, changing key success factors, and changes in the number and composition of the strategic groups comprising the industry.
B) because of newly-emerging industry threats and industry opportunities that alter the composition of the industry's strategic groups.
C) as an industry moves naturally through successive stages of the industry life-cycle.
D) because forces are in motion that create pressures or incentives for industry participants (competitors, customers, suppliers) to alter their actions.
E) All of these.

Answer: D   Difficulty: Medium

71. The task of driving forces analysis is to
    A) develop a comprehensive list of all the underlying causes of changing industry conditions.
    B) predict which new driving forces will emerge next.
    C) scan the environment in an effort to spot budding trends and conditions that may become driving forces in the future.
    D) identify the specific factors causing fundamental industry and competitive adjustments and assess the impact these changes will have on the industry.
    E) All of these are part of driving forces analysis.

    Answer: D   Difficulty: Medium

72. Which of the following is <u>not</u> generally a "driving force" capable of producing fundamental changes in industry direction or in the industry's competitive structure?
    A) Changes in the long-term industry growth rate
    B) Increasing globalization of the industry
    C) Product innovation and technological change
    D) Ups and downs in the economy
    E) New government regulations or significant changes in government policy toward the industry

    Answer: D   Difficulty: Medium

73. Which of the following are most <u>unlikely</u> to qualify as driving forces?
    A) Changes in the long-term industry growth rate, the entry or exit of major firms, and changes in cost and efficiency
    B) Increasing globalization of the industry and product innovation
    C) The Internet and the new and expanded e-commerce opportunities and threats it breeds in the industry
    D) Falling entry barriers, mounting competition from substitutes, and fundamental changes in the make-up of the industry's strategic group map
    E) Marketing innovations, new government regulations or significant changes in government policy toward the industry, and changes in who buys the industry's product and how they use it

    Answer: D   Difficulty: Medium

74. Increasing globalization of the industry can be a driving force because
    A) the products of foreign competitors represent important substitute products and thus add to the potential for chronic excess capacity conditions.
    B) foreign producers typically have lower costs, greater technological expertise, and more product innovation capabilities than domestic firms.
    C) it tends to increase rivalry among industry members and often shifts the pattern of competition among an industry's major players, favoring some and disadvantaging others.
    D) the transfer of technology from one country to another increases scale economies, lowers experience curve effects, and increases the competition from substitute products.
    E) market growth rates go up, product innovation speeds up, and some firms are likely to exit the industry.

    Answer: C   Difficulty: Medium

75. Driving forces analysis
    A) indicates to managers what newly-developing external factors will have the greatest impact on the industry over the next several years.
    B) addresses what the impact and consequences of each driving force will be.
    C) prompts managers to think about the kind of strategy needed to respond to the driving forces and their impact on the industry.
    D) All of these.
    E) None of these.

    Answer: D Difficulty: Easy

76. An industry's driving forces
    A) are generally determined by competitive pressures, the sizes of strategic groups, and the power of rival firms' competitive strategies.
    B) work to modify the current industry situation in important ways and to alter existing competitive pressures.
    C) frequently cause a leveling off of industry growth and a reduction in the bargaining power of buyers.
    D) are normally triggered by ups and downs in the economy, higher or lower inflation rates, higher or lower interest rates, or important new strategic alliances.
    E) can be triggered by the efforts of rival firms to employ significantly new or different offensive strategies, by growing competitive pressures from substitute products, and greater seller-supplier collaboration.

    Answer: B Difficulty: Medium

77. Which of the following are not likely to be driving forces capable of inducing fundamental changes in industry and competitive conditions?
    A) Changes in who buys the product and how they use it, changes in the long-term industry growth rate, and changes in cost and efficiency.
    B) Entry or exit of major firms, product innovation, and marketing innovation.
    C) Increases in the economic power and bargaining leverage of customers and suppliers, growing supplier-seller collaboration, and growing buyer-seller collaboration.
    D) Growing buyer preferences for differentiated products instead of mostly standardized or identical products.
    E) Changes in economies of scale and experience curve effects brought on by changes in manufacturing technology, increasing globalization of the industry, and new Internet capabilities.

    Answer: C Difficulty: Hard

78. In analyzing driving forces, the strategist's role is to
    A) identify the driving forces, evaluate their impact on industry and competitive conditions, and craft an appropriate strategic response.
    B) predict future marketing innovations and how fast the industry is likely to globalize and be impacted by the Internet.
    C) evaluate what stage of the life cycle the industry is in and when it is likely to move to the next stage.
    D) determine who is likely to exit the industry and what changes can be expected in the industry's strategic group map.
    E) forecast fluctuations in product demand and how buyer needs will most likely change.

    Answer: A Difficulty: Easy

79. Which one of the following is <u>least</u> likely to qualify as a driving force?
   A) Changes in cost or efficiency
   B) Process innovation and product innovation
   C) Changes in long-term market growth
   D) Entry or exit of major firms
   E) An attempt by one or more industry rivals to shift to a different strategic group

   Answer: E   Difficulty: Medium

80. Which of the following is <u>most</u> likely to qualify as a driving force?
   A) Increases in price-cutting by rival sellers and the launch of major new advertising campaigns by one or more rivals
   B) Wildly successful introduction of innovative new products by one or more industry rivals that force other rivals to respond quickly or lose a major share of their customers to the innovating rival(s)
   C) An increase in the prices of substitute products
   D) Predictable and regular changes in technology
   E) Decisions by one or more outsiders not to attempt to enter the industry

   Answer: B   Difficulty: Medium

Environmental Scanning

81. Environmental scanning concerns
   A) how to identify key success factors ahead of rivals.
   B) a way to raise management's consciousness about potential industry developments that could, in time, pose new opportunities or threats or otherwise significantly alter industry and competitive conditions.
   C) an attempt to determine which strategic groups have a sustainable competitive advantage.
   D) a way to measure industry attractiveness.
   E) a way to detect new changes in the strength of the five competitive forces.

   Answer: B   Difficulty: Hard

Strategic Groups and Strategic Group Mapping

82. A strategic group
   A) consists of those companies in an industry which are growing at about the same rate and having similar product line breadth.
   B) includes all rival firms which are trying to sell to the same type of customer.
   C) consists of those rival firms with similar competitive approaches and market positions.
   D) consists of those firms whose market shares are about the same size.
   E) is made up of those firms which have comparable market shares, profitability, and rates of return on investment.

   Answer: C   Difficulty: Medium

83. A strategic group consists of those firms in an industry that
   A) have comparable product line breadth.
   B) are utilizing about the same emphasis on each distribution channel.
   C) place comparable emphasis on the same key success factors.
   D) employ similar competitive approaches and occupy similar positions in the market.
   E) have comparable market shares and profitability.

   Answer: D Difficulty: Medium

84. The concept of strategic groups is relevant to industry and competitive analysis because
   A) firms in the same strategic groups tend to be close competitors.
   B) entry barriers and competitive conditions vary from strategic group to strategic group.
   C) the existence of multiple strategic groups generally increases competitive rivalry in an industry.
   D) the profit potential of firms in different strategic groups is often different.
   E) All of these.

   Answer: E Difficulty: Medium

85. In mapping strategic groups
   A) any two variables can be used as axes for the map.
   B) it is important for as many groups to fall above the diagonal as below the diagonal; otherwise the variables used as axes can be assumed to be highly correlated.
   C) the best variables to use as axes for the map are those that reveal the most about how rivals have positioned themselves to compete against one another in the marketplace.
   D) the objective is to identify all of the features that are common to each rival firm's strategy.
   E) it is important to use strategic variables that can be measured quantitatively; this permits the sizes of the circles on the map to be drawn in proportion to the combined sales of firms in each strategic group.

   Answer: C Difficulty: Hard

86. With the aid of a strategic group map, strategic analysts
   A) can readily identify the entry and exit barriers for each strategic group.
   B) can pinpoint precisely which firms are in viable strategic groups and which are not.
   C) can identify which competitive forces are strong and which are weak.
   D) can measure accurately whether across-group rivalry is stronger than within-group rivalry, or vice versa.
   E) may be able to pinpoint the strengths and weaknesses in each strategic group's position, and then use these to predict how members of each group will probably respond to new competitive pressures or industry conditions.

   Answer: E Difficulty: Hard

87. Strategic group mapping is a technique for determining
   A) how many rivals are pursuing a low-cost producer strategy and how many are pursuing focus or differentiation strategies.
   B) which companies have the biggest market share and who the industry leader really is.
   C) the different competitive positions that rival firms occupy in an industry.
   D) which firms are good at the most key success factors.
   E) which companies are the most profitable.

   Answer: C   Difficulty: Medium

88. Using strategic group maps to divide industry members into strategic groups
   A) is an excellent way to determine how many rivals are pursuing low-cost, focus, best-cost, or differentiation strategies.
   B) allows industry analysts to better understand the pattern of competition in complex industries and to pinpoint which companies are in closest competition with each other.
   C) is an excellent way to determine an industry's key success factors.
   D) which firms are doing the best job of responding to the industry's driving forces.
   E) helps identify which companies in the industry are the most profitable.

   Answer: B   Difficulty: Hard

89. The best strategic variables to choose as axes for a strategic group map are
   A) market share and profitability.
   B) those which expose the major differences in how rivals have positioned themselves to compete against one another in the marketplace.
   C) those which also qualify as key success factors.
   D) those which separate the most profitable firms in an industry from the least profitable firms.
   E) those that best expose which firms are competitively successful and those which are not.

   Answer: B   Difficulty: Medium

90. Which of the following pairs of variables are least likely to be useful in drawing a strategic group map?
   A) Geographic coverage and degree of vertical integration
   B) Brand name reputation and distribution channel emphasis
   C) Product quality and product line breadth
   D) Level of profitability and size of market share
   E) Price/quality range and appeal to different buyer groups or buyer segments

   Answer: D   Difficulty: Medium

91. Some strategic groups are usually more favorably positioned than others in the sense that
    A) their current profits are bigger and their market shares are bigger.
    B) they have bigger scale economies and experience curve effects.
    C) their prices are lower.
    D) they have better future profit prospects, perhaps because the industry's driving forces and competitive pressures in the marketplace favor them while disadvantaging others.
    E) they attract more customers.

    Answer: D Difficulty: Hard

92. Which of the following is not an appropriate guideline for developing a strategic group map for a given industry?
    A) The variables chosen as axes for the map should indicate big differences in how rivals have positioned themselves to compete in the marketplace.
    B) The variables chosen as axes for the map can be either quantitative or qualitative.
    C) The variables chosen as axes for the map should be highly correlated.
    D) Several maps should be drawn if more than one pair of variables prove useful in depicting the competitive positions of industry members.
    E) The sizes of the circles on the map should be drawn proportional to the combined sales of the firms in each strategic group.

    Answer: C Difficulty: Hard

Competitor Analysis

93. The payoff of competitor analysis is improved ability to predict
    A) how a rival will respond to changing industry and competitive conditions.
    B) whether a rival is likely to initiate a fresh strategic move.
    C) how much a rival can be pushed before being provoked into retaliation.
    D) the meaning and intent of a rival's new strategic move and how seriously it should be taken.
    E) All of these.

    Answer: E Difficulty: Medium

94. The manner in which rival firms employ various competitive weapons to try to outmaneuver one another
    A) helps determine whether the industry's driving forces will be strong or weak.
    B) shapes the "rules of competition" in the industry and determines the requirements for competitive success.
    C) determines which rivals will be in which strategic group.
    D) depends on how much bargaining power that suppliers and customers have.
    E) varies according to the strength of the five competitive forces.

    Answer: B Difficulty: Hard

95. One of the benefits of doing first-rate competitor analysis is to
   A) learn who the industry's current major contenders are.
   B) ascertain which rivals are favorably or unfavorably positioned to gain market ground, why there is potential for some firms to do better or worse than other rivals, and what moves various rivals are likely to make next.
   C) determine which company has the best strategy and how it can copy most of what the strategy leader is doing.
   D) determine which rival has the worst strategy and how it can avoid making the same strategy mistakes.
   E) All of these.

   Answer: B   Difficulty: Hard

96. In evaluating who the industry's major players are going to be on down the road, it is usually relevant to consider
   A) whether the current major contenders for industry leadership are well-positioned for the future.
   B) which firms in the industry are currently gaining ground and which are losing ground and why.
   C) the degree to which the various industry rivals possess the skills, competencies, resources, and capabilities that will be needed to compete successfully in the future.
   D) why there is potential for particular industry rivals to do better or worse than others.
   E) All of these.

   Answer: E   Difficulty: Easy

97. Gathering competitive intelligence about rival firms can provide strategically useful clues and predictions about
   A) how a rival will likely react to industry trends and broader environmental conditions.
   B) which rivals will initiate what kinds of fresh strategic moves and why.
   C) what each rival would probably do in response to certain strategic moves of other firms.
   D) the meaning and intent of a new strategic move by a particular rival and how seriously it should be taken.
   E) All of these.

   Answer: E   Difficulty: Easy

Key Success Factors

98. The key success factors in an industry
   A) are those things that most affect industry members' ability to prosper in the marketplace—the particular strategy elements, product attributes, resources, competencies, competitive capabilities, and business outcomes that spell the difference between success and failure.
   B) are usually the same from industry to industry, although some variation can be expected if the industry's driving forces are unusually potent.
   C) hinge on how many firms are pursuing low-cost, differentiation, focus, and best-cost strategies.
   D) depend on which rivals are in which strategic group and whether many rivals are trying to move from one group to another.
   E) vary from industry to industry based on such factors as how many firms are in the industry, what their market shares are, who has what kind of competitive advantage, and the make-up of each rival firm's competitive strategy.

   Answer: A   Difficulty: Medium

99. In identifying an industry's key success factors, strategists should
   A) try to single out all factors which play a major role in industry growth.
   B) consider on what basis customers choose between competing brands and what resources and competitive capabilities firms need to be competitively successful.
   C) consider whether the number of strategic groups is increasing or decreasing, whether entry barriers are rising or falling, and whether industry driving forces are powerful or relatively weak.
   D) consider what it will take to overtake the company with the industry's overall best strategy.
   E) All of these.

   Answer: B Difficulty: Medium

100. An industry's key success factors
   A) are a function of market share, entry barriers, economies of scale, experience curve effects, and industry profitability.
   B) vary according to whether an industry has high or low long-term attractiveness.
   C) consist of the three or four biggest determinants of financial and competitive success in an industry and, thus, point to the things any firm in the industry must be competent at doing or concentrate on achieving.
   D) can be determined from studying the "winning" strategies of the industry leaders and ruling out as potential key success factors the strategy elements of those firms considered to have "losing" strategies.
   E) depend on the relative competitive strengths of the industry leaders and how vulnerable they are to competitive attack.

   Answer: C Difficulty: Medium

101. Which of the following is not a good example of a marketing-related key success factor?
   A) Product R & D capabilities and expertise in product design
   B) A well-trained, effective sales force
   C) Breadth of product line and product selection
   D) Merchandising skills
   E) Attractive styling/packaging

   Answer: A Difficulty: Hard

102. A good example of a manufacturing-related key success factor is
   A) scientific research expertise.
   B) high labor productivity.
   C) low distribution costs.
   D) accurate filling of buyer orders.
   E) ability to deliver rapidly.

   Answer: B Difficulty: Hard

103. A good example of a technology-related key success factor is
    A) low-cost product design.
    B) product and process innovation capability.
    C) quality control know-how.
    D) having superior systems for tracking costs.
    E) ability to develop efficient inventory control systems.

    Answer: B   Difficulty: Easy

Industry Attractiveness

104. Evaluating long-term industry attractiveness involves
    A) sizing up overall industry and competitive conditions to determine whether the industry's future profit prospects are above average, average, or below average.
    B) an assessment of which firms in the industry have the best competitive strategies.
    C) determining the overall strength of the five competitive forces.
    D) constructing a strategic group map and assessing the attractiveness of the competitive position of each strategic group to determine the overall attractiveness of all the strategic groups.
    E) using value chain analysis to determine the relative cost positions of rival firms and to learn who the industry's low-cost producer is.

    Answer: A   Difficulty: Medium

105. Evaluating long-term industry attractiveness involves a consideration of which of the following factors?
    A) The industry growth rate, whether competition will become stronger or weaker, and whether the industry's future profit prospects are above average, average, or below average
    B) An assessment of which firms in the industry have the best and worst competitive strategies, whether the number of strategic groups in the industry is increasing or decreasing, and how big a factor economies of scale and experience curve effects are
    C) Determining the overall strength of the five competitive forces, the overall attractiveness of the various strategic groups, how many key success factors the industry has, and the resources needed to be competent at each one of these KSFs
    D) Analyzing the industry's driving forces, constructing a strategic group map and assessing the attractiveness of the competitive position of each strategic group, and sizing up whether the industry leaders are competitively vulnerable
    E) All of these.

    Answer: A   Difficulty: Medium

106. Evaluating long-term industry attractiveness usually does not involve a consideration of which of the following factors?
   A) The industry growth rate, whether competitive pressures will likely grow stronger or weaker, and whether the industry's future profit prospects are above average, average, or below average
   B) An assessment of the degrees of business risk and uncertainty in the industry's future
   C) Whether the industry's future profitability will be favorably or unfavorably affected by the prevailing driving forces
   D) The severity of the problems confronting the industry as a whole
   E) How many driving forces and key success factors the industry has, whether the industry's prices are rising or falling faster than the overall inflation rate, and whether the industry's product is strongly or weakly differentiated

   Answer: E   Difficulty: Medium

107. The most "ideal" competitive condition from an industry attractiveness perspective is where
   A) both suppliers and customers occupy strong bargaining positions.
   B) rivalry among sellers is strong.
   C) there are no good substitutes for the industry's product.
   D) entry barriers are low.
   E) None of the above really enhance industry attractiveness.

   Answer: C   Difficulty: Hard

108. The competitive structure of an industry tends to be "unattractive" from the standpoint of future profitability when
   A) rivalry among sellers is very strong.
   B) entry barriers are relatively low.
   C) competition from substitutes is strong.
   D) the industry's customers have strong bargaining power over the terms and conditions of sale.
   E) All of these.

   Answer: E   Difficulty: Easy

109. The competitive structure of an industry is unattractive from a profit-making perspective when
   A) the industry's driving forces are strong and there are more than three key success factors.
   B) there are few opportunities for achieving scale economies and experience curve effects are minimal.
   C) capital requirements are large, entry barriers are fairly high, and companies must spend heavily on advertising to retain customer loyalty and maintain a strong brand image.
   D) entry barriers are low, competition from substitutes is strong, both suppliers and customers are able to exercise considerable bargaining leverage, and rivalry among competing sellers is vigorous.
   E) there is only one strategic group in the industry, the industry's driving forces are strong, there are only two key success factors, and the industry's products are strongly differentiated.

   Answer: D   Difficulty: Medium

Short Answer Questions

110. What are the seven key questions which form the framework of industry and competitive analysis?

   Difficulty: Medium

111. Explain the meaning and significance of each of the following:
   a.) driving forces
   b.) strategic group mapping
   c.) the experience curve
   d.) key success factors
   e.) long-term industry attractiveness
   f.) environmental scanning
   g.) competitive strategy

   Difficulty: Medium

112. Draw and briefly describe the five forces model of competition.

   Difficulty: Medium

113. Identify and briefly discuss any four of the factors that influence the strength of competitive rivalry among member firms.

   Difficulty: Medium

114. Competitive markets are economic battlefields. True or False. Explain.

   Difficulty: Easy

115. Not all buyers of an industry's product are likely to possess the same degree of bargaining power or leverage over the terms and conditions under which they purchase the product. True or False. Explain.

   Difficulty: Medium

116. Discuss the conditions that tend to make potential entry a strong competitive force.

   Difficulty: Medium

117. Identify and briefly describe any five of the major sources of entry barriers.

Difficulty: Hard

118. What conditions cause substitute products to be a strong competitive force?

Difficulty: Hard

119. What conditions cause suppliers to be a strong competitive force?

Difficulty: Hard

120. What conditions tend to give customers a high degree of bargaining power?

Difficulty: Hard

121. What is the analytical value of constructing a strategic group map?

Difficulty: Hard

122. What is the analytical value of studying competitors and trying to predict what moves rivals will make next?

Difficulty: Medium

123. What is the strategy-making value of identifying an industry's key success factors?

Difficulty: Medium

124. What are some of the major factors that enter into an assessment of whether an industry does or does not have long-term attractiveness?

Difficulty: Hard

125. Can an industry be attractive to one company and unattractive to another company? Why or why not?

Difficulty: Medium

Chapter 4: Evaluating Company Resources and Competitive Capabilities

Multiple Choice Questions

What Company Situation Analysis Involves

1. Which of the following is <u>not</u> a component of company situation analysis?
   A) Evaluating how well the present strategy is working
   B) Environmental scanning to determine a company's best customers
   C) An assessment of whether the company's costs and prices are competitive
   D) Evaluating the company's competitive strength and competitive position
   E) Pinpointing what strategic issues the company's management needs to address

   Answer: B Difficulty: Easy

2. The components of company situation analysis include
   A) evaluating whether the company's present strategy is better than the strategies of its closest rivals based on such performance measures as earnings per share, ROE, dividend payout ratio, and average annual increase in the common stock price.
   B) a SWOT analysis.
   C) an assessment of whether the company has the industry's most efficient and effective value chain.
   D) an evaluation of the company's key success factors vis-a-vis the key success factors of close rivals.
   E) an assets/liabilities assessment aimed at determining what new acquisitions the company would be well advised to make in order to strengthen its financial performance and overall balance sheet position.

   Answer: B Difficulty: Easy

3. The <u>least</u> important step of company situation analysis is
   A) conducting a competitive strength assessment.
   B) deciding how well the present strategy is working.
   C) identifying the key strategic issues which company management needs to address in crafting the company's strategy.
   D) determining the company's resource strengths and weaknesses and its external opportunities and threats.
   E) None of these is inherently less essential or less important than the others.

   Answer: E Difficulty: Medium

4. Which of the following is the <u>most</u> essential and important component of company situation analysis?
   A) Assessing the company's cost position in relation to competitors.
   B) Conducting a SWOT analysis.
   C) Evaluating the company's competitive position and competitive strengths and weaknesses vis-à-vis close rivals.
   D) Assessing the effectiveness of the current strategy.
   E) None of these is inherently more essential or important than the others.

   Answer: E Difficulty: Medium

Evaluation of How Well a Company's Present Strategy Is Working

5. Assessing a company's situation from a strategic perspective should logically begin with
   A) an evaluation of the company's competitive strengths and weaknesses.
   B) an evaluation of the company's future profit prospects and current financial position.
   C) an identification of the present strategy and how well it is working (as measured by key performance indicators).
   D) doing an environmental scan to assess emerging company threats and opportunities.
   E) a five forces analysis of the company's competitive capabilities.

   Answer: C   Difficulty: Medium

6. To identify a company's strategy, one should consider
   A) whether it is striving to be a low-cost leader or stressing ways to differentiate its product offering from those of rivals.
   B) whether it is concentrating on serving a broad spectrum of customers or a narrow market niche.
   C) how many stages of the industry's total value chain it operates in.
   D) the nature of the company's functional and operating strategies.
   E) All of the above.

   Answer: E   Difficulty: Easy

7. Good evidence of how well a firm's present strategy is working includes
   A) how many core competencies the firm has and whether it has more core competencies than close rivals.
   B) whether the firm's strategy takes the industry's driving forces into account and is built around the industry's key success factors.
   C) the trend in the firm's profits and return on investment, whether its market share is rising or falling, whether its sales revenues are growing faster or slower than the industry as a whole, its image and reputation with customers, and the size of the firm's profit margins relative to other rivals.
   D) whether the firm is customarily a first-mover or a late-mover and whether it is the market share leader.
   E) whether the firm is fully integrated or only partially integrated.

   Answer: C   Difficulty: Medium

8. Relevant criteria for determining whether a company's present strategy is working well include
   A) whether the company's competitive assets exceed its competitive liabilities.
   B) whether the company is in the industry's best strategic group.
   C) trends in the firm's profits and return on investment, whether its market share is rising or falling, whether its sales revenues are growing faster or slower than the industry as a whole, its image and reputation with customers, and the size of the firm's profit margins relative to other rivals.
   D) whether a SWOT analysis of the company's strategy comes out positive or negative.
   E) All of the above are quite pertinent criteria.

   Answer: C   Difficulty: Medium

9. One can evaluate how well an organization's current strategy is working, in part, by looking at
    A) whether the firm's market share is rising or falling.
    B) the size of the firm's profit margins relative to those of its rivals.
    C) trends in the company's stock price and whether the strategy is producing larger or smaller gains in shareholder value relative to the gains of other companies in the industry.
    D) its image and reputation with customers.
    E) All of these.

    Answer: E Difficulty: Medium

10. Which one of the following is not really pertinent in evaluating how well an organization's current strategy is working?
    A) Whether sales revenues are growing faster or slower than the industry as a whole
    B) Whether it has more competitive assets than competitive liabilities or vice versa
    C) Trends in the company's stock price and whether the strategy is producing larger or smaller gains in shareholder value relative to the gains of other companies in the industry.
    D) Whether its profit margins are rising or falling and how large they are relative to those of its rivals
    E) Whether it is regarded as a leader in one or more of the relevant factors on which buyers base their choice of which brand to purchase

    Answer: B Difficulty: Medium

SWOT Analysis

11. Identifying and assessing a company's resource strengths and weaknesses and its external opportunities and threats is called
    A) SWOT analysis.
    B) WOTS-up analysis.
    C) environmental scanning.
    D) strategic mapping of the company's future prospects.
    E) TOWS analysis.

    Answer: A Difficulty: Easy

12. SWOT analysis is a helpful tool for
    A) predicting whether the company's value chain is cost competitive.
    B) seeing how closely a firm's strategy is matched to its resource capabilities and deficiencies, its market opportunities, and the external threats to its future well-being.
    C) evaluating whether a company is competitively stronger than its closest rivals.
    D) seeing how closely a firm's strategy is matched to the industry's key success factors.
    E) assessing the pros and cons of backward and forward vertical integration.

    Answer: B Difficulty: Easy

13. The value of SWOT analysis in evaluating a company's situation is that
    A) it highlights those areas in the company's value chain where important differences can occur between its costs and the costs of competing firms.
    B) it assists strategy-makers in crafting a strategy that is well-matched to the company's resources and capabilities, its market opportunities, and the external threats to its future well-being.
    C) it enables a company to assess its overall competitive position relative to its key rivals.
    D) it allows a company to compare its market share, measures of profitability, and sales with its key competitors.
    E) it helps strategy-makers create a strong fit between the company's resource strengths and the industry's key success factors.

    Answer: B   Difficulty: Medium

Company Resource Strengths and Weaknesses

14. A company strength can relate to
    A) a skill or important expertise.
    B) its intellectual capital, physical assets, organizational assets, and intangible assets.
    C) an achievement or attribute that puts the company in a position of market advantage.
    D) its partnerships or alliances with other organizations having expertise or capabilities that enhance its own competitiveness.
    E) All of these.

    Answer: E   Difficulty: Easy

15. A company strength can relate to
    A) its physical and/or organization assets, its intellectual capital, its competitive capabilities, an achievement or attribute that puts the company in a position of market advantage, or its partnerships or alliances with other organizations.
    B) its ability to move from one strategic group to another, whether it has more shareholders than rival firms, and whether its product line is broader than those of close rivals.
    C) the capabilities it has for shifting back and forth between one value chain and another, how often it does strategic cost analysis, and whether it benchmarks its costs at least annually.
    D) whether it has more collaborative partnerships and strategic alliances with other organizations than do its close rivals.
    E) All of these.

    Answer: A   Difficulty: Medium

16. From a strategy-making perspective, a company's resource strengths are important because of
    A) their potential for providing the firm with an experience-based cost advantage.
    B) their potential for serving as the cornerstones of strategy and the building of competitive advantage.
    C) the extra muscle they provide in making a success out of forward integration.
    D) the added ability they provide in insulating the firm against the impact of the industry's driving forces.
    E) All of these.

    Answer: B   Difficulty: Easy

17. Company strengths and competitive capabilities can emerge from
    A) the regularity and effectiveness with which different parts of the organization team together and collaborate on such things as continuous product innovation, shortening the time it takes to bring new products to market, improving customer service, and so on.
    B) partnering with key suppliers or others having valuable expertise and technological know-how.
    C) the possession of competitively valuable core competencies.
    D) such intangibles as a well-known brand name, a positive work climate and culture, and a loyal, dedicated work force.
    E) All of these.

    Answer: E Difficulty: Easy

18. The best example of a company strength is
    A) having been in business longer than rivals.
    B) being totally self-sufficient such that the company does not have to rely in any way on key suppliers, partnerships with outsiders, or strategic alliances.
    C) having a reputation as a technological leader and a product innovator.
    D) having a shorter value chain than rivals.
    E) being less vertically integrated than rivals.

    Answer: C Difficulty: Medium

19. Which of the following is not a good example of a company strength?
    A) Having fewer suppliers and a shorter value chain than close rivals.
    B) Having partnerships or alliances that enhance that company's own competitiveness and capabilities.
    C) A reputation for having more intellectual capital than rivals.
    D) Having a well-known brand name and enjoying the confidence of customers.
    E) Charging lower prices than rivals.

    Answer: A Difficulty: Medium

20. From a strategy perspective, a company weakness
    A) represents a problem that needs to be turned into a strength because otherwise the company will be competitively vulnerable.
    B) is something that the company lacks or does poorly (in comparison to rivals) or a condition that puts it at a disadvantage.
    C) makes it hard, if not impossible, to craft a winning strategy.
    D) usually stems from having a missing link or links in the industry value chain.
    E) causes the company to fall into a lower strategic group than it otherwise could compete in.

    Answer: B Difficulty: Medium

2₁. A company's internal weaknesses can relate to
   A) a deficiency of intellectual capital.
   B) something that it lacks or does poorly (in comparison to rivals).
   C) deficiencies in technological know-how.
   D) missing or weak competitive capabilities in key areas of the value chain.
   E) All of these.

   Answer: E   Difficulty: Easy

22. Which of the following is not a potential resource weakness or competitive deficiency?
   A) Having a single, unified functional strategy instead of several distinct functional strategies
   B) Less productive R & D efforts than rivals
   C) Lack of a strong market image and reputation
   D) Higher overall unit costs relative to rivals
   E) Too narrow a product line relative to rivals

   Answer: A   Difficulty: Medium

23. Sizing up company resource strengths and weaknesses
   A) essentially involves constructing a strategic balance sheet where the company's resource strengths represent competitive assets and its weaknesses represent competitive liabilities.
   B) is called SWOT analysis.
   C) is called competitive strength assessment.
   D) should include an assessment of how many of the industry's key success factors represent company strengths and how many represent company weaknesses.
   E) entails deciding whether the company's strategy is a strength (competitive asset) or weakness (competitive liability).

   Answer: A   Difficulty: Medium

Core Competencies and Competitive Capabilities

24. When a company has the ability to perform a competitively important value chain activity better than other competitively important value chain activities, it is said to have
   A) a distinctive competence.
   B) a core competence.
   C) a key activity in its value chain that holds promise for strong product differentiation.
   D) a key success factor.
   E) a company competence in that activity.

   Answer: B   Difficulty: Easy

25. When a company has gained real proficiency in performing some internal activity, it is said to have
   A) a competitive edge over rival.
   B) a competitive asset.
   C) a distinctive competence.
   D) a core competence.
   E) a company competence.

Answer: E   Difficulty: Medium

26. The difference between a company competence and a core competence is that
   A) a company competence refers to a company's best-executed functional strategy and a core competence refers to a company's best-executed business strategy.
   B) a company competence refers to a company's best-executed value chain activity whereas a core competence refers to a company's best-executed strategic activity.
   C) a company competence is a competitively-relevant activity which a firm performs especially well relative to other internal activities, whereas a core competence is an activity that a company has learned to perform proficiently.
   D) a company competence represents real proficiency in performing an internal activity whereas a core competence is a competitively-relevant activity which a firm performs especially well relative to other internally-performed activities.
   E) a core competence usually resides in a company's technology and physical assets (state-of-the-art plants and equipment, attractive real estate locations, modern distribution facilities, and so on) whereas a company competence usually resides in a company's base of intellectual capital.

Answer: D   Difficulty: Medium

27. The difference between a core competence and a distinctive competence is that
   A) a distinctive competence refers to a company's best-executed functional strategy and a core competence refers to a company's best-executed operating strategy.
   B) a core competence usually resides in a company's base of intellectual capital whereas a distinctive competence stems from the superiority of a company's physical and tangible assets.
   C) a core competence is a competitively-relevant activity which a firm performs especially well in comparison to the other activities it performs, whereas a distinctive competence is a competitively-relevant activity which a firm performs especially well in comparison to its competitors.
   D) a core competence represents a resource strength whereas a distinctive competence is achieved by having more resource strengths than rival companies.
   E) a core competence usually resides in a company's technology and physical assets (state-of-the-art plants and equipment, attractive real estate locations, modern distribution facilities, and so on) whereas a distinctive competence usually resides in a company's know-how, expertise, and intellectual capital.

Answer: C   Difficulty: Medium

28. A core competence
    A) adds to a company's arsenal of competitive capabilities and competitive assets and is a genuine resource strength
    B) typically resides in a company's people (skills and knowledge) and in its capabilities, not in its assets on the balance sheet.
    C) is sometimes the product of effective collaboration among different organizational units and/or of individual resources teaming together.
    D) All of these.
    E) None of the above is correct; they apply to a distinctive competence, not a core competence.

    Answer: D Difficulty: Medium

29. A core competence
    A) gives a company competitive capability and is a genuine company strength and resource.
    B) typically resides in the physical and tangible assets on a company's balance sheet.
    C) is seldom the product of cross-department or cross-functional collaboration.
    D) is more difficult for rivals to copy than a distinctive competence.
    E) All of these.

    Answer: A Difficulty: Medium

30. When a company performs some activity truly well in comparison to its competitors, it is said to have
    A) an internal resource strength.
    B) a competitive asset.
    C) a distinctive competence.
    D) a core competence.
    E) a company competence.

    Answer: C Difficulty: Medium

31. Which of the following does not represent a potential core competence?
    A) The ability to manufacture virtually defect-free products
    B) The capability to develop new products in a more or less continuing stream
    C) Know-how in creating and operating a system for filling customer orders accurately and swiftly
    D) Being more vertically integrated than rivals
    E) The capability to get newly developed products to the marketplace within a relatively short period of time

    Answer: D Difficulty: Easy

32. A distinctive competence
    A) is something a company does especially well in comparison to its competitors.
    B) represents a competitively superior company resource.
    C) is a basis for building competitive advantage.
    D) holds potential for being the cornerstone of a company's strategy.
    E) All of the above.

    Answer: E Difficulty: Easy

33. A company competence becomes a meaningful "competitive capability" when
   A) it helps differentiate a company from its competitors, customers deem the competence valuable and beneficial, and it enhances a company's competitiveness.
   B) it cannot be copied by rivals except at considerable expense and over a period of several years of trying.
   C) it is competitively superior to the resource strengths of rivals.
   D) it is not easily trumped by the different resources/capabilities of rivals.
   E) All of these.

   Answer: A Difficulty: Medium

34. For a particular company resource/capability to qualify as a basis for competitive advantage, it should
   A) be hard for competitors to copy.
   B) be durable and long-lasting (not lose its value quickly because of new developments).
   C) really be competitively superior to the essentially equivalent type of resource/capability of rivals.
   D) not be easily trumped by the different resources/capabilities of rivals.
   E) All of these.

   Answer: E Difficulty: Easy

35. For a particular company resource/capability to qualify as a basis for competitive advantage, it should
   A) be hard for competitors to copy, be durable and long-lasting, and not be easily trumped by the different resources/capabilities of rivals.
   B) be something that a company does internally rather than in collaborative arrangements with outsiders.
   C) be patentable.
   D) be an industry key success factor and occupy a prime position in the company's value chain.
   E) All of these.

   Answer: A Difficulty: Easy

36. Which one of the following is not a condition for a particular company resource to qualify as a basis for competitive advantage?
   A) Be hard for competitors to copy.
   B) Provide avenues for enhancing a company's image in product innovation and product quality.
   C) Be durable and long-lasting (not lose its value quickly because of new developments).
   D) Really be competitively superior to the comparable resources/capabilities possessed by rivals.
   E) Not be easily trumped by the different resources/capabilities of rivals.

   Answer: B Difficulty: Medium

37. If a company doesn't possess a competitively superior resource,
    A) it may still derive considerable competitive vitality, even competitive advantage, if it has a collection of adequate to good resources which, in combination, have competitive power in the marketplace.
    B) it is unlikely to survive in the marketplace and should exit the industry.
    C) all potential for competitive advantage is lost.
    D) it is virtually blockaded from using offensive strategies and must resort to relying on defensive strategies.
    E) its best strategic option is to revise its value chain in hopes of creating a better match with its resources.

    Answer: A Difficulty: Medium

38. A company's strategy should
    A) be tailored to fit its resource capabilities, taking both its resource strengths and its resource deficiencies into account.
    B) be aimed at those market opportunities that offer potential for profitable growth and competitive advantage.
    C) be built around exploiting and leveraging company resources and capabilities.
    D) generally not place heavy demands on value chain activities where company resources are weak or unproven.
    E) All of these.

    Answer: E Difficulty: Medium

Company Opportunities and Threats

39. The external opportunities which are <u>most</u> significant to a company are the ones which
    A) increase market share.
    B) reinforce its overall business strategy.
    C) offer important avenues for profitable growth, have the potential to achieve competitive advantage, and match up well with the firm's financial resources and competitive capabilities.
    D) correct its internal weaknesses and resource deficiencies.
    E) help defend against the external threats to its well-being.

    Answer: C Difficulty: Medium

40. The industry opportunities most relevant to a particular company are those that
    A) offer important avenues for profitable growth.
    B) provide a strong defense against industry threats and help promote greater diversification.
    C) hold the most potential for the company to build sustainable competitive advantage.
    D) provide avenues for taking market share away from close rivals and enhance a company's image as a leader in product innovation and product quality.
    E) Both A and C.

    Answer: E Difficulty: Medium

41. The industry opportunities most relevant to a particular company are those that
    A) offer important avenues for profitable growth, are well-suited to a company's resource capabilities, and hold the most potential to build competitive advantage.
    B) provide a strong defense against industry threats and help promote greater diversification of revenues and profits.
    C) hold the most potential for the company to be a first mover.
    D) provide avenues for taking market share away from close rivals and enhance a company's image as a leader in product innovation and product quality.
    E) offset a company's biggest weaknesses and offer the company a chance to raise entry barriers.

    Answer: A Difficulty: Medium

42. Which of the following is not an example of an external threat to a company's future profitability?
    A) The lack of a distinctive competence
    B) New legislation that entails burdensome and costly government regulations
    C) Shifts in consumer lifestyles and buyer preferences away from using the industry's product to using alternative products instead
    D) The entry of powerful new competitors into the company's primary markets
    E) The emergence of new technologies that could erode demand for the industry's and the company's product

    Answer: A Difficulty: Easy

43. Which of the following is not an example of an external threat to a company's well-being?
    A) The threat of a hostile takeover
    B) The lack of a well-known brand name with which to attract new customers and help retain existing customers
    C) Shifts in consumer lifestyles and buyer preferences away from using the industry's product to using alternative products instead
    D) The potential for political upheaval in foreign countries where the company has facilities
    E) Growing bargaining power on the part of the company major customers and major suppliers

    Answer: B Difficulty: Easy

44. Tailoring strategy to a company's external opportunities and threats entails
    A) pursuing market opportunities well-suited to the company's resources and capabilities.
    B) building a resource base that helps defend against external threats to the company's business.
    C) catering to the needs and preferences of long-time, loyal buyers
    D) trying to insulate the enterprise from the five competitive forces and from the industry's driving forces
    E) Both A and B.

    Answer: E Difficulty: Hard

Value Chains, Strategic Cost Analysis, Benchmarking

45. Disparities in costs among rival competitors can arise from differences in:
    A) prices paid for raw materials.
    B) marketing costs such as advertising expenditures.
    C) rival firms' exposure to inflation and changes in foreign exchange rates.
    D) basic technology and the age of plants and equipment.
    E) All of these

    Answer: E Difficulty: Easy

46. A company's value chain concerns
    A) the market value of its competitive assets and the extent to which this value can be transferred to shareholders on a tax-free basis.
    B) the primary activities it performs in creating customer value and the related support activities.
    C) how many steps it takes to get a product from the raw materials stage into the hands of end-users.
    D) the activities it performs in creating and developing its distinctive competencies.
    E) the manner in which it seeks to create and enhance shareholder value.

    Answer: B Difficulty: Medium

47. A company's value chain
    A) shows the linked set of primary and support activities it performs in the course of trying to create a profit and deliver value to shareholders in the form of higher dividends and a higher stock price.
    B) depicts the internally performed activities associated with creating and enhancing the company's competitive assets.
    C) shows the linked set of primary and support activities it performs in the course of trying to deliver value to its customers.
    D) concerns the basic process the company goes through in performing R&D and developing new products.
    E) shows all of the costs it incurs in manufacturing and distributing its products or services and whether the price it charges is sufficient to cover these costs and earn a profit.

    Answer: C Difficulty: Medium

48. Value chain analysis
    A) is a tool for identifying how a firm's internal operating costs compare with the averages of the costs of other firms in the industry for each of several production activities.
    B) helps identify an industry's key success factors.
    C) indicates whether it is more advantageous to pursue a differentiation strategy or to strive for low-cost leadership.
    D) is a tool for identifying the separate activities, functions, and business processes that a company performs in designing, producing, marketing, distributing, and supporting a product or service.
    E) is a tool for helps managers ascertain whether the company is doing a good job of building shareholder value through the internal activities it performs.

    Answer: D Difficulty: Medium

49. The relative cost positions of industry rivals can vary substantially because of
    A) differences in basic technology, the age of plants and equipment, and wages paid to labor.
    B) learning and experience curve effects.
    C) differences in rival firms' exposure to rates of inflation and changes in foreign exchange rates.
    D) differences in marketing costs, sales and promotion expenditures, and advertising expenses.
    E) All of these.

    Answer: E Difficulty: Easy

50. One of the most telling signs of whether a company's market position is strong or precarious is
    A) whether its product is strongly or weakly differentiated from rivals.
    B) whether its prices and costs are competitive with rivals.
    C) the size of its market share relative to rivals, particularly the industry leaders.
    D) the opinions of buyers regarding which seller has the best product quality and customer service.
    E) whether it has few or many strategic issues and problems that need to be addressed.

    Answer: B Difficulty: Medium

51. The primary analytic tool of strategic cost analysis is
    A) benchmarking.
    B) a value chain identifying the activities, functions, and business processes that have to be performed in designing, producing, marketing, distributing, and supporting a product or service.
    C) activity-based costing.
    D) a cost chain that separates the variable cost drivers from the fixed cost drivers.
    E) cost-driver analysis.

    Answer: B Difficulty: Medium

52. The key part and also the hardest part of strategic cost analysis is
    A) laying out a complete set of cost projections for the next three years to see how future costs are going to change.
    B) learning how the company's costs for various value chain activities compare with the estimated costs of competitors for these same activities.
    C) linking the company's cost projections with industry cost projections.
    D) determining where the company is on the experience curve as compared to competitors.
    E) determining which of a company's value chain activities is performed most efficiently and thus holds potential for gaining a cost advantage over rival companies.

    Answer: B Difficulty: Hard

53. Strategic cost analysis focuses on
    A) comparisons of the costs of different types of competitive strategies.
    B) the make-up of a firm's cost structure (all the way from the inception of raw materials and components production to the price paid by ultimate end-users) as compared to the costs of its rivals.
    C) the cost advantages of forward vertical integration as compared to backward vertical integration.
    D) how to achieve the position of being the low-cost producer in the industry.
    E) benchmarking the costs of purchasing needed items from alternative suppliers, so as to keep the firm's materials and components costs below those of competitors.

    Answer: B Difficulty: Medium

54. Strategic cost analysis focuses on
    A) identifying which competitor is the industry's low-cost producer and learning how the low-cost leader achieved its low cost position.
    B) the make-up of a firm's cost structure (all the way from the inception of raw materials and components production to the price paid by ultimate end-users).
    C) determining the cost of each element of the company's strategy so that management can make informed decisions about which parts of the company's strategy are cost effective and which are not.
    D) comparing how a company's unit costs stack up against the unit costs of key competitors activity by activity, thereby pinpointing which internal activities are a source of cost advantage or disadvantage.
    E) determining the costs of different types of competitive strategies so that management will be in position to choose the most cost-effective strategy.

    Answer: D Difficulty: Hard

55. Strategic cost analysis and the construction of value chains can add much to the picture of a company's strategic situation, particularly as concerns
    A) who has the best strategy.
    B) who is gaining market share at the expense of which rivals.
    C) what kind of competitive advantage is strongest.
    D) whether the company has a cost advantage/disadvantage vis-à-vis major competitors and which activities in the value chain are the source of the cost advantage or disadvantage.
    E) the costs of different types of competitive strategies which management is considering.

    Answer: D Difficulty: Medium

56. Accurately assessing a company's cost competitiveness in end-use markets requires
    A) a full understanding of the costs of different types of competitive strategies which management is considering.
    B) knowledge of how the costs of a company's competitive strategy compare against the costs of the competitive strategies employed by rival firms.
    C) knowledge of the costs of internally performed activities and also costs in the value chains of both suppliers and forward channel allies plus knowledge of how all these costs compare against the costs that make up the value chain systems employed by rival firms.
    D) careful study of the experience curve and economy-of-scale segments across the entire industry value chain.
    E) a full understanding of the costs of each piece of a company's competitive strategy.

    Answer: C Difficulty: Hard

57. Benchmarking concerns
   A) doing cross-company comparisons of how basic functions and processes in the value chain are performed and comparing the costs of these activities.
   B) checking how many of the company's objectives have been achieved and determining the sizes of the variances above or below the targeted performance level.
   C) studying how a company's resource strengths stack up against the resource strengths of rival companies.
   D) studying how a company's competitive capabilities stack up against the competitive capabilities of selected companies known to have world class competitive capabilities.
   E) None of the above accurately describe what benchmarking is about.

   Answer: A   Difficulty: Medium

58. Benchmarking
   A) is inherently unethical because it involves snooping around to learn what competitors' costs are.
   B) can be ethical if certain practices are dutifully observed.
   C) is ethical only if it is done entirely by disinterested third parties and with the full concurrence of all the companies involved.
   D) is seldom done by most firms because of the borderline ethical considerations which it involves abilities.
   E) is a good concept in theory but is rarely undertaken in the real world because of the difficulties in getting all of the needed data and information.

   Answer: B   Difficulty: Medium

59. The three main areas in the value chain where significant differences in relative costs of competing firms can occur include
   A) age of plants and equipment, number of employees, and advertising costs.
   B) operating-level activities, functional area activities, and line of business activities.
   C) supplier-related activities, manufacturing-related activities, wholesale distribution and retailing activities.
   D) human resource activities (particularly labor costs), vertical integration activities, and diversification activities.
   E) variable cost activities, fixed cost activities, and support activities.

   Answer: C   Difficulty: Hard

60. The options for attacking cost disadvantages in the distribution portion of the industry value chain include
   A) shifting to a more economical distribution strategy, including the possibility of forward integration.
   B) trying to make up the difference by initiating cost savings earlier in the value chain.
   C) pushing for more favorable terms with distributors and other forward channel allies.
   D) All of these.
   E) None of these; the most effective option is to shift to a new strategy and to cut price to offset the cost disadvantage.

   Answer: D   Difficulty: Medium

61. The options for attacking the high costs of items purchased from suppliers include
    A) trying to negotiate more favorable supply prices and/or switching to lower priced substitute inputs.
    B) pursuing horizontal integration and/or forward vertical integration.
    C) shifting into the production of substitute products and/or from a low-cost leadership strategy to a differentiation or focus strategy.
    D) cutting product quality and trying to detour the cost disadvantage by cutting selling prices and win a bigger market share.
    E) shifting to a best-cost provider or a low-cost leader strategy.

    Answer: A   Difficulty: Easy

62. The options for attacking the high costs within a company's own portion of the industry value chain include
    A) investing in cost-saving technology and productivity-enhancing equipment.
    B) redesign of the product.
    C) forward and/or backward vertical integration to capture cost savings.
    D) initiating cost-savings in externally-performed value chain activities.
    E) All of these.

    Answer: E   Difficulty: Medium

63. Which of the following are options for attacking the high costs of items purchased from suppliers?
    A) Pursue backward integration to manage the costs of items purchased from suppliers downward
    B) Negotiate for better prices from suppliers
    C) Decrease the quality of the components being purchased
    D) To compensate, seek out cost savings in other parts of the overall cost chain
    E) All of the above are possible options

    Answer: E   Difficulty: Medium

64. A company's best and most logical strategic options for attacking cost disadvantages in the forward portion of the industry value chain include
    A) changing to a more economical distribution strategy, including the possibility of forward vertical integration.
    B) pursuing backward vertical integration.
    C) boosting the productivity of company employees and replacing aging equipment with state-of-the-art equipment.
    D) using lower-priced parts and components to overcome the distribution cost disadvantage.
    E) collaborating more closely with suppliers to reduce the costs of purchased supplies.

    Answer: A   Difficulty: Medium

65. Determining whether a company's prices and costs are competitive
    A) requires looking at the activities and costs of competitively relevant suppliers and forward channel allies(distributors/dealers), as well as the costs of internally performed activities.
    B) is best indicated by comparing a company's costs activity by activity against the costs of key rivals, so as to learn which value chain activities are a source of cost advantage or disadvantage.
    C) is best indicated by comparing the number of activities in a company's value chain against the number of activities in the value chains of key rivals.
    D) requires (1) using activity-based costing to determine whether the costs of a company's fixed cost activities, variable cost activities, overhead activities, and managerial activities are above or below these same activities of close rivals and (2) comparing whether buyers pay more for the company's product than they do for rivals' products.
    E) involves the use of activity-based costing to determine which value chain activities are the major cost drivers and which are the minor cost drivers.

    Answer: B Difficulty: Hard

66. Activity-based costing
    A) entails breaking down the broad categories of traditional accounting expenses (employee compensation and benefits, purchased supplies, depreciation, R&D, maintenance, and so on) into the costs of performing each of the specific primary and support activities in the company's value chain.
    B) involves using benchmarking techniques to develop cost estimates for each value chain activity for each major rival.
    C) is a powerful tool for determining a company's value chain and separating primary activities from support activities.
    D) involves determining which value chain activities are the major cost drivers and which are the minor cost drivers.
    E) is a tool for identifying the activities that cause a company's product to be strongly differentiated from the products of rivals.

    Answer: A Difficulty: Medium

67. Which of the following is not one of the objectives of benchmarking?
    A) To understand the best practices in performing an activity
    B) To learn how best practice companies achieve lower costs
    C) To help construct an industry value chain
    D) To develop cross-company comparisons of the costs of performing specific activities
    E) To take actions to improve a company's cost competitiveness when benchmarking reveals that its costs of performing an activity are out of line with what other companies have achieved

    Answer: C Difficulty: Medium

68. A manager's best tool for determining whether a company is performing particular functions or activities in a cost-effective manner is
    A) value chain analysis.
    B) activity-based costing.
    C) cost driver analysis.
    D) economy-of-scale and experience curve analysis.
    E) benchmarking.

    Answer: E Difficulty: Medium

69. Creating competitively valuable capabilities typically involves
    A) integrating the knowledge and skills of individual employees.
    B) leveraging the economies of learning and experience.
    C) effectively coordinating related value chain activities in ways that lower costs or produce greater flexibility or reduce response times.
    D) exerting efforts to develop dominating expertise over rivals in performing one or more value chain activities critical to customer satisfaction and market success.
    E) All of these.

    Answer: E Difficulty: Medium

70. Developing the skills, competencies, and capabilities to perform competitively crucial value chain activities better than competitors
    A) is one of the most dependable ways for a company to build sustainable competitive advantage.
    B) helps neutralize the impact of the five competitive forces.
    C) is one of the best ways for a company to counteract the industry's driving forces.
    D) allows a company to move into a higher strategic group.
    E) helps neutralize external threats to a company's well-being.

    Answer: A Difficulty: Medium

71. How well a company manages its value chain activities relative to competitors
    A) determines whether a company is likely to have the capability to move from a disadvantaged strategic group to a more favorably situated strategic group.
    B) is often a key to gaining the resources strengths needed to pursue the industry's most attractive opportunities.
    C) determines the speed with which it can build intellectual capital and achieve a distinctive competence.
    D) is often a key to building valuable competencies and capabilities and leveraging them into competitive advantage.
    E) determines how well it will be able to neutralize the impact of the company's resource weaknesses and competitive liabilities.

    Answer: D Difficulty: Medium

Competitive Strength Assessment

72. The value of doing competitive strength assessment is to
    A) determine how good the company's core competencies are.
    B) learn if the company's opportunities are better than rivals' opportunities.
    C) learn whether a company has more competitive capabilities than key rivals.
    D) learn how the company ranks relative to rivals on each important measure of competitive strength and each industry key success factor and determine whether the company has a net competitive advantage or disadvantage vis-à-vis major rivals.
    E) determine whether a company's resource strengths are sufficient to allow it to earn bigger profits than rivals.

    Answer: D Difficulty: Medium

73. Competitive strength assessment entails
    A) determining how good the company's competitive capabilities are relative to those possessed by key rivals.
    B) ranking the company against major rivals on each important measure of competitive strength and each industry key success factor in order to determine whether the company has a net competitive advantage or disadvantage vis-à-vis major rivals.
    C) analyzing whether a company has more core competencies than key rivals.
    D) analyzing whether the company's strategy is better than rivals' strategies and who has the biggest competitive advantage.
    E) determining whether a company's future profit prospects are better than those of its rivals.

    Answer: B Difficulty: Medium

74. Calculating competitive strength ratings for a company and comparing them against strength ratings for its key competitors helps indicate
    A) which weaknesses and vulnerabilities of competitors that the company might be able to attack successfully.
    B) the net competitive costs of opposing an attack from one of these rival companies.
    C) the strategic intent of major competitors and their capabilities for launching a competitive offensive.
    D) who has the best value chain.
    E) what the industry's key success factors are and what the most relevant indicators of competitive strength are.

    Answer: A Difficulty: Medium

75. A weighted competitive strength assessment is generally analytically superior to an unweighted strength assessment because
    A) a weighted ranking identifies which competitive advantages are most powerful.
    B) an unweighted ranking doesn't discriminate between companies with high and low market shares.
    C) it singles out which competitor has the best core competencies.
    D) with an unweighted rating scheme the competitor with the biggest market share is likely to get the highest competitive strength rating.
    E) all of the various measures of competitive strength are not equally important.

    Answer: E Difficulty: Easy

76. The essence of a competitive strength assessment involves comparing a company with its key rivals on the basis of
   A) who has the best prices and lowest costs.
   B) industry key success factors and telling measures of competitive strength or weakness.
   C) who has the most resource strengths, competencies, and competitive capabilities.
   D) who has the biggest market shares.
   E) who has the best value chain.

   Answer: B   Difficulty: Easy

77. A weighted competitive strength analysis is conceptually stronger than an unweighted analysis because
   A) it provides a more accurate assessment of the strength of competitive forces.
   B) it eliminates the bias introduced for those firms have large market shares.
   C) the different measures of competitive strength are unlikely to be equally important.
   D) the results provide a more reliable measure of what competitive moves rivals are likely to make next.
   E) it provides better analytical balance between the measures of competitive strength and the measures of competitive weakness.

   Answer: C   Difficulty: Medium

78. In a weighted competitive strength analysis, each strength measure is assigned a weight based on
   A) whether the company being rated has a relatively high or low market share.
   B) the importance the measure has in building a sustainable competitive advantage.
   C) its perceived importance in shaping competitive success in the marketplace.
   D) whether the company being rated has a relatively high or low competitive advantage.
   E) what it takes to provide better analytical balance between the companies with high ratings and the companies with low ratings and thus get the sum of the weights to add up to 1.0.

   Answer: C   Difficulty: Medium

79. Calculating competitive strength ratings for rival firms using the industry's most telling measures of competitive strength or weakness
   A) is a way of determining which competitor has the greatest overall competitive advantage in the marketplace and which competitor has the greatest overall competitive disadvantage.
   B) is a technique for benchmarking the industry's competitors from highest to lowest in terms of competitive capability.
   C) is a way of gauging which competitor has the best value chain and overall approach to creating customer value.
   D) is a reliable way of determining which rival has the most valuable distinctive competencies.
   E) helps identify which industry rivals are best able to insulate themselves from the industry's driving forces.

   Answer: A   Difficulty: Medium

Addressing Strategic Issues

80. Identifying the strategic issues that company managers need to address is an important situation analysis component because
    A) without a precise fix on what the issues are, managers are not prepared to start crafting a strategy.
    B) a good strategy must include actions to deal with all the strategic issues that need to be addressed.
    C) it calls for managers to draw upon all the prior analysis of both the internal and external environment, put the company's overall situation in perspective, and get a grip on exactly where they need to focus their attention.
    D) All of these.
    E) None of these, because this is the least important step of situation analysis and can be omitted without great loss of understanding.

    Answer: D Difficulty: Easy

81. Identifying the strategic issues that company managers need to address involves
    A) using the results of both company situation analysis and industry and competitive analysis.
    B) developing a "worry list" of "how to...", "whether to....", and "what to do about....."
    C) locking in on what challenges the company has to overcome in order to be financially and competitively successful in the years ahead.
    D) evaluating whether the company's present strategy will be adequate for protecting and improving the company's market position in light of the industry's competitive forces and driving forces.
    E) All of the above.

    Answer: E Difficulty: Easy

82. Identifying the strategic issues that company managers need to address involves
    A) using the results of industry and competitive analysis.
    B) developing a "worry list" of "how to...", "whether to....", and "what to do about....."
    C) using cost-driver analysis to determine whether the company's costs are competitive with those of key rivals.
    D) using what has been learned from evaluating the company's present strategy, SWOT analysis, and the analysis of the company's competitiveness to help lock in on what challenges the company has to overcome in order to be financially and competitively successful in the years ahead..
    E) All of the above except C.

    Answer: E Difficulty: Medium

Short Answer Questions

83. Identify and briefly discuss the relevance of each of the five questions that form the framework of company situation analysis.

    Difficulty: Medium

84. Briefly discuss the meaning and significance of each of the following terms:
    a.) SWOT analysis
    b.) core competence
    c.) strategic cost analysis
    d.) company value chain
    e.) industry value chain
    f.) a weighted competitive strength assessment
    g.) distinctive competence
    h.) benchmarking
    i.) activity-based costing

    Difficulty: Medium

85. How can one tell whether a company's present strategy is working well?

    Difficulty: Medium

86. What is the value of SWOT analysis?. How does it contribute to the task of crafting strategy?

    Difficulty: Medium

87. What is the difference between a company competence and a core competence? What is the difference between a core competence and a distinctive competence? How do a company's core and distinctive competencies fit into the strategy-making picture?

    Difficulty: Medium

88. Why do rival companies not incur the same costs in producing the same product?

    Difficulty: Medium

89. If a firm is at a cost disadvantage with rivals because its internal costs are higher than rivals, what strategic moves can it make to restore cost parity? Use the concepts of value chain analysis to support your answer.

    Difficulty: Hard

90. Draw a typical company value chain and briefly discuss its analytical value in the strategy-making process.

    Difficulty: Hard

91. Explain how a company develops a competitive capability.

    Difficulty: Hard

92. Explain why a weighted competitive strength assessment is conceptually superior to an unweighted one.

    Difficulty: Medium

93. What is benchmarking and why is it a strategically important analytical tool? Is it ethical? Why or why not?

    Difficulty: Medium

94. The ability of a company to perform competitively crucial value chain activities better than rivals is one of the keys to sustainable competitive advantage. True or False? Explain and defend your answer.

    Difficulty: Medium

95. In determining the various strategic issues that a company needs to address, managers need to consider both the results of industry and competitive analysis and the results of company situation analysis. True or False? Explain and defend your answer.

    Difficulty: Medium

Chapter 5: Strategy and Competitive Advantage

Multiple Choice Questions

Competitive Strategy and Competitive Advantage

1. A company has competitive advantage whenever
    A) it is the acknowledged market share leader.
    B) it is the industry's most active user of offensive strategies.
    C) it has greater financial resources than its rivals.
    D) it has a strong brand name reputation, prefers offensive strategies to defensive strategies, and has a strong balance sheet.
    E) it has an edge over rivals in attracting customers and defending against competitive forces.

    Answer: E   Difficulty: Medium

2. A company can be said to have competitive advantage if
    A) it is the acknowledged market share leader and has greater financial resources than its rivals.
    B) it is the industry's most active user of offensive strategies and earns the largest profits of any firm in the industry.
    C) it has an edge over rivals in attracting customers and defending against competitive forces.
    D) it is not vulnerable to preemptive strikes by rivals and has a stron brand name reputation with which to defend against offensive attacks from challengers.
    E) All of the above are clear signals of competitive advantage.

    Answer: C   Difficulty: Medium

3. A company's competitive strategy is best described as
    A) the business approaches and initiatives it undertakes to attract customers and fulfill their expectations, to withstand competitive pressures, and to strengthen its market position.
    B) the sum of its functional area strategies—its R&D strategy, its production strategy, its sales and marketing strategy, its distribution strategy, and so on.
    C) its collection of offensive and defensive strategies to improve its market position.
    D) the composite of its pricing strategy, its product line strategy, its quality strategy, its customer service strategy, and its advertising strategy.
    E) the combination of actions it employs to outmaneuver its rivals in the marketplace.

    Answer: A   Difficulty: Medium

4. The heart and soul of building competitive advantage entails
    A) building a brand name image that buyers trust.
    B) delivering superior value to buyers and building competencies and resource strengths in performing value chain activities that rivals cannot readily match.
    C) erecting a defense capable of warding off the strategic offensives of challenger firms.
    D) finding effective and efficient ways to improve the company's market position.
    E) being the industry's most active user of clever and fresh offensive strategies.

    Answer: B   Difficulty: Medium

5. The appeal of a competitive advantage is that it enables a company to
   A) charge a premium price for its product/service.
   B) better cope with competitive forces, enjoy an edge over rivals in attracting customers, and enhance its profitability.
   C) become the market share leader.
   D) boost customer loyalty.
   E) have the best reputation and brand image in the industry.

   Answer: B   Difficulty: Medium

Generic Competitive Strategies

6. Which of the following is not one of the generic types of competitive strategy?
   A) A low-cost leadership strategy
   B) A broad differentiation strategy
   C) A best-cost provider strategy
   D) Focused low-cost
   E) Market share leadership

   Answer: E   Difficulty: Easy

7. The generic types of competitive strategies include
   A) build market share, maintain market share, and slowly surrender market share.
   B) be the dominant leader, be a content follower, and aggressively overhaul and reposition.
   C) low-cost leadership, broad differentiation, best-cost provider, focused low-cost, and focused differentiation.
   D) single-business concentration, vertical integration, and diversification.
   E) a price leader strategy, a price follower strategy, a technology leader strategy, a technology follower strategy, and a middle-of-the-road strategy.

   Answer: C   Difficulty: Medium

Low-Cost Provider Strategies

8. A low-cost leader's basis for competitive advantage is
   A) lower prices than rival firms.
   B) using a low cost/low price approach to gain the biggest market share.
   C) high buyer switching costs.
   D) lower overall costs than competitors.
   E) a well-known reputation among buyers for charging the best prices in the industry.

   Answer: D   Difficulty: Medium

9. How valuable a low-cost leader's cost advantage is depends on
   A) its sustainability.
   B) the leader's ability to convert the cost advantage into gaining the biggest market share.
   C) the leader's ability to convert the cost advantage into the absolute lowest possible costs.
   D) the leader's ability to combine the cost advantage with a reputation for good quality.
   E) the leader's ability to convert the cost advantage into a well-known reputation among buyers for charging the lowest prices in the industry.

   Answer: A   Difficulty: Medium

10. A low-cost leader can achieve superior profit performance by
    A) using the low-cost edge to underprice competitors and attract price sensitive buyers in large enough numbers to increase total profits.
    B) refraining from price-cutting and use the low-cost advantage to earn a bigger profit margin on each unit sold.
    C) going all out to use its cost advantage to capture a dominant share of the market.
    D) spending heavily on advertising to promote its cost advantage and the fact the it charges the lowest prices in the industry—it can then use this reputation for low prices to build very strong customer loyalty, gain repeat sales year after year, and earn sustained profits over the long-term.
    E) Both A and B.

    Answer: E   Difficulty: Medium

11. The basic approaches to achieving a cost advantage include
    A) revamping the firm's value chain to bypass some cost—producing activities altogether—usually eliminating activities that produce little value added insofar as customers are concerned and/or doing a better job than competitors of performing value chain activities efficiently and of managing the cost-drivers.
    B) pursuing both backward and forward integration so as to maximize scale economies and gain full control of the cost-drivers across the entire industry value chain.
    C) being a first-mover in adopting the latest state-of-the-art technologies, especially those relating to the Internet and e-commerce business approaches.
    D) using offensive strategies to retaliate against rivals that attempt to imitate the firm's own cost-saving moves.
    E) All of these.

    Answer: A   Difficulty: Medium

12. A competitive strategy of striving to be the low-cost provider is particularly attractive when
    A) buyers are not very price sensitive.
    B) most rivals are trying to be best-cost providers.
    C) there are many ways to achieve product differentiation that have value to buyers.
    D) buyers are large, have significant power to bargain down prices, use the product in the same ways, and have common user requirements.
    E) most rivals are pursuing focused low-cost or focused differentiation strategies.

    Answer: D   Difficulty: Medium

13. Which of the following is not a "cost-driver" that a company can manage to help achieve a low-cost advantage?
    A) Value chain activities that present opportunities for scale economies
    B) Shifting away from use of distributors and dealers as a way to access buyers and, instead, pursuing a sell-direct distribution approach—thereby economizing on distribution-related costs
    C) The percentage of capacity utilization
    D) The cost of key resource inputs
    E) Performing linked value chain activities in a cooperative and coordinative fashion

    Answer: B Difficulty: Hard

14. Which of the following is not a way that companies can achieve a low-cost advantage by reconfiguring the makeup of their value chains?
    A) Pursuing backward or forward integration to detour suppliers or buyers with considerable bargaining power and leverage
    B) Shifting to e-business technologies
    C) Simplifying product designs and stripping away frills and extras
    D) Reengineering core business processes
    E) Focusing on a limited product line to eliminate costs and activities associated with many product versions and/or shifting to an economical manufacturing process that accommodates efficient build-to-order product customization

    Answer: A Difficulty: Medium

15. Which of the following is not one of the primary ways to achieve cost advantage by reconfiguring the make-up of the value chain?
    A) Reengineering core business processes to cut out needless steps and low value-added activities
    B) Lowering the specifications for purchased materials and bargaining hard with suppliers for lower prices on purchased parts and components
    C) Shifting to e-business technologies
    D) Simplfying the product design and/or shifting to a more streamlined technological and manufacturing process
    E) Finding ways to bypass the use of raw materials or components that are costly

    Answer: B Difficulty: Hard

16. A strategy to be the industry's overall low-cost provider tends to work best when
    A) there are many differences among the various buyers and buyer segments regarding the product attributes that meet their requirements and expectations.
    B) there are many market segments and market niches, such that it is feasible for a low-cost leader to dominate the niche where buyers want a budget-priced product.
    C) price competition is especially vigorous and the offerings of rival firms are essentially identical, standardized, commodity-like products.
    D) most rivals are employing differentiation, focused, or best-cost provider strategies—such that company can more easily be a standout as a low-cost leader.
    E) the bargaining power of both suppliers and buyers is strong, entry barriers are low, and there is considerable diversity in how buyers use the product.

    Answer: C Difficulty: Medium

17. In which of the following circumstances is a strategy to be the industry's overall low-cost provider <u>not</u> particularly well matched to the market situation?
    A) When the offerings of rival firms are essentially identical, standardized, commodity-like products
    B) When there are few ways to achieve differentiation that have value to buyers
    C) When price competition is especially vigorous
    D) When buyers have high switching costs because of their of their special needs and requirements
    E) When entry barriers are low and industry newcomers are active in using the appeal of low prices to attract buyers and build a customer base

    Answer: D Difficulty: Medium

18. A strategy to be the industry's overall low-cost provider tends to be more appealing than a differentiation or best-cost or focus/market niche strategy when
    A) there are many ways to achieve product differentiation that buyer find appealing.
    B) buyer use the product in a variety of different ways and have high switching costs in changing from one seller's product to another.
    C) the offerings of rival firms are essentially identical, standardized, commodity-like products.
    D) entry barriers are high, competition from substitutes is relatively weak, and the market is comprised of many distinct segments with varying buyer needs and expectations.
    E) the bargaining power of both suppliers and buyers is strong.

    Answer: C Difficulty: Medium

19. Successful low-cost providers
    A) typically have cost-conscious corporate cultures featuring broad employee participation in continuous cost improvement efforts and are committed to ongoing efforts to benchmark costs against best-in-class performers of an activity.
    B) usually are the industry leaders in market share and profitability.
    C) generally achieve their cost advantage by revamping their value chains rather than by controlling the cost drivers.
    D) prefer offensive strategies to defensive strategies and usually are the most profitable firms in their industry.
    E) All of these.

    Answer: A Difficulty: Easy

20. An industry's lowest-cost provider is in a better position than rivals to
    A) defend itself against the pressures imposed by competition from substitute products.
    B) compete on the basis of low price and to defend itself in price wars.
    C) earn the highest profits of any company in the industry.
    D) protect itself against the negative impacts of the industry's driving forces.
    E) win the biggest market share (because of its ability to underprice rivals).

    Answer: B Difficulty: Medium

21. A low-cost provider strategy can defeat a differentiation strategy
   A) when buyers are pretty much satisfied with a standard product and do not see extra product attributes as worth paying extra money to obtain.
   B) when buyer switching costs are high, most buyers have moderate to weak bargaining power, and buyers are looking for a good-to-excellent product at a bargain price.
   C) if differentiators ignore the need to signal value and depend only on the "real" bases of differentiation.
   D) when entry barriers are low, no close rivals are pursuing a low-cost provider strategy, and buyers have only moderate expectations regarding product durability and the seller's after-the-sale service capabilities.
   E) when technology is advancing rapidly and new product generations are introduced several times a year.

   Answer: A Difficulty: Hard

22. A low-cost leadership strategy tends to be more successful when
   A) the industry's product is a standardized commodity.
   B) buyers are looking for a good-to-excellent product at a bargain price.
   C) the industry is composed of more than three strategic groups, at least one of which is pursuing full vertical integration.
   D) entry barriers are low and substitute products are making strong market inroads.
   E) key suppliers have substantial bargaining power.

   Answer: A Difficulty: Hard

23. Achieving a cost advantage over rivals entails
   A) concentrating on a narrow portion of the value chain and abandoning all other activities that create costs.
   B) being a first-mover in pursuing backward and forward integration and controlling as much of the value chain as possible.
   C) outmanaging rivals in controlling the cost drivers and finding creative ways to cut cost-producing activities out of the value chain.
   D) being a heavy user of offensive strategies and a light user of defensive strategies.
   E) producing a standard product, redesigning the product infrequently, and having minimal advertising.

   Answer: C Difficulty: Medium

24. If an organization is successful in achieving low-cost producer status in its respective industry, this means
   A) it will be able to sell more of its product/service than its key competitors and be the market share leader.
   B) it has achieved lower overall per unit costs for its product/service than its competitors.
   C) it has lower total costs on its income statement than do its competitors.
   D) it will be able to earn a higher rate of return on investment than its competitors.
   E) it will earn greater total profits than any of its rivals.

   Answer: B Difficulty: Easy

25. The products of a company pursuing a low-cost leadership strategy would likely
    A) be designed with good-to-excellent attributes so as to provide customers with more value for the money.
    B) incorporate a good basic design with few frills, acceptable quality, and a limited number of models/styles to select from.
    C) include many product variations and wide selection and be of average or better quality.
    D) emphasize a few chosen differentiating features to help set off its image with buyers.
    E) be customized to fit the specialized needs of the company's target group of customers.

    Answer: B Difficulty: Medium

26. Being the overall low-cost producer in an industry has the attractive advantage of
    A) guaranteeing that the company will have the biggest competitive edge of any firm in the industry because its customers will have high switching costs.
    B) ensuring that the firm will earn the largest profits of any firm in the industry.
    C) putting a firm in position to compete offensively on the basis of low price and to defend against price war conditions should they arise.
    D) giving the firm's product the most buyer appeal.
    E) blocking the entry of new firms into the industry.

    Answer: C Difficulty: Medium

27. Being the low-cost provider in an industry
    A) gives a company ability to wield heavy influence in setting the industry's price floor.
    B) helps protect profit margins against the bargaining of powerful customers for lower prices.
    C) makes it harder for a new entrant to take away customers.
    D) provides a defense against the attempts of substitutes to gain a market inroad.
    E) All of these.

    Answer: E Difficulty: Easy

28. Which of the following is not one of the pitfalls of a low-cost provider strategy?
    A) Overly aggressive price-cutting
    B) Trying to set the industry's price ceiling
    C) Not emphasizing avenues of cost advantage that can be kept proprietary
    D) Becoming too fixated on cost reduction
    E) Having the basis for the firm's cost advantage undermined by cost-saving technological breakthroughs that can be readily adopted by rival firms

    Answer: B Difficulty: Easy

Differentiation Strategies

29. To be successful with a differentiation strategy, a company has to
    A) study buyer needs and behavior very carefully to learn what buyers consider as important, what they think has value, and what they are willing to pay for.
    B) incorporate a greater number of differentiating features into its product/service than rivals.
    C) strive to raise buyer switching costs.
    D) outspend rivals on advertising and promotion in order to inform and convince buyers of the value of its differentiating attributes.
    E) concentrate on providing a top-of-the-line product to consumers.

    Answer: A   Difficulty: Medium

30. Broad differentiation strategies are well-suited for market situations where
    A) there are many ways to differentiate the product or service and these differences are perceived by some buyers to have value.
    B) most buyers use the product in the same ways and have common user requirements.
    C) buyers are susceptible to clever advertising and have low switching costs.
    D) barriers to entry are high and suppliers have a low degree of bargaining power.
    E) price competition is especially vigorous.

    Answer: A   Difficulty: Hard

31. Differentiation strategies are an attractive competitive approach whenever
    A) buyer needs and preferences are too diverse to be fully satisfied by a standardized product or by sellers with identical capabilities.
    B) most buyers use the product in the same ways and have common user requirements.
    C) buyers have low switching costs and are adamant about a product meeting their expectations regarding quality and durability.
    D) barriers to entry are high, suppliers have a low degree of bargaining power, and price competition is especially vigorous.
    E) buyer switching costs are low, entry barriers are low, few rivals have a strong brand name reputation, and the industry's products are weakly differentiated.

    Answer: A   Difficulty: Hard

32. The price premium commanded by a broad differentiation strategy is
    A) a function of the difference between the actual value to the buyer and the buyer's perceived value.
    B) a reflection of the value actually delivered to the buyer and the value perceived by the buyer (even if not actually delivered).
    C) dependent upon whether the seller does a good job of signaling value through packaging, offering a wide selection of premium accessories, and promoting use of the product by prestigious buyers.
    D) dependent on how frequently buyers repurchase the product and whether they are sophisticated or unsophisticated.
    E) dependent on whether buyers are easily swayed by clever advertising into paying more for a product than it is really worth.

    Answer: B   Difficulty: Hard

33. A differentiation-based competitive advantage
    A) nearly always is attached to quality and service aspects.
    B) generally results from especially effective marketing and advertising.
    C) requires developing a distinctive competence that buyers consider valuable.
    D) requires an ability to develop product features that will command the biggest price premium in the industry.
    E) usually is linked to product innovation, technological superiority, product quality and reliability, comprehensive customer service, and/or unique competitive capabilities.

    Answer: E   Difficulty: Hard

34. The ways a product's value is signaled to buyers can be as important as actual value when
    A) the differences between rival brands are readily visible and objectively measured.
    B) buyers are making their first-time purchases, repurchase is infrequent, and the nature of the differentiation is subjective and hard to quantify.
    C) repurchase is frequent, buyers are experienced in using the product, and buyer switching costs are high.
    D) buyers are sophisticated and shop hard for the best product for the money.
    E) buyers have very little bargaining power, low switching costs, and purchase the product infrequently.

    Answer: B   Difficulty: Hard

35. Successful differentiation allows a firm to
    A) have the best value chain in the industry.
    B) command a premium price for its product and/or increase unit sales (because of the attraction of its differentiating product attributes and/or gain buyer loyalty to its brand.
    C) outcompete firms using any other strategy and to become the acknowledged industry leader.
    D) set the ceiling on the price that rival firms can charge and still retain their customers.
    E) All of the above.

    Answer: B   Difficulty: Hard

36. Differentiation enhances a company's total profits whenever
    A) additional buyers are won over by the differentiating product attributes.
    B) the company has more differentiating attributes than any other rival pursuing a differentiation strategy.
    C) the extra price the product commands outweighs the added costs of achieving the differentiation and unit sales increase.
    D) buyer loyalty to the brand is enhanced (because buyers are strongly attracted to the differentiating features and bond with the company and its product).
    E) it is difficult for rivals to copy the differentiating features.

    Answer: C   Difficulty: Hard

37. The key to a profitable differentiation strategy is
    A) to make the nature of the differentiation subjective and hard to quantify and to concentrate on those market segments where buyer repurchase is infrequent.
    B) differentiating on the basis of product attributes and features that are not available to a best-cost producer.
    C) making sure that the differentiating features appeal to sophisticated and prestigious buyers.
    D) to keep the costs of differentiating below the price premium that the differentiation approach commands and to incorporate differentiating features that boost unit sales.
    E) preventing rivals from imitating the differentiating features by raising buyer switching costs.

    Answer: D   Difficulty: Hard

38. Using a broad differentiation strategy to produce an attractive competitive advantage is least likely to be based on
    A) developing a superior performing product.
    B) offering buyers a product which is superior in quality and reliability as compared to rivals' brands.
    C) giving consumers comprehensive support services.
    D) providing buyers with a continuing stream of better-designed, better-performing, and more stylish products.
    E) charging a lower price than rivals.

    Answer: E   Difficulty: Easy

39. The production emphasis of a company pursuing a broad differentiation strategy usually involves
    A) a search for continuous cost reduction without sacrificing acceptable quality and essential features.
    B) strong efforts to be a leader in manufacturing process innovation.
    C) above-average expenditures for new product R&D and efforts to build-in whatever features that buyers are willing to pay for.
    D) aggressive pursuit of economies of scale and experience curve effects.
    E) developing a distinctive competence in zero-defect manufacturing techniques.

    Answer: C   Difficulty: Medium

40. The marketing emphasis of a company pursuing a broad differentiation strategy usually is
    A) to underprice rival brands with comparable features.
    B) to charge a premium price to more than cover the extra costs of differentiating features.
    C) to out-advertise rivals.
    D) to emphasize differentiating features that are inexpensive to incorporate.
    E) to communicate the product's ability to serve the customer's every need.

    Answer: B   Difficulty: Medium

41. A differentiation strategy is more likely to result in competitive advantage when the approaches to differentiation
    A) are based on features and capabilities that are hard or expensive for rivals to copy.
    B) are based on product attributes rather than a company's unique skills, competencies, and capabilities.
    C) incorporate product features which clever ads can promote as being highly virtuous or desirable.
    D) are not costly to incorporate.
    E) will be especially attractive to upscale buyers.

    Answer: A   Difficulty: Medium

42. A differentiation strategy works best in situations where
    A) there are many ways to differentiate a product or service that are perceived by buyers to have value.
    B) buyer needs and uses of the product are very similar.
    C) buyers have strong brand loyalty and low switching costs.
    D) barriers to entry are low and buyers have a low degree of bargaining power.
    E) price competition is especially vigorous.

    Answer: A   Difficulty: Medium

43. Achieving a differentiation-based competitive advantage typically involves
    A) incorporating product attributes and user features that lower a buyer's overall cost of using the product.
    B) incorporating features that raise the performance a buyer gets from using the product.
    C) incorporating features that enhance buyer satisfaction in noneconomic or intangible ways.
    D) delivering value to customers via competitive capabilities that rivals don't have or can' afford to match.
    E) All of the above are viable ways of building competitive advantage via differentiation.

    Answer: E   Difficulty: Easy

44. The pitfalls of a differentiation strategy include
    A) trying to differentiate on the basis of attributes or features that do not lower a buyer's costs or oenhance a buyer's well being, as perceived by the buyer.
    B) overdifferentiating so that price is too high relative to competitors or so that the features and attributes incorporated exceed buyer needs and requirements.
    C) trying to charge too high a price premium for the differentiating features.
    D) ignoring the need to signal value.
    E) All of these.

    Answer: E   Difficulty: Medium

45. Which of the following is <u>not</u> a pitfall of pursuing a differentiation strategy?
    A) Trying to strongly differentiate the company's product from those of rivals rather than be content with weak product differentiation
    B) Overdifferentiating so that price is too high relative to competitors or so that the features and attributes incorporated exceed buyer needs and requirements
    C) Trying to charge too high a price premium for the differentiating features
    D) Not understanding or identifying what buyers consider as value
    E) Ignoring the need to signal value

    Answer: A   Difficulty: Medium

Best-Cost Provider Strategies

46. A firm pursuing a best-cost provider strategy
    A) seeks to be the low-cost provider in the largest and fastest growing (or best) market segment.
    B) tries to have the best cost (as compared to rivals) for each activity in the industry's value chain.
    C) tries to outcompete a low-cost provider by attracting buyers on the basis of charging the best price.
    D) combines a strategic emphasis on low cost with a strategic emphasis on more than minimally acceptable product attributes (quality, service, features, performance) and aims at giving customers more value for the money.
    E) can generally outcompete companies pursuing differentiation strategies by charging a lower price.

    Answer: D   Difficulty: Medium

47. Best-cost provider strategies
    A) deliver superior value to buyers by having the best cost (as compared to rivals) for each activity in the industry's value chain.
    B) are an attractive way to outcompete companies pursuing focused and broad differentiation strategies because a best-cost provider is in position to charge a lower price.
    C) seek to attract buyers on the basis of charging the best price.
    D) aim at giving customers more value for the money.
    E) deliver superior value to buyers by offering them the lowest switching costs.

    Answer: D   Difficulty: Medium

48. Best-cost provider strategies are appealing in those market situations where
    A) buyer diversity makes product differentiation the norm and where many buyers are sensitive to both price and product caliber.
    B) a company is caught between competitors who have low-costs and competitors who have appealing product differentiation.
    C) buyer switching costs are high, many buyers have strong bargaining power, buyers have common user requirements, and seller's products are weakly differentiated.
    D) there are numerous buyer segments, buyer needs are diverse across these segments, only a few of the segments are growing rapidly, and seller's products are strongly differentiated.
    E) buyers are not value conscious.

    Answer: A   Difficulty: Medium

49. The strategic objective of a best-cost producer is to
   A) outmatch the resource strengths of both low-cost producers and differentiators.
   B) position the company outside the competitive arena of low-cost producers and differentiators.
   C) meet or exceed buyer expectations on product attributes while beating their expectations on price.
   D) deliver superior value to buyers by doing such a good job of cost control that it ends up with the best cost (as compared to rivals) in performing each activity in its value chain.
   E) identify and concentrate on those differentiating features that are inexpensive to incorporate.

   Answer: C Difficulty: Medium

50. The competitive advantage of a best-cost producer is
   A) convincing buyers to pay a premium for the attributes/features incorporated in its product.
   B) an ability to match close rivals on key product attributes and beat them on cost and on price.
   C) being able to take market share away from rivals by convincing buyers that its differentiating features are better than those of rivals.
   D) delivering superior value to buyers by lowering their switching costs.
   E) delivering superior value to buyers by doing a better job than rivals of controlling the cost drivers.

   Answer: B Difficulty: Medium

51. The most powerful competitive approach a company can employ is
   A) to strive relentlessly to become a lower and lower cost provider of a higher and higher caliber product, with the intent to approach becoming the absolute lowest cost provider of the industry's best overall product.
   B) to be the industry's low-cost leader.
   C) to pursue broad differentiation and be the provider of the industry's very best product.
   D) dominate the company's target market niche with a focus strategy keyed to low cost.
   E) dominate the company's target market niche with a focus strategy keyed to differentiation.

   Answer: A Difficulty: Medium

52. A best-cost provider strategy can defeat a low-cost provider strategy when
   A) buyers are pretty much satisfied with a standard product and do not see extra product attributes as worth paying extra money to obtain.
   B) buyers are looking for a good-to-excellent product at a bargain price.
   C) differentiators ignore the need to signal value and depend only on the "real" bases of differentiation.
   D) entry barriers are low, no other close rivals are pursuing a best-cost provider strategy, and buyers have moderate to low expectations regarding product performance and customer service.
   E) new product generations are introduced several times a year, buyer switching costs are high, and many buyers have considerable bargaining power.

   Answer: B Difficulty: Hard

Focus and Market Niche Strategies

53. Focus strategies based either on low-cost or differentiation are especially appropriate for situations where
    A) the market is comprised of distinctly different buyer groups who either have different needs or use the product in different ways.
    B) most other rival firms are using a best-cost producer strategy.
    C) buyers have strong bargaining power and entry barriers are low.
    D) most industry rivals have weakly differentiated products and buyers have moderate to strong bargaining power.
    E) a number of industry participants are also using some type of focus strategy.

    Answer: A   Difficulty: Easy

54. What sets focus strategies apart from low-cost leadership and differentiation strategies is
    A) their suitability for market situations comprised of distinctly different buyer groups who either have different needs or use the product in different ways.
    B) their concentrated attention on serving the needs of buyers in a narrow piece of the overall market.
    C) their basis for competitive advantage.
    D) their suitability for market situations where most industry rivals have weakly differentiated products and buyers have moderate to strong bargaining power.
    E) their objective of striving to deliver more value for the money.

    Answer: B   Difficulty: Easy

55. The aim of a focus strategy is
    A) building a value-based competitive advantage.
    B) creating the capability to simultaneously serve the specialized needs of buyers in a variety of distinct and different market segments.
    C) to do a better job of serving the needs and expectations of buyers in the target market niche than other competitors in the industry.
    D) to position a company between low-cost leaders and differentiators.
    E) to dominate the target segment on the basis of providing buyers with a top-of-the-line premium product that is unmatched by any other competitor in the industry.

    Answer: C   Difficulty: Easy

56. A focuser's basis for competitive advantage is
    A) nearly always created in the distribution channel portion of the industry value chain.
    B) lower costs than competitors in serving the target market niche or else an ability to outmatch other competitors in offering niche members something they perceive is better suited to their own unique tastes and preferences.
    C) grounded in being fully vertically integrated and in position to perform all of the value chain activities needed to serve the target niche.
    D) based on the target market niche being too small to be of interest to any other competitor.
    E) delivering more value for the money than other competitors.

    Answer: B   Difficulty: Medium

57. A focused strategy based on differentiation depends on there being a market segment where buyers are looking for
    A) the best value at the best price.
    B) an upscale product at an attractively low price.
    C) low switching costs.
    D) special product attributes or seller capabilities.
    E) a top-of-the-line or world class product.

    Answer: D   Difficulty: Medium

58. A focused strategy based on low-cost cannot be successful unless there is a market segment where
    A) buyers are looking for the best value at the best price.
    B) buyers are looking for a budget-priced product.
    C) buyers are price sensitive and are attracted to brands with low switching costs.
    D) demand is growing rapidly and a company can achieve a big enough volume to fully capture all the available scale economies.
    E) buyer requirements and expectations are less costly to satisfy as compared to other parts of the market.

    Answer: E   Difficulty: Medium

59. Which of the following do not represent market circumstances where a focus strategy is attractive?
    A) When it is costly or difficult for multi-segment competitors to put the capabilities in place to meet the specialized needs of the target market niche and at the same time satisfy the expectations of their mainstream customers.
    B) When the industry has many different segments and market niches, thereby allowing a focuser to pick an attractive niche suited to its resource strengths and capabilities.
    C) When industry leaders do not see that having a presence in the niche is crucial to their own success.
    D) When few, if any, other rivals are attempting to concentrate on the same market niche.
    E) When buyers are not strongly brand loyal, niche members are not sensitive to increased prices, and the industry is comprised of only a few market niches—all of which are experiencing strong growth.

    Answer: E   Difficulty: Medium

60. The attractiveness of a differentiation-based focus strategy is greatest when
    A) the industry has fast-growing segments that are quite profitable.
    B) other rivals concentrating on the same target segment are using focused low-cost strategies.
    C) buyers in the target segment require specialized expertise or customized product attributes and the focuser's skills, competencies, and capabilities are well suited to meeting these requirements.
    D) buyers in the target market niche are not extremely price sensitive and have low switching costs.
    E) there are not many opportunities for differentiation in the main part of the market (outside the target market niche).

    Answer: C   Difficulty: Medium

61. A focus or market niche strategy can be competitively attractive because
    A) the focuser's specialized competencies and capabilities in serving the target market niche give it strength in countering challenges from larger multi-segment competitors (who may not be easily able to put the capabilities in place to meet the specialized needs of the target market niche and at the same time satisfy the expectations of their mainstream customers).
    B) the focuser's specialized competencies and capabilities in serving the target market niche act as an entry barrier and give it some measure of protection from other firms wanting to horn in on the niche.
    C) rivalry in the niche may be weaker than in the broader market if there are relatively few players competing in the niche.
    D) difficulties in matching the focuser's competitive capabilities in serving buyers in the target market niche present a hurdle that the sellers of substitute products must overcome in order to be a factor in the niche.
    E) All of the above make a focus strategy attractive from the standpoint of contending with competitive forces.

    Answer: E Difficulty: Medium

62. The risks of a focused strategy include
    A) the chance that competitors outside the niche will find effective ways to match the focuser in satisfying the needs and expectations of niche members.
    B) the potential over time for the specialized needs of niche buyers to shift towards many of the same product attributes and capabilities desired by buyers in the mainstream portion of the market.
    C) the potential for the segment to become so attractive that it is soon inundated with competitors, intensifying rivalry and splintering sales, profits, and growth prospects.
    D) the potential for segment growth to slow to such a small rate that a focuser's prospects for future sales and profit gains become unacceptably dim.
    E) All of these.

    Answer: E Difficulty: Easy

Cooperative Strategies and Competitive Advantage

63. Alliances and partnerships have become an important component of the strategies of many companies because
    A) collaboration with outsiders is essential in developing new technologies and new products in virtually every industry.
    B) collaborative arrangements with other companies are often a necessity in racing against rivals to build a strong global presence and/or to stake out a strong position in the industries of the future.
    C) they represent cheaper and faster ways of getting things done, thus allowing firms with good alliances to achieve low-cost leadership and first-mover advantages.
    D) they have proved to be a powerful way to build loyalty and goodwill among customers with diverse needs and expectations.
    E) collaboration is effective in minimizing the impact of external threats to a company's well-being and helping insulate a firm from the five competitive forces.

    Answer: B Difficulty: Medium

64. Growing use of strategic alliances and collaborative partnerships is
   A) a clever way for firms to circumvent prohibitions against anticompetitive behavior since competitors cal ally with one another in efforts to raise prices and neutralize the bargaining power of large customers.
   B) being driven chiefly by the need of companies to keep their personnel abreast of rapidly advancing technology.
   C) changing the basis of competition from company against company to groups of companies against groups of companies.
   D) most pervasive among companies that are striving to catch up to the technological leaders in their respective industries.
   E) being driven chiefly by the need of companies to improve supply chain efficiency.

   Answer: C   Difficulty: Medium

65. Companies racing against rivals for global market leadership often utilize alliances and collaborative partnerships with companies in foreign countries in order to
   A) combat the bargaining power of foreign suppliers and foreign buyers, help defend against the competitive threat of substitute products produced by foreign rivals, and avoid the need to acquire the needed competitive capabilities by merging with or acquiring foreign companies.
   B) build a bigger customer base quickly, help raise needed financial capital from foreign banks, share the business risk with foreign companies, and win stronger brand name recognition among foreign buyers.
   C) get into critical country markets quickly and accelerate the process of building a potent global presence, gain inside knowledge about unfamiliar markets and cultures, and access valuable skills and competencies that are concentrated in particular geographic locations.
   D) retaliate against foreign competitors that are merging with or acquiring their major domestic rivals.
   E) exercise better control over the cost drivers in foreign markets, help revamp the global industry value chain, and enhance their chances of achieving global low-cost leadership.

   Answer: C   Difficulty: Medium

66. Companies racing to stake out a strong position in an industry of the future often utilize alliances and collaborative partnerships in order to
   A) combat the bargaining power of suppliers and buyers, help defend against the competitive threat of substitute products, and avoid the need to acquire the needed competitive capabilities by merging with or acquiring other companies.
   B) raise entry barriers into the newly emerging industry, build a bigger customer base, help raise needed financial capital, and reduce overall business risk.
   C) help master new technologies and build new expertise and competencies faster than would be possible through internal efforts, establish a bigger and stronger beachhead for participating in the target industry, and expand their opportunities in the target industry by melding their capabilities with the resources and expertise of partners.
   D) help defeat competitors that are employing broad differentiation strategies and enhance their chances of achieving low-cost leadership by exercising better control over industry cost drivers.
   E) All of the above.

   Answer: C   Difficulty: Medium

67. Which one of the following is <u>not</u> a strategically beneficial reason why a company may enter into strategic partnerships or cooperative arrangements with key suppliers, distributors, or makers of complementary products?
   A) To open up or improve access to new markets
   B) To learn from one another in performing joint research, to share technological know-how, and/or to collaborate on developing mutually interesting technology or new products
   C) To lessen competition (cooperating with rivals is often more profitable than competing against them)
   D) To improve supply chain efficiency
   E) To fill gaps in their technical and manufacturing expertise

   Answer: C Difficulty: Hard

68. The Achilles heel of collaborative partnerships and strategic alliances is
   A) that partners will not fully cooperate or share all they know, preferring instead to guard their most valuable information and protect their more valuable know-how.
   B) the danger of becoming dependent on other companies for essential skills and capabilities over the long-term, thereby weakening the firm's competitiveness and ability to be a master of its own destiny.
   C) the added time and expense of engaging in collaborative efforts.
   D) having to compromise the company's own priorities and strategies in reaching agreements with partners.
   E) not having full control of creating the company's own competitive advantage in the company's own way.

   Answer: B Difficulty: Hard

69. Which of the following is <u>not</u> a typical reason that many alliances prove unstable or break apart?
   A) Diverging objectives and priorities
   B) An inability to work well together
   C) The emergence of more attractive technological paths that are better pursued alone or with other partners
   D) Disagreement over how the divide the profits from their joint venture
   E) Marketplace rivalry between one or more allies

   Answer: D Difficulty: Medium

Merger and Acquisition Strategies

70. Which of the following is <u>not</u> a typical reason for pursuing mergers and acquisitions?
   A) Alliances and partnerships sometimes do not go far enough in providing a company with access to the needed resources and capabilities—merger or acquisition allows tighter integration and more in-house control and autonomy
   B) To reduce costs
   C) The need to strengthen a company's position in its existing markets
   D) To avoid having to share the profits with allies and joint venture partners
   E) To create a more attractive lineup of products and services, achieve wider geographic coverage, and gain the advantages of combined financial and organizational resources

   Answer: D Difficulty: Medium

71. Mergers with or acquisitions of companies having attractive resources and capabilities
    A) can be a superior strategic alternative to forming alliances or partnerships with these same companies.
    B) are typically a lesser drain on a company's financial resources than forming strategic alliances and collaborative partnerships.
    C) come apart and fail to produce the desired benefits about four times more frequently than do strategic alliances with resource-rich companies.
    D) are seldom a superior strategic alternative to forming alliances or partnerships with these same companies because of the financial drain of using the company's cash resources to accomplish the merger or acquisition.
    E) are much more suitable for helping a firm outrace rivals to build positions in newly emerging industries than they are in helping a company win the race for global market leadership.

    Answer: A   Difficulty: Medium

72. Merger and acquisition strategies
    A) are nearly always a superior strategic alternative to forming alliances or partnerships with these same companies.
    B) are well suited for situations where alliances and partnerships do not go far enough in providing a company with access to the needed resources and capabilities, can be a good means for opening up new market opportunities, and may offer considerable cost-saving opportunities (perhaps helping to transform otherwise high-cost companies into a competitor with average or below-average costs).
    C) produce the desired benefits about four times more frequently than do strategic alliances.
    D) seldom are a superior strategic alternative to forming alliances or partnerships with these same companies because of the financial drain of using the company's cash resources to accomplish the merger or acquisition.
    E) are much more suitable for helping a company strengthen its position in existing markets than they are in helping a company outrace rivals to build positions in newly emerging industries or win the race for global market leadership.

    Answer: B   Difficulty: Medium

Strategies to Vertically Integrate or Deintegrate

73. Vertical integration strategies
    A) extend a company's competitive scope within the same industry by expanding the firm's range backward into sources of supply and/or forward toward end-users of the product.
    B) are one of the best options for helping companies win the race for global market leadership.
    C) offer the potential to expand a company lineup of products and services.
    D) are a particularly effective means for enhancing a company's ability to expand into additional geographic markets, particularly the markets of foreign countries.
    E) are a particularly effective way for a company to revamp its value chain and eliminate low value-added activities.

    Answer: A   Difficulty: Hard

74. The best reason to invest company resources in vertical integration (either forward or backward) is to
    A) expand into foreign markets.
    B) broader the firm's product line.
    C) gain a first mover advantage over rivals in revamping the industry value chain.
    D) substantially strengthen the company's competitive position.
    E) either avoid being dependent on wholesalers/retailers who have no strong allegiance to the company's brand and who push "what sells" and makes them the most money or else avoid being dependent on powerful suppliers of crucial inputs.

    Answer: D Difficulty: Medium

75. A good example of vertical integration is
    A) a large public accounting firm (like DeloitteTouche or Arthur Andersen) acquiring a small local or regional public accounting firm.
    B) a large supermarket chain getting into convenience food stores.
    C) a crude oil refiner purchasing a firm engaged in drilling and exploring for oil.
    D) a hospital opening up a nursing home for the aged.
    E) a railroad company acquiring a trucking company specializing in long-haul freight.

    Answer: C Difficulty: Medium

76. Which of the following is not a potential advantage of backward vertical integration?
    A) Reduced vulnerability to powerful suppliers that raise prices at every opportunity
    B) Fewer disruptions in the supply and delivery of crucial materials and components
    C) Generating sufficient cost savings to justify the additional investment in bringing supply chain activities in-house (a possibility when suppliers have big profit margins and entry barriers into a supplier's business are low or can be hurdled)
    D) A reduced level of overall business risk because of performing more value chain activities in-house and controlling a bigger portion of the overall chain
    E) Allowing the firm to build or strengthen its competencies, better master key skills or strategy-critical technologies, or add features that deliver greater customer value

    Answer: D Difficulty: Hard

77. Which of the following is typically the most strategically important advantage of forward vertical integration into the activities of distributors and retailers?
    A) Being able to control the forward distribution portion of the industry value chain
    B) Fewer disruptions in the delivery of the company's products to end-users
    C) Avoiding being dependent on independent distributors/retailers who have no strong allegiance to the company's brand and who push "what sells" and makes them the most money
    D) Being able to capture the profit margins of companies in the forward portion of the industry value chain
    E) Allowing the firm access to greater economies of scale

    Answer: C Difficulty: Hard

78. Which of the following is not a strategic disadvantage of vertical integration?
    A) It boosts a firm's capital investment in the industry and thus increases business risk if the industry becomes unattractive later.
    B) It locks a firm in to using internal sources of supply (which later may prove more costly or less flexible than outsourcing).
    C) It reduces the opportunity for achieving greater product differentiation.
    D) Taking on more value chain activities may require radically different skills and business capabilities than the firm possesses.
    E) It can reduce a company's manufacturing flexibility, lengthening the time it takes to make model or design changes and bring new products to market.

    Answer: C   Difficulty: Medium

Unbundling and Outsourcing Stratgies

79. Outsourcing pieces of the value chain presently performed in-house so as to narrow the boundaries of the business makes strategic sense when
    A) an internal value chain activity can be performed better or more cheaply by outside specialists.
    B) it allows a company to concentrate on its core business and do what it does best.
    C) the activity is not crucial to the firm's ability to achieve competitive advantage and won't hollow out its technical know-how, competencies, or capabilities.
    D) it reduces the company's risk exposure to changing technology and/or changing buyer preferences.
    E) All of these.

    Answer: E   Difficulty: Medium

80. Which of the following is not a good strategic reason to outsource value chain activities presently performed in-house?
    A) When an internal value chain activity can be performed better or more cheaply by outside specialists
    B) When it allows a company to concentrate on its core business and do what it does best
    C) When the activity is not crucial to the firm's ability to achieve sustainable competitive advantage and won't hollow out its technical know-how, competencies, or capabilities
    D) When outsourcing the activity causes a company to lose its status of being fully integrated
    E) When it helps streamline company operations by increasing organization flexibility, cutting design-to-market cycle time, speeding decision-making, or cutting coordination costs

    Answer: D   Difficulty: Medium

81. Relying on outsiders to perform certain value chain activities offers such strategic advantages as
    A) obtaining higher quality and/or cheaper components or services.
    B) improving the company's ability to innovate.
    C) enhancing the firm's strategic flexibility.
    D) increasing the firm's ability to assemble diverse kinds of expertise speedily and efficiently.
    E) All of the above.

    Answer: E   Difficulty: Easy

82. Relying on outsiders to perform certain value chain activities offers such strategic advantages as
    A) helping the company to become partially integrated instead of being fully integrated.
    B) improving the company's ability to innovate, enhancing the firm's strategic flexibility, and obtaining higher quality and/or cheaper components or services.
    C) speeding the company's entry into foreign markets.
    D) permitting greater use of e-business technologies.
    E) giving the firm more direct control over the cost drivers.

    Answer: B Difficulty: Medium

83. The biggest pitfall of relying on outsiders to perform certain value chain activities is
    A) causing the company to become partially integrated instead of being fully integrated.
    B) hollowing out a firm's own capabilities and losing touch with activities and expertise that contribute fundamentally to the firm's competitiveness and market success.
    C) hurting a company's R&D capability.
    D) putting the company in the position of being a late mover instead of an early mover.
    E) giving the firm less direct control over the cost drivers.

    Answer: B Difficulty: Medium

Using Offensive Strategies to Build Competitive Advantage

84. Which of the following is <u>not</u> one of the basic types of strategic offensives?
    A) Simultaneous initiatives on many fronts
    B) Guerrilla offensives
    C) Initiatives to move from one strategic group to another
    D) Initiatives to capitalize on competitors' weaknesses
    E) Preemptive strikes

    Answer: C Difficulty: Medium

85. After a firm has built up a competitive advantage (usually via a successful competitive offensive), there's a benefit period during which the fruits of the advantage can be enjoyed; the length of the benefits period is crucial because
    A) it determines how long the firm will have to recoup the investment made in creating the advantage.
    B) it indicates how long the firm has to earn whatever added profits are yielded by the competitive advantage.
    C) during the benefit period the firm is vulnerable to preemptive strikes undertaken by rivals trying to retaliate for having lost out in winning a competitive advantage of their own.
    D) it determines how long the company will enjoy the status of being the industry leader.
    E) it determines how long the company will enjoy the status of being the most competitive firm in the industry.

    Answer: A Difficulty: Medium

86. When a company has built a competitive advantage,
    A) competent, resourceful rivals can be counted on to counterattack with initiatives of their own to try to close the competitive gap.
    B) its rivals are forced to use defensive strategies to avoid being driven from the marketplace.
    C) some rivals are likely to launch preemptive strikes or guerilla offensives in retaliation for having lost out in winning a competitive advantage of their own.
    D) its closest rivals will almost certainly have to resort to aggressive price-cutting to try to offset their competitive disadvantage.
    E) it is in the strongest position to launch additional offensive strategies to continue to defeat rivals by an ever wider margin.

    Answer: A   Difficulty: Medium

Attacking Competitor Strengths and Weaknesses

87. Which one of the following is not an example of an offensive initiative to match or exceed competitor strengths?
    A) Coming up with an equally good product and charging a lower price
    B) Launching a preemptive strike on a strong rival's biggest geographic stronghold
    C) Developing product features that will especially appeal to the customers of strong rivals
    D) Expanding the product line to match a strong rival model for model
    E) Trying to pioneer the next-generation technology to make a strong rival's products and/or production process obsolete

    Answer: B   Difficulty: Medium

88. Aggressive price-cutting works best as an offensive strategy when
    A) the aggressor is using a focus strategy keyed to differentiation.
    B) the products of rival firms are strongly differentiated.
    C) the aggressor is not the market share leader.
    D) the aggressor has a cost advantage or else has more financial resources and can outlast rivals in a war of attrition.
    E) the aggressor uses the element of surprise and employs guerrilla warfare tactics.

    Answer: D   Difficulty: Medium

89. Offensive initiatives to match or exceed competitor strengths make sense when
    A) a company's major rivals have been successful with a best-cost producer strategy.
    B) a company's major rivals have been successful with broad differentiation strategies.
    C) a company's major rivals utilize frequent guerrilla attacks.
    D) strong rivals have important competitive advantages that threaten a company's long-term market position and profitability.
    E) a company's market share is stagnating and the company is not growing faster than the market as a whole.

    Answer: D   Difficulty: Medium

90. Attacking the strengths of rivals can be an attractive offensive option if
   A) a firm has either a superior product or superior organizational resources and capabilities.
   B) a company is the industry's low-cost producer.
   C) a company is the industry's market share leader.
   D) a company is the industry's best-cost producer.
   E) the company is willing to rely mainly on preemptive strikes or else launch simultaneous initiatives on many fronts.

   Answer: A   Difficulty: Medium

End-Run Offensives to Move to Less Contested Ground

91. An example of an end-run offensive is
   A) launching a new product very quickly in order to beat competitors to the marketplace.
   B) trying to create new segments by introducing products with creatively different attributes and performance features that better meet buyer needs.
   C) investing considerable sums in advertising for new product introductions.
   D) imitating market leaders' products at lower prices.
   E) refusing to disclose any development details prior to new product introduction.

   Answer: B   Difficulty: Hard

92. An offensive strategy that avoids direct assault on entrenched competitors and aims at being the first to occupy new ground is best described as
   A) a competitive gap strategy.
   B) a preemptive strategy.
   C) an offensive strategy to attack competitor weaknesses.
   D) a guerrilla offensive strategy.
   E) an end run offensive.

   Answer: E   Difficulty: Easy

93. Which of the following is not an example of an end-run offensive?
   A) Launching initiatives to build strong positions in geographic areas where close rivals have little or no market presence
   B) Trying to create new segments by introducing products with creatively different attributes and performance features that better meet buyer needs
   C) Introducing innovative products that redefine the market and the terms of competition
   D) Being the first company to cut price and boost advertising when buyer demand begins to slow down
   E) Leapfrogging into next-generation technologies to supplant existing technologies, products, and/or services

   Answer: D   Difficulty: Hard

Simultaneous Initiatives on Many Fronts

94. Launching a series of offensive initiatives across many fronts simultaneously
    A) can throw a rival off balance, diverting its attention in many directions and forcing it to try to protect many pieces of its customer base at the same time.
    B) have their best chance of success when a company employs a differentiation strategy and can blitz the market with a wave of new product features.
    C) are most likely to succeed when the main offensive feature is a sharply lower price that grabs buyers' attention.
    D) works best if the targets of the offensive are firms prone to use guerilla-style competitive tactics.
    E) is an attractive option when a firm is fully integrated and can launch its initiatives all along the whole industry value chain.

    Answer: A   Difficulty: Medium

Preemptive Strikes

95. Preemptive strike strategies entail
    A) an offensive attack on a narrow, well-defined market segment that is weakly defended by competitors.
    B) moving first to secure an advantageous position that rivals are foreclosed or discouraged from duplicating.
    C) concentrating one's competitive strengths and resources against the weaknesses of rivals.
    D) pitting one's own competitive strengths head-on against the strengths of rivals.
    E) leapfrogging into next-generation products and technologies, thus forcing rivals to play catch-up.

    Answer: B   Difficulty: Easy

96. Preemptive strikes involve
    A) trying to out-focus rivals by appealing to customers in every attractive growth segment.
    B) moving first to secure an advantageous position that rivals are foreclosed or discouraged from duplicating.
    C) initiating price-cuts in areas where weak rivals are the strongest.
    D) using a best-cost provider approach to block off the market leaders.
    E) filing lawsuits to block competitors from investing in different technological processes and new plant capacity.

    Answer: B   Difficulty: Easy

Using Defensive Strategies to Protect Competitive Advantage

97. Which one of the following is not a way to block the avenues open to challenger firms?
    A) Adding new features or models and otherwise broadening its product line to close off gaps and vacant niches
    B) Broadening and deepening the company's complement of skills, expertise, core competencies, and competitive capabilities
    C) Launching guerilla attacks on the market positions of would-be challengers
    D) Lengthening warranty periods, patenting alternative technologies, and offering free training and support services
    E) Granting dealers and distributors attractive volume discounts in order to discourage them from handling the lines of rivals

    Answer: C   Difficulty: Medium

98. Which one of the following is <u>not</u> a defensive option for protecting a company's market share and competitive position?
   A) Adding new features or models and otherwise broadening the product line to close off vacant niches and gaps to would-be challengers
   B) Keeping prices attractively low on those models that most closely match competitors' offerings
   C) Running comparison ads that call attention to weaknesses in rivals' products
   D) Enhancing the flexibility of the company's resources and competencies so that they can be rapidly re-deployed or adapted to meet either new market conditions or fresh challenges by rivals
   E) Convincing dealers and distributors to handle its product line exclusively

   Answer: C   Difficulty: Hard

99. Which of the following is a potential defensive move to ward off challenger firms?
   A) Raising the financing offered to dealers and/or buyers
   B) Signaling challengers that retaliation is likely in the event that launch an attack
   C) Offering free or low-cost training to users of the firm's product
   D) Maintaining a participation in alternative technologies
   E) All of these.

   Answer: E   Difficulty: Hard

First-Mover Advantages and Disadvantages

100. Being first to initiate a particular move can have a high payoff when
   A) pioneering helps build up a firm's image and reputation with buyers.
   B) customer loyalty accrues to the firm that wins over first-time buyers.
   C) moving first can produce an absolute cost advantage over rivals.
   D) moving first can constitute a preemptive strike, making imitation extra hard or unlikely.
   E) All of these.

   Answer: E   Difficulty: Easy

101. Because when to make a strategic move can be just as important as what move to make, a company's best option with respect to timing is
   A) to be the first mover.
   B) to be a fast follower.
   C) to be a late mover (because it is cheaper and easier to imitate the successful moves of the leaders and moving late allows a company to avoid the mistakes and costs associated with trying to be a pioneer—first mover disadvantages usually overwhelm first-mover advantages).
   D) to be the last mover-playing catch-up is usually fairly easily and nearly always much cheaper than any other option.
   E) to carefully weigh the first-mover advantages against the first mover disadvantages and act accordingly.

   Answer: E   Difficulty: Easy

102. First-mover disadvantages arise when
    A) the costs of pioneering are much higher than being a follower and only negligible experience curve effects accrue to the leader.
    B) technological change is rapid and following rivals find it easy to leapfrog the pioneer with next-generation products of their own.
    C) the pioneer's skills, know-how, and products are easily copied or even bested by late-movers.
    D) customer loyalty to the pioneer is low.
    E) All of these.

    Answer: E   Difficulty: Medium

Short Answer Questions

103. What is the difference between competitive strategy and business strategy? What is the primary objective of competitive advantage? Why is competitive advantage an important strategy-making consideration?

    Difficulty: Medium

104. Describe the strategy of striving to be the industry's overall low cost provider. What are its pros and cons?

    Difficulty: Medium

105. What are the pros and cons of a differentiation strategy?

    Difficulty: Medium

106. What are the pros and cons of a market niche strategy?

    Difficulty: Medium

107. What are the distinctive features of a broad differentiation strategy?

    Difficulty: Medium

108. What are the distinctive features of a best-cost producer strategy?

    Difficulty: Medium

109. What are the distinctive features of a focused differentiation strategy?

    Difficulty: Medium

110. What are the approaches a company can take to become a low-cost producer in its industry?

Difficulty: Medium

111. Under what circumstances is a low-cost leadership strategy attractive?

Difficulty: Medium

112. Under what circumstances is a differentiation strategy attractive?

Difficulty: Medium

113. Under what circumstances is a focused or market niche strategy attractive?

Difficulty: Medium

114. What are the pitfalls of pursuing a low-cost leadership strategy?

Difficulty: Medium

115. What are the strategic advantages and disadvantages of a vertical integration strategy?

Difficulty: Hard

116. What are the advantages of strategic alliances and collaborative partnerships with key suppliers?

Difficulty: Hard

117. What are the merits of strategic alliances and collaborative partnerships for companies racing for global market leadership? Under what circumstances do they make sense? How do they contribute to competitive advantage?

Difficulty: Hard

118. What are the merits of strategic alliances and collaborative partnerships for companies racing against rivals to build a strong position in emerging industries of the future? Under what circumstances do they make sense? How do they contribute to competitive advantage?

Difficulty: Hard

119. Under what sorts of circumstances are mergers with or acquisitions of other companies a better solution than entering into partnerships or alliances with these companies? How do mergers and/or acquisitions contribute to enhancing a company's position?

Difficulty: Hard

120. What are the merits of outsourcing the performance of certain value chain activities as opposed to performing them in-house? Under what circumstances does outsourcing make good strategic sense?

Difficulty: Hard

121. What kinds of strategic moves are required to build competitive advantage? Why do competitive advantages, once built, tend to erode? What does it take to sustain a competitive advantage?

Difficulty: Medium

122. Identify and briefly explain any three of the six types of offensive strategies.

Difficulty: Medium

123. Identify and briefly explain what is meant by each of the following terms:
   a.) a broad differentiation strategy
   b.) a focused differentiation strategy
   c.) preemptive strike
   d.) an end-run offensive
   e.) a best-cost producer strategy
   f.) a focused low cost strategy
   g.) a cooperative strategy
   h.) vertical integration strategy
   i.) a first-mover advantage

Difficulty: Hard

124. What are the merits of mounting an offensive strategy that attacks competitor weaknesses as opposed to competitor strengths?

Difficulty: Hard

125. What is the purpose of defensive strategy? Give at least five examples of defensive moves?

Difficulty: Hard

126. What are the strategic advantages of being a first-mover? What are the strategic advantages of being a follower or "late-mover"?

Difficulty: Medium

Chapter 6: Strategies for Competing in Globalizing Markets

Multiple Choice Questions

Why Companies Expand into Foreign Markets

1. The reasons why companies opt to expand outside their home market include
   A) gaining access to more customers for the company's products/services.
   B) to spread its business risk across a bigger number of country markets.
   C) a competitive need to achieve lower costs.
   D) a desire to leverage its competencies and capabilities.
   E) All of these.

   Answer: E   Difficulty: Easy

2. Which of the following is <u>not</u> a typical reason for companies to expand into the markets of foreign countries?
   A) To gain market access to a greater number of customers for the company's products/services
   B) To enable the pursuit of a global strategy
   C) To achieve lower costs and enhance the firm's competitiveness
   D) To capitalize on company competencies and capabilities
   E) To spread business risk across a bigger number of country markets

   Answer: B   Difficulty: Medium

3. Which of the following is <u>not</u> a typical reason for companies to expand into the markets of foreign countries?
   A) To gain market access to a greater number of customers for the company's products/services
   B) To build the profit sanctuaries necessary to wage guerilla warfare against global challengers endeavoring to invade its home market
   C) To achieve lower costs and enhance the firm's competitiveness
   D) To capitalize on company competencies and capabilities
   E) To spread business risk across a bigger number of country markets

   Answer: B   Difficulty: Medium

4. A company is said to be an international (or multinational) competitor when
   A) it competes in a majority of the world's different country markets.
   B) it has operations on all of the world's major continents.
   C) it competes in a select few foreign markets (and perhaps has only modest ambitions to enter additional country markets).
   D) it competes in 15 or fewer country markets and employs an international strategy.
   E) it employs an international strategy.

   Answer: C   Difficulty: Medium

5. A company is said to be a global competitor when
   A) it competes in a majority of the world's different country markets.
   B) it has or is pursuing a market presence on most continents and in virtually all of the world's major countries.
   C) it has long range strategic intentions to compete in as many as 50 country markets.
   D) it competes in 15 or more country markets and employs a global strategy.
   E) it employs a global strategy.

   Answer: B Difficulty: Easy

6. The difference between a company that competes "internationally" and a company that competes "globally" is that
   A) a global competitor has a presence in a majority of the world's different country markets and an international competitor has a presence in fewer than 10 countries.
   B) the former competes in a select few foreign markets (and perhaps has only modest ambitions to enter additional country markets) while the latter has or is pursuing a market presence on most continents and in virtually all of the world's major countries.
   C) an international competitor has a market presence on a few continents and a global competitor has a market presence on all of the world's continents.
   D) an international competitor has a market presence in a few major countries of the world and a global competitor has a market presence in virtually all of the major countries of the world.
   E) an international competitor has an international strategy and a global competitor has a global strategy.

   Answer: B Difficulty: Medium

Cross-Country Differences in Cultural, Demographic, and Market Conditions

7. One of the biggest strategic challenges to competing in the international arena is
   A) figuring out what kinds of strategic adjustments it will take to be responsive to cross-country differences in cultural, demographic, and market conditions.
   B) whether to charge the same price in all country markets.
   C) how many foreign firms to license to produce and distribute the company's products.
   D) whether to offer a mostly standardized product worldwide or whether to customize the company's offerings in each different country market.
   E) Both A and D.

   Answer: E Difficulty: Easy

8. Which of the following is not an accurate aspect of competing in the markets of foreign countries?
   A) A multi-country strategy is generally superior to a global strategy
   B) There are country-to-country differences in consumer buying habits and buyer tastes and preferences
   C) A company must contend with country-to-country variations in host government restrictions and requirements and fluctuating exchange rates
   D) Product designs suitable for one country are often inappropriate in another
   E) Market growth rates vary from country to country

   Answer: A Difficulty: Easy

9. Competing in the markets of foreign countries entails dealing with such factors as
   A) fluctuating exchange rates, country-to-country variations in host government restrictions and requirements, and big variations in market growth rates from country to country.
   B) important country-to-country differences in consumer buying habits and buyer tastes and preferences.
   C) whether to customize the company's offerings in each different country market or whether to offer a mostly standardized product worldwide.
   D) the fact that product designs suitable for one country are sometimes inappropriate in another.
   E) All of these.

   Answer: E   Difficulty: Easy

10. Competing in the markets of foreign countries entails dealing with such factors as
    A) big variations in market growth rates from country to country, important country-to-country differences in consumer buying habits and buyer tastes and preferences, and the fact that product designs suitable for one country are sometimes inappropriate in another.
    B) country-to-country variations in host government restrictions and requirements and fluctuating exchange rates.
    C) whether to customize the company's offerings in each different country market or whether to offer a mostly standardized product worldwide.
    D) in which countries to locate company operations for maximium locational advantage (given country-to-country variations in wages rates, worker productivity, energy costs, tax rates, and the like).
    E) All of these.

    Answer: E   Difficulty: Easy

11. One important concern a company has in maneuvering to achieve competitive advantage in foreign markets is
    A) gaining access to low transportation costs in exporting its goods to foreign countries.
    B) how fast it can build a strong network of local distributors and dealers to get its products into the marketplaces of foreign countries.
    C) how well it capitalizes on country-to-country cost variations and locates its foreign activities in those countries where its costs will be lowest (or where it can gain other important locational advantages that enhance its competitiveness).
    D) focusing its efforts in those countries where there is an absence of significant trade barriers.
    E) developing the expertise to minimize the impact of fluctuating exchange rates.

    Answer: C   Difficulty: Medium

Multicountry Competition versus Global Competition

12. Market features and industry characteristics that work against globally competitive market conditions include
    A) low international transportation costs.
    B) low barriers to gaining access to distribution channels in different countries.
    C) different product preferences and buyer requirements from country to country.
    D) the absence of significant trade barriers in the markets of most of the world's countries.
    E) the absence of a need for intensive customer service on a locality-by-locality basis.

    Answer: C   Difficulty: Medium

13. The defining characteristic of global competition is
    A) minimal cross-country trade restrictions.
    B) a worldwide price for the product.
    C) common user requirements from country to country.
    D) a market situation where competitive conditions across national markets are linked strongly enough to form a true international or world market and where leading competitors compete head to head in many different countries.
    E) All of the above are important characteristics of a globally competitive market.

    Answer: D   Difficulty: Medium

14. The characteristics of a market where global competition prevails include
    A) a market situation where competitive conditions across national markets are linked strongly enough to form a true international or world market and where leading competitors compete head to head in many different countries.
    B) minor cost variations among countries, minimal cross-country trade restrictions, a worldwide price for the product, and common user requirements from country to country.
    C) an industry made up of companies from various parts of the world that operate in the same part of the industry value chain.
    D) an industry made up of companies that utilize the same basic type of competitive strategy and where these companies compete head to head in many different countries.
    E) None of the above accurately captures the character of a globally competitive market.

    Answer: A   Difficulty: Hard

15. In global competition
    A) rival companies compete for having the biggest share of the world market, but only occasionally compete head-to-head in different countries.
    B) a firm's overall competitive advantage typically grows out of the advantages generated at its home base.
    C) a company's market strength depends mainly on its market share in foreign country markets; its market share in its home market and its portfolio of home-based competencies, capabilities, and resource strengths have little impact on its global competitiveness.
    D) the industry leaders are foreign companies; domestic companies play only a minor role.
    E) the markets in various countries are part of the world market and competitive conditions across country markets are strongly linked together.

    Answer: E   Difficulty: Medium

16. A global competitor's market strength
    A) is proportional to the number of countries in which it competes.
    B) depends on the number of country markets in which it either has a market leading position or is in the ranks of the leaders (in top five in market share).
    C) is directly proportional to its portfolio of country-based competitive advantages.
    D) hinges primarily on the strength of its brand name recognition across the world.
    E) hinges primarily on the size of its global market share and whether it enjoys global low-cost leadership.

    Answer: C   Difficulty: Medium

17. Multi-country or multi-domestic competition refers to situations where
    A) global markets are fragmented, no domestic companies have king-sized market shares, and each national market has many competitors.
    B) each country market is self-contained—competition in one national market is independent of competition in other national markets and, as a consequence, there is strictly speaking no "international market" or "world market."
    C) domestic rivals pursue market niche strategies and do not compete internationally.
    D) domestic companies have a competitive disadvantage in competing with foreign rivals that operate in many different countries.
    E) most competitors operate in more than two country markets and usually in more than five.

    Answer: B   Difficulty: Medium

18. Multi-domestic or multi-country competition is characterized by
    A) a situation where the arena in which competition among rival companies takes place is one of several neighboring countries rather than a single country or the world market as a whole.
    B) a situation where competition is mainly among the domestic companies of a few neighboring countries (five countries at most).
    C) extensive trade restrictions, sharply fluctuating exchange rates, and high tariff barriers in many country markets that work against the formation of a true world market.
    D) a market situation where competition among domestic companies predominates and foreign competitors are a minor factor.
    E) a situation where there is no international or global market, just a collection of self-contained country markets.

    Answer: E   Difficulty: Medium

19. One good way to distinguish between multicountry competition and global competition is that
    A) in multicountry competition rivalry is primarily among companies in several neighboring countries whereas in global competition the arena in which rivalry takes place is the world market.
    B) in multicountry competition rival companies vie mainly for "national market championships" whereas in global competition the grand prize is the "world market championship."
    C) in multicountry competition rivals have domestic-based competitive advantages or disadvantages whereas in global competition rivals have global-based competitive advantages or disadvantages.
    D) multicountry competition prevails when extensive trade restrictions from country to country preclude companies from operating in many different country markets whereas global competition prevails when cross-border trade restrictions are sufficiently low that companies can readily compete in many different countries.
    E) in multicountry competition rivals are in domestic strategic groups whereas in global competition rival companies are positioned in global strategic groups.

    Answer: B   Difficulty: Medium

Strategy Options for Entering and Competing in Foreign Markets

20. The strategic approaches to competing in foreign markets include
    A) a global focus strategy.
    B) maintaining a national (one-country) production base and exporting goods to foreign markets.
    C) licensing foreign firms to produce and distribute one's products.
    D) a custom-tailored country-by-country approach based on meeting the particular needs of particular buyers in each target country.
    E) All of the above.

    Answer: E   Difficulty: Easy

21. Which of the following is <u>not</u> one of the competitive strategy options for competing in the markets of foreign countries?
    A) Using a dominant firm leadership strategy in each country market to counter the impact of fluctuating exchange rates
    B) Maintaining a national (one-country) production base and exporting goods to foreign markets
    C) A global best-cost strategy
    D) A custom-tailored country-by-country approach based on meeting the particular needs of particular buyers in each target country
    E) A global focus strategy

    Answer: A   Difficulty: Easy

22. Which of the following are generic strategy options for competing in foreign markets?
    A) Maintain a national (one-country) production base and exporting goods to foreign markets
    B) Global low-cost, global differentiation, global best-cost, and global focus strategies
    C) Franchising and licensing strategies
    D) A multicountry strategy (where a company pursues a custom-tailored country-by-country approach in accordance with local competitive conditions and buyer tastes and preferences)
    E) All of these

    Answer: E   Difficulty: Medium

23. Which of the following are <u>not</u> generic strategy options for competing in foreign markets?
    A) An export strategy
    B) Global low-cost, global differentiation, global best-cost, and global focus strategies
    C) Cross-market subsidization strategies and home-field advantage strategies
    D) A multicountry strategy
    E) Franchising and licensing strategies

    Answer: C   Difficulty: Medium

Export, Licensing, and Franchising Strategies

24. Using domestic plants as a production base for exporting goods to selected foreign country markets
    A) can be an excellent initial strategy to test the international waters and learn if market positions can be established in foreign markets.
    B) can be a competitively successful strategy when a company is focusing on vacant market niches in each foreign country and does not have to compete head-to-head against strong host country competitors.
    C) works well when a firm does not have the financial resources to employ cross-market subsidization.
    D) is usually a weak strategy when competitors are pursuing multi-country strategies.
    E) can be a powerful strategy if foreign rivals have their plants located in countries that are not in the world's major markets.

    Answer: A   Difficulty: Medium

25. The advantages of using a export strategy to build a customer base in foreign markets include
    A) minimizing risk and capital requirements.
    B) being able to minimize shipping costs and avoid tariffs.
    C) being cheaper and more cost effective than licensing and franchising.
    D) being cheaper and more cost effective than a multicountry strategy.
    E) being more suited to accommodating local buyer tastes than a global strategy.

    Answer: A   Difficulty: Medium

26. The advantages of using a franchising strategy to pursue opportunities in foreign markets include
    A) having franchisees bear most of the costs and risks of establishing foreign locations and requiring the franchiser to expend only the resources to recruit, train, and support franchisees.
    B) being particularly well suited to the global expansion efforts of banking and e-commerce enterprises.
    C) helping build multiple profit sanctuaries and employ cross-market subsidization when needed.
    D) being well suited to companies with patented technology.
    E) being well suited to the global expansion efforts of local companies in emerging country markets.

    Answer: A   Difficulty: Medium

27. The advantages of using a licensing strategy to participate in foreign markets include
    A) being more suited to accommodating local buyer tastes than a multicountry strategy
    B) being able to avoid shipping costs, tariffs, and foreign taxes.
    C) allowing the company to achieve first-mover advantages.
    D) being able to leverage the company's technical know-how or patents without committing significant additional resources to markets that are unfamiliar, present uncertainty, or are politically volatile.
    E) All of these.

    Answer: D   Difficulty: Medium

Multi-Country Strategies

28. A multicountry strategy
   A) is very risky, given fluctuating exchange rates and the propensity of foreign governments to impose tariffs on imported goods.
   B) is usually defeated by a global differentiation strategy.
   C) is one where a firm tailors its competitive strategy to buyer needs and other relevant conditions in each target national market where it elects to compete.
   D) is generally an inferior strategy when one or more foreign competitors is pursuing a global low-cost strategy.
   E) can defeat a global strategy if the multicountry strategist concentrates its efforts exclusively in the markets where it has profit sanctuaries.

   Answer: C Difficulty: Medium

29. The strength of a multicountry strategy is that
   A) it matches a company's competitive approach to host country circumstances, country by country.
   B) each country strategy is almost totally different from and unrelated to other country strategies.
   C) the plants located in different countries can be operated independent of one another, thus promoting greater achievement of scale economies.
   D) it avoids host country ownership requirements and import quotas.
   E) there is considerable cross-country coordination—the strategic moves undertaken in one country are tightly linked to the moves undertaken in the other countries.

   Answer: A Difficulty: Medium

30. A multicountry strategy is preferable to a global strategy when
   A) host governments enact regulations requiring that products sold locally meet strictly-defined manufacturing specifications or performance standards that are largely unique to that particular country.
   B) the industry is characterized by big economies of scale and strong experience curve effects.
   C) entry barriers are low, the firm has limited financial capital, market conditions in many countries are volatile and uncertain, and there are big differences in production costs from country to country (because of wage rates, worker productivity, and the prices of parts and components).
   D) market growth rates vary considerably from country to country.
   E) a big majority of the company's rivals are pursuing global strategies, have multiple profit sanctuaries, and are prone to employ cross-market subsidization tactics.

   Answer: A Difficulty: Medium

31. The weaknesses of a multi-country strategy are that
   A) it is especially vulnerable to fluctuating exchange rates and it can usually be defeated by companies employing cross-market subsidization tactics.
   B) each country's strategy is different from the strategies employed in other countries and it is harder to build multiple profit sanctuaries.
   C) it presents a firm with greater exposure to increases in tariffs and restrictive trade barriers than does a global strategy.
   D) it is less conducive to building competitive advantage by transferring company competencies and resources across country boundaries and it does not promote building a single, unified competitive advantage.
   E) it is unsuitable for the markets of emerging countries and it can usually be defeated by companies using export strategies or global strategies.

   Answer: D   Difficulty: Medium

32. The product-line strategy of a firm using a multi-country strategic approach would likely entail
   A) a narrow product line, focused on identified international market niches.
   B) mostly standardized products sold worldwide.
   C) customizing the firm's products and features offered in each country to meet the needs and preferences of buyers in each country.
   D) competing in many buyer segments with a broad product line (many models and varieties) so that buyers in each target national market would be able to select the item that best met their individual needs.
   E) creating a different value chain for each country.

   Answer: C   Difficulty: Easy

33. The marketing and distribution strategy of a firm pursuing a multi-country approach would likely be
   A) coordinated on a worldwide basis to hold down costs.
   B) adapted to the buying habits, practices, and culture of each host country.
   C) adapted only minimally to host country situations if required, so as to permit achievement of scale economies in shipping, distribution, and sales promotion.
   D) standardized across all countries to hold down distribution costs.
   E) None of the above.

   Answer: B   Difficulty: Medium

34. A company pursuing a multicountry strategy in a globally competitive industry is potentially vulnerable to competition from rivals pursuing a global low-cost leadership strategy and intent on global dominance because
   A) it has no cross-market subsidization defense in important country markets.
   B) it cannot appeal to host country governments for trade protection against the unfair competitive practices of global competitors.
   C) it is likely to have a cost disadvantage owing to its having many small plants and short production runs to turn out specialized products country-by-country.
   D) globally competitive companies are likely to have more profit sanctuaries than multi-country strategists.
   E) a global low-cost leadership strategy typically results in company having a stronger brand image than companies employing a multi-country strategy.

   Answer: C   Difficulty: Hard

Global Strategies

35. Employing a global strategy involves
    A) competing in essentially same basic manner in all countries where the firm does business (only minor country-to-country differences exist).
    B) selling in many, if not all, of the nations where there is significant buyer demand.
    C) integrating and coordinating the company's moves worldwide.
    D) All of the above.
    E) Just A and C are correct.

    Answer: D Difficulty: Easy

36. A global strategy is preferable to a multicountry strategy when
    A) host governments enact regulations requiring that products sold locally meet strict manufacturing specifications or performance standards.
    B) country-to-country differences are small enough to be accommodated with the framework of a global strategy.
    C) there are difficulties in crafting country strategies that are considerably different from and unrelated to the strategies in other countries.
    D) market growth rates vary considerably from country to country.
    E) a big majority of the company's rivals are pursuing multicountry strategies.

    Answer: B Difficulty: Easy

37. Which of the following is not a barrier to using a global strategy in world markets?
    A) Getting access to distribution channels in various countries
    B) The prohibitive cost of international advertising
    C) High international distribution and transportation costs such that domestic producers have a significant cost advantage over foreign manufacturers
    D) An absence of demand for the product in many countries
    E) The wants and needs of buyers vary considerably from country to country

    Answer: B Difficulty: Easy

38. The product-line strategy of a firm using a global strategy would likely entail
    A) a narrow selection of models and styles, with each model/style focused on identified international market niches.
    B) producing and marketing mostly standardized products worldwide, with some customization where and when necessary.
    C) producing the various products at plants scattered around the world.
    D) competing with a broad product line (many models and varieties) so that buyers in each target national market would be able to select the item that best met their individual needs.
    E) creating a different product lineup for each country.

    Answer: B Difficulty: Easy

39. The production strategy of a firm using a global strategy would likely entail
   A) a narrow selection of models and styles, with each model/style focused on identified international market niches.
   B) locating plants on the basis of maximum competitive advantage—in countries where manufacturing costs can be kept low *or* close to major markets to economize on shipping costs *or* use of a few world-scale plants to capture maximum scale economies and experience curve effects, as most appropriate.
   C) producing the various products at plants scattered around the world.
   D) producing a broad product line (many models and varieties) so that buyers in each target national market would be able to select the item that best met their individual needs.
   E) creating a different product lineup for each major area of the world (Europe, North America, Latin America, and the Asian Pacific).

   Answer: B   Difficulty: Hard

40. The competitive approach of a firm pursuing a global strategy
   A) entails little or no strategy coordination across countries.
   B) usually involves cross-subsidizing the prices in those markets where there are significant country-to-country differences in the product attributes that customers are most interested in.
   C) is essentially the same in all country markets where it competes but it may nonetheless allow for minor country-by-country variations where necessary to satisfy buyers.
   D) involves using a worldwide differentiation strategy, with the incorporated product attributes varying according to buyer preferences in each country market.
   E) involves using a worldwide low-cost strategy, with the basic product attributes varying according to buyer preferences in each country market.

   Answer: C   Difficulty: Easy

41. The production strategy of a firm using a global approach to competing would likely
   A) involve locating plants in whatever countries and geographic areas that offered the maximum competitive advantage.
   B) be determined by the host country government's standards or product specifications.
   C) involve plants scattered across many host countries so as to minimize cross-border transportation and shipping costs.
   D) be based on extensive market research to determine whether to make a standardized or a differentiated product for each country market.
   E) involve scattering the company's plants geographically because of the limited need for cross-border coordination.

   Answer: A   Difficulty: Medium

42. The organizational structure of a firm pursuing a global strategy is likely to involve
   A) forming subsidiary companies in each host country and making sure each country subsidiary operates in a manner tailored to fit host country conditions very closely.
   B) a global organization structure where corporate headquarters retains control over major strategic decisions and where there's extensive cross-country coordination of strategy-related decisions and activities.
   C) having manufacturing plants and sales and marketing offices in each country where it operates.
   D) giving country managers full responsibility and authority over the firm's operations in their assigned country.
   E) All of the above except B.

   Answer: B Difficulty: Medium

43. A global strategy can defeat a multi-country strategy when
   A) a multinational rival can accommodate the necessary local responsiveness within a global strategy approach and still retain a cost edge.
   B) host governments lower trade restrictions and tariff barriers in an effort to pursue a free trade policy.
   C) buyers believe foreign firms make higher quality products than domestic firms.
   D) it is based on achieving a differentiation-based competitive advantage as opposed to a focus-based competitive advantage.
   E) the global strategist operates across more stages of the industry value chain and also has more strategic alliances than the multi-country strategist.

   Answer: A Difficulty: Medium

44. A global strategist has potential competitive advantage over a multicountry strategist when
   A) economies of scale from operating world-scale plants give it a cost edge over a multicountry strategist's numerous small plants and short production runs.
   B) it has more profit sanctuaries and can resort to cross-market subsidization if and when needed in order to wage offensives in markets where the multicountry strategist is strong.
   C) the necessary tailoring of a firm's product offering to meet the different country-to-country buyers can still be accommodated within a global strategy.
   D) local governments do not pursue a policy of protectionism for locally-based producers.
   E) All of these.

   Answer: E Difficulty: Medium

Pursuing Competitive Advantage by Competing Multinationally

45. For a company to gain competitive advantage (or offset domestic disadvantages) by expanding into foreign markets, it needs to
    A) build multiple profit sanctuaries, fully capture scale economies, compete in both developed and emerging country markets, and pursue some type of global strategy.
    B) use export, licensing, or franchising strategies so as to minimize risk and capital investment.
    C) disperse buyer-related activities to all countries where it sells its product.
    D) disperse its activities among various countries in a manner that lowers costs or else helps achieve greater product differentiation, efficiently and effectively transfer its domestic competencies and capabilities to its operations in foreign markets, and/or work to deepen/broaden its resource strengths and capabilities.
    E) avoid competing in countries with high tariffs and trade restrictions, be aggressive in forming strategic alliances with foreign partners, employ some form of global strategy, and have expertise in managing the impacts of fluctuating exchange rates.

    Answer: D   Difficulty: Hard

Locating Operations in the Most Advantageous Countries

46. Dispersing activities to many locations worldwide can be competitively advantageous when
    A) transportation costs are high and there are diseconomies of large size in production and or distribution.
    B) dispersing buyer-related activities gives the firm a service-based competitive edge over rivals who don't have the resources or capabilities to disperse buyer-related activities to the same degree.
    C) trade barriers make it too expensive to operate from a central location.
    D) dispersement acts as a hedge against fluctuating exchange rates, supply interruptions, and adverse political developments.
    E) All of the above.

    Answer: E   Difficulty: Medium

47. A multinational or global competitor can pursue sustainable competitive advantage by
    A) locating its various value chain activities in whichever countries prove most advantageous.
    B) aligning and coordinating cross-border activities in ways that a domestic-only competitor cannot.
    C) using the same types of competencies, resource strengths and capabilities in country after country, ideally resulting in the company achieving dominating depth in one or more competitively valuable areas.
    D) being adept at cross-border transfer of skills, expertise, competencies, and capabilities.
    E) All of the above.

    Answer: E   Difficulty: Easy

48. To use location to build competitive advantage, a firm must consider whether
    A) the location will allow the firm to capitalize on country-specific buyer demands.
    B) a foreign-based plant can operate autonomously with little coordination from headquarters.
    C) to concentrate each activity it performs in a few select countries or disperse performance of the activity to many nations and in which countries to locate particular activities.
    D) the host country can supply the necessary raw materials and components or whether the firm will have to import items.
    E) to concentrate all of its value chain activities in one country (where low cost can be achieved) or whether to locate value chain activities close to the customer (to minimize transportation and logistics costs).

    Answer: C Difficulty: Medium

49. In which of the following circumstances is it unnecessary for a firm to concentrate its activities in a limited number of locations in order to build competitive advantage in multinational markets?
    A) When the costs of manufacturing or other activities are significantly lower in a few particular geographic locations than in others
    B) When a company has competitively superior patented technology that it can license to foreign partners
    C) When there is a steep learning or experience curve associated with performing an activity in a single location
    D) When certain locations have superior resources, allow better coordination of related activities, or offer other valuable advantages
    E) When there are significant scale economies in performing the activity

    Answer: B Difficulty: Medium

50. The competitive advantage opportunities that a global competitor can gain by dispersing performance of its activities across many nations include
    A) being able to shift production from one country to another to take advantage of exchange rate fluctuations, lower wage rates, energy costs, or trade restrictions.
    B) being in better position to choose where and how to challenge rivals.
    C) shortening delivery times to customers by having geographically scattered distribution facilities.
    D) locating buyer-related activities (such as sales, advertising, after-sale service and technical assistance) close to buyers.
    E) All of these.

    Answer: E Difficulty: Medium

51. The classic reason for locating an activity in a particular country is
    A) low cost.
    B) to escape paying tariffs and/or to escape high taxes.
    C) to be close to customers.
    D) to avoid strong competition.
    E) to achieve faster growth.

    Answer: A Difficulty: Medium

52. Dispersing particular value chain activities across many countries rather than concentrating them in a select few countries can be more advantageous when
    A) buyer-related activities need to take place close to buyers.
    B) high transportation costs and trade barriers make it uneconomical to operate from one or just a few locations.
    C) it helps hedge against the risks of exchange rate fluctuations, supply disruptions, and adverse political developments.
    D) there are diseconomies of scale in trying to operate from a single location.
    E) All of these.

    Answer: E   Difficulty: Medium

Cross Border Transfer of Competencies and Capabilities

53. Transferring a company's core competencies and resource strengths from one country market to another is
    A) a good way for a domestic company to leverage its competitive capabilities, expand into foreign markets, and grow its sales and profits plus it can help a company broaden and deepen its capabilities, perhaps even building dominating depth in some competitively valuable area and thereby earning a competitive edge over certain rivals.
    B) best accomplished with a multicountry strategy as opposed to a global strategy.
    C) feasible only with a global strategy; it can't be done with a multicountry strategy.
    D) unlikely to produce as good a competitive advantage as dispersing activities to the most advantageous country locations since low costs are a more important competitive asset than strong competencies and capabilities.
    E) can help companies based in emerging countries to defend their home base market against the invasion by global giants.

    Answer: A   Difficulty: Hard

Profit Sanctuaries

54. Profit sanctuaries
    A) are usually the result of having formed strong strategic alliances with important foreign-based rivals.
    B) refer to a government-protected home market where is company is safe from having to compete against potentially strong foreign rivals.
    C) are generally the result of a distinctive competence in product innovation.
    D) are country markets where a company earns substantial profits because it has a strong or protected market position.
    E) are usually possessed by firms whose strategic intent is dominance of their home market.

    Answer: D   Difficulty: Medium

55. A nation becomes a company's profit sanctuary when the company
    A) is the market share leader in that country market.
    B) is allied with one of that nation's major companies and, together, the two allies are able to achieve the leading market share in that nation.
    C) earns a substantial portion of its profits from sales in that nation due either to its strong competitive position or to the protection it enjoys from host country trade barriers.
    D) locates the performance of all its value chain activities in that country because of exceptional profit opportunities.
    E) earns over 50% of its total profits from its operation in that country.

    Answer: C   Difficulty: Medium

56. Profit sanctuaries are
    A) best created through successful strategic alliances with important foreign-based rivals that allow the allies to win a dominant market share in particular country markets.
    B) a source of competitive advantage over companies that do not have a profit sanctuary and, as a rule, the more profit sanctuaries a company has the better.
    C) almost always created by convincing host governments to erect high trade barriers to protect domestic firms from foreign competitors.
    D) most likely to result from locating company activities in those nations where it enjoys lower costs than key rivals.
    E) more easily created and sustained in the markets of emerging countries than in the markets of the world's major industrialized and wealthiest countries.

    Answer: B   Difficulty: Medium

The Competitive Power of Cross-Market Subsidization

57. To successfully use cross-market subsidization to wage a strategic offensive in selected country markets, a company needs to
    A) have one or more profit sanctuaries.
    B) convince host governments to allow it to compete against the countries' domestic firms on the basis of a lower price.
    C) enter into strategic alliances with foreign firms and subsidize their resource weaknesses with its own resource strengths.
    D) develop ways to subsidize its resource weaknesses in the target countries with its resource strengths other country markets.
    E) utilize the power of the Internet to effectively divert the resource strengths and capabilities it has in some countries to help wage the strategic offensive in the target country markets.

    Answer: A   Difficulty: Medium

58. A purely domestic company is vulnerable to competition from a multinational rival with multiple profit sanctuaries because
    A) it can't overcome trade barriers in the major country markets of the world.
    B) of the multinational competitor's cross-market subsidization capabilities.
    C) it can't hope to match the multinational competitor's lower costs.
    D) it is at a market share disadvantage, the multinational competitor has a stronger brand name image, and access to greater economies of scale.
    E) it can't hope to match the multinational competitor's resource strengths in production, marketing, and distribution.

    Answer: B   Difficulty: Hard

59. Cross-market subsidization refers to
    A) the practice of getting a company's home government to help finance and otherwise subsidize its entry into the markets of foreign countries.
    B) using cross-border transfer of a company's skills and expertise as a basis for successfully overcoming the barriers to entering new country markets.
    C) supporting competitive offensives in one market with resources and profits diverted from operations in other markets.
    D) the practice of shifting company resources from nations where a company has big profit sanctuaries to nations where it has smaller profit sanctuaries.
    E) deliberately operating at a loss in some country markets in order to help grow the size of a company's profit sanctuary in a competitively crucial country market.

    Answer: C   Difficulty: Hard

60. Cross-market subsidization is a particularly powerful competitive weapon when used by
    A) firms whose primary strategic objective is achieving or maintaining domestic dominance in their home market.
    B) a domestic-only competitor with a protected profit sanctuary in its home market.
    C) firms with strong strategic alliances in several different national markets.
    D) competitors pursuing global strategies as opposed to multicountry strategies.
    E) a global or multinational firm with multiple profit sanctuaries.

    Answer: E   Difficulty: Medium

61. One way that domestic-only competitors can ward off competitive attacks from aggressive global competitors with multiple profit sanctuaries is by
    A) getting their local government to outlaw cross-market subsidization.
    B) getting their local governments to pass anti-dumping legislation and strongly enforce such laws when foreign companies are suspected of unreasonably low-balling prices in their home market.
    C) growing the size of their home base profit sanctuary and shifting to a global low-cost strategy.
    D) pursuing full vertical integration and building a distinctive competence in each of the key value chain activities.
    E) by shifting to a focused differentiation strategy and concentrating on providing an upscale product/service to customers willing to pay a premium price.

    Answer: B   Difficulty: Hard

Strategic Alliances and Joint Ventures with Foreign Partners

62. Strategic alliances and cooperative agreements between domestic and foreign firms are a potentially fruitful means for the partners to
    A) enter additional country markets and compete on a more global scale while still preserving their independence.
    B) gain better access to scale economies in production and/or marketing.
    C) fill competitively important gaps in their expertise, capabilities, or resource base.
    D) share distribution facilities and dealer networks in all or most of the countries where they have operations, thus mutually strengthening their access to buyers.
    E) All of these.

    Answer: E   Difficulty: Medium

63. Which of the following is <u>not</u> a potential benefit of cooperative arrangements between foreign and domestic companies?
    A) Gaining wider access to attractive country markets
    B) Gaining better access to scale economies in production and/or marketing
    C) Filling competitively important gaps in their technical expertise and/or knowledge of local markets
    D) Greater ability to build multiple profit sanctuaries and share the resulting profits
    E) Share distribution facilities and dealer networks in all or most of the countries where they have operations, thus mutually strengthening their access to buyers

    Answer: D   Difficulty: Medium

64. Strategic alliances between domestic and foreign firms are more effective
    A) in building multiple profit sanctuaries than in achieving competitive advantage.
    B) in giving the partners locational advantages than in facilitating cross-border resource transfers.
    C) in helping establish a new beachhead of opportunity than in achieving and sustaining global leadership.
    D) in pursuing a multi-country strategy as compared to a global strategy.
    E) in pursuing a global strategy as compared to a multi-country strategy.

    Answer: C   Difficulty: Hard

65. The problems and risks of strategic alliances between domestic and foreign firms do <u>not</u> include
    A) the time-consuming delays associated with building trust, overcoming language and cultural barriers and building an effective working relationship.
    B) the potential for deep differences of opinion to emerge about how to proceed or what the objectives of the alliance are.
    C) becoming overly dependent on another company for essential skills and expertise.
    D) making it harder to pursue a multi-country strategy as compared to a global strategy.
    E) a slow and cumbersome decision-making process.

    Answer: D   Difficulty: Hard

66. To make the most of strategic alliances between domestic and foreign firms, companies need to consider such factors as
    A) whether to emphasize a competitive advantage based on low cost or differentiation, whether to pursue building one or more profit sanctuaries, and how soon it will take to achieve global leadership.
    B) what partner to pick, how to make the alliance mutually beneficial, how to build in assurances that each partner will live up to its commitments, and how best to manage the learning process.
    C) how to divide profits, how long the alliance should last, which partner should be in total control, and where the headquarters for the alliance should be located.
    D) whether to pursue a multi-country strategy or a global strategy, which countries to focus marketing attention on, whether to concentrate on profits or market share, how many countries to compete in, and which rivals to target.
    E) who will own the patent rights to any innovations, whose dealers and distributors to utilize, how to allocate R&D costs, and how to divide up control over the various activities comprising the alliance-related value chain.

    Answer: B Difficulty: Hard

Competing in Emerging Foreign Markets

67. Companies racing for global market leadership
    A) generally have to build beachheads in the markets of emerging countries.
    B) are well-advised to avoid all the risks and problems of competing in emerging country markets.
    C) seldom have the resource capabilities it takes to be effective in competing in emerging country markets and usually are at a strong competitive disadvantage to the domestic market leaders.
    D) can usually be expect to earn sizable profits quickly in emerging country markets.
    E) usually encounter the lowest entry barriers in emerging country markets.

    Answer: A Difficulty: Hard

68. Companies that elect to compete in the markets of emerging countries
    A) can usually expect to encounter very low entry barriers.
    B) typically achieve high profit levels very quickly because it is relatively easy to overpower the unsophisticated and resource-poor domestic firms that have been accustomed to serving local buyers.
    C) usually find that competing on the basis of premium quality is superior to competing on the basis of low price.
    D) have to be very sensitive to local conditions, be willing to invest in developing the market for their product over the long term, and be patient in earning a profit.
    E) typically encounter weaker competitive forces than they do in the markets of the world's most industrialized and wealthy countries.

    Answer: D Difficulty: Hard

Strategies for Local Companies in Emerging Markets

69. Foreign companies that elect to compete in the markets of emerging countries
    A) can usually expect to encounter very low entry barriers.
    B) typically achieve high profit levels very quickly because it is relatively easy to overpower the unsophisticated and resource-poor domestic firms that have been accustomed to serving local buyers.
    C) usually find that competing on the basis of premium quality is superior to competing on the basis of low price.
    D) have to be very sensitive to local conditions, be willing to invest in developing the market for their product over the long term, and be patient in earning a profit.
    E) typically encounter weaker competitive forces than they do in the markets of the world's most industrialized and wealthy countries.

    Answer: D   Difficulty: Hard

70. The basic strategy options for local companies in competing against global challengers include
    A) focused differentiation, focused low cost, and low-cost leadership strategies.
    B) export strategies, low-cost leadership strategies, best-cost provider strategies, cross-market subsidization strategies, and home-field advantage strategies.
    C) transferring expertise and capabilities to cross-border markets, relying on home-field advantages, contending on a more global level, and dodging rivals by shifting to a new business model or a defendable market niche.
    D) franchising strategies, multicountry strategies keyed to product superiority, global low-cost leadership strategies, and cross-market subsidization strategies.
    E) relocating key value chain activities to countries where costs are lower, relying upon scale economies to underprice global rivals, out-advertising global rivals, promoting anti-dumping legislation, seeking to build multiple profit sanctuaries in emerging country markets, and market niche or focus strategies.

    Answer: C   Difficulty: Medium

71. If industry pressures for globalization are weak, the best strategy options for a local company in competing against global challengers include
    A) dodging rivals by shifting to a new business model or a defendable market niche.
    B) export strategies, entering into alliances and/or joint ventures with one or more foreign companies having globally competitive strengths, and home-field advantage strategies.
    C) export strategies, licensing strategies, franchising strategies, and cross-market subsidization strategies.
    D) transferring the company's expertise and capabilities to cross-border markets and relying on home-field advantages.
    E) offensives aimed at the global challengers' strengths, promoting anti-dumping legislation, seeking to build profit sanctuaries in neighboring country markets, and/or launching some type of guerilla warfare strategy.

    Answer: D   Difficulty: Medium

72. If industry pressures for globalization are strong, the best strategy options for a local company in competing against global challengers include
A) moving to enter foreign markets and beginning to contend on a more globalized basis or else dodging rivals by shifting to a new business model or a defendable market niche.
B) export strategies, guerilla warfare strategies, preemptive strike strategies, and offensives aimed at the global challengers' weaknesses.
C) export strategies, licensing strategies, franchising strategies, offensives aimed at the global challengers' strengths, and cross-market subsidization strategies.
D) relying on home-field advantage strategies or else trying to transfer the company's expertise and capabilities to markets in countries where its resources and strengths will be competitively valuable.
E) relocating key value chain activities to neighboring countries where costs are lower, promoting anti-dumping legislation, employing cross-market subsidization strategies, selling out to a global entrant, and/or launching some type of global strategy to contend with the global challengers on a more global basis.

Answer: A   Difficulty: Medium

Short Answer Questions

73. Briefly discuss the special features of competing in foreign markets.

Difficulty: Hard

74. Discuss in some detail the difference between a multi-country strategy and a global strategy and give the pros and cons of each.

Difficulty: Hard

75. What circumstances call for use of a multi-country strategy for competing in international markets? When is a global strategy "superior" to a multi-country strategy?

Difficulty: Medium

76. Identify and briefly describe any four of the six generic strategic options for competing in foreign markets.

Difficulty: Easy

77. What are the pros and cons of using strategic alliances to try to enhance a company's ability to compete in foreign markets?

Difficulty: Medium

78. Discuss why a company desirous of competing in foreign country markets needs to pay close attention to the advantages of cross-border transfer of competencies and capabilities. Is such transfer often a key to competitive advantage? Why or why not?

Difficulty: Medium

79. Explain what a profit sanctuary is and why it is a competitive plus.

Difficulty: Medium

80. Explain why a company desirous of competing in foreign markets needs to pay careful attention to where it locates it value chain activities.

Difficulty: Hard

81. Under what circumstances is it advantageous for a company desiring to compete in foreign markets to concentrate its activities in a select few locations?

Difficulty: Medium

82. Under what circumstances is it advantageous for a company desiring to compete in foreign markets to disperse its activities across many countries?

Difficulty: Medium

83. Briefly discuss the advantages of entering into a strategic alliance with foreign companies. What are the risks and disadvantages?

Difficulty: Medium

84. Explain why a global competitor with multiple profit sanctuaries is well positioned to outcompete a domestic competitor whose only profit sanctuary is its home market.

Difficulty: Medium

85. Identify and explain the significance of each of the following terms and concepts:
   a.) global strategy
   b.) profit sanctuary
   c.) multicountry strategy
   d.) cross-market subsidization

Difficulty: Medium

86. Identify and briefly describe a local company's strategic options in competing against global challengers if industry pressures for globalization are weak

   Difficulty: Medium

87. Identify and briefly describe a local company's strategic options in competing against global challengers if industry pressures for globalization are strong.

   Difficulty: Medium

88. Identify five things a company needs to consider or do if it is to make the most of strategic alliances with foreign partners.

   Difficulty: Medium

Chapter 7: New Business Models and Strategies for the Internet Economy

Multiple Choice Questions

The Internet: Technology and Participants

1. Everyday use of the Internet by business and consumers has had the effect of
   A) making the Internet an important new distribution channel.
   B) giving business an important new technological tool for better performing some value chain activities and bypassing others.
   C) altering the strength of the five competitive forces.
   D) spawning entirely new industries.
   E) All of these.

   Answer: E   Difficulty: Easy

2. The Internet can be most accurately characterized as
   A) a series of interconnected computers with the capacity to exchange data and information.
   B) an integrated network of banks of servers and high speed computers, digital switches and routers, telecommunications equipment and lines, and individual users' computers.
   C) a series of individual users' computers which are wired to banks of servers loaded with easily accessible data and information.
   D) a globally wired e-commerce system that represents "the next big thing" because of its power to transform the world.
   E) a giant bank of servers and high-speed computers that depend on the providers of communications services to quickly relay data and information from one individual user's computer to another user's PC anywhere in the world.

   Answer: B   Difficulty: Medium

3. The supply side of the Internet Economy consists of
   A) the makers of specialized communications components and equipment.
   B) providers of communications services.
   C) the suppliers of computer components and computer hardware and the developers of specialized software.
   D) an assortment of e-commerce enterprises.
   E) All of the above.

   Answer: E   Difficulty: Easy

4. The supply side of the Internet Economy consists of
   A) the makers of specialized communications components and equipment, the providers of communications services, the suppliers of computer components and computer hardware, the developers of specialized software, and an assortment of e-commerce enterprises.
   B) the providers of Internet hardware and Internet communications services.
   C) the suppliers of computer components and computer hardware, the developers of specialized software, and e-commerce enterprises (including Internet service providers).
   D) an assortment of Internet service providers, computer makers, software providers, and e-commerce enterprises.
   E) the providers of Internet hardware and Internet communications services, computer makers, and an assortment of e-tailers.

   Answer: A   Difficulty: Medium

5. Which one of the following least qualifies as being an impact of the Internet and Internet technology?
   A) Raising profitability
   B) Creating an important new distribution channel
   C) Giving businesses an important tool for improving the performance of value chain activities
   D) Spawning entirely new industries
   E) Altering the strength of competitive forces

   Answer: A   Difficulty: Medium

6. In situations where there is vigorous competition among alternative technologies for building various components of the Internet infrastructure, rival companies can seek to win the battle for technological supremacy by
   A) investing aggressively in R&D to win the technological race against rivals.
   B) forming strategic alliances with potential customers, suppliers, and those with complementary technologies to try to win consensus for the favored technological approaches and industry standards.
   C) hedging the company's technological bets by investing resources in two or more of the competing technologies so as to be better able to shift to another technological approach should it win out.
   D) acquiring other companies with complementary technological expertise so as to broaden and deepen the company's technological capabilities and thereby drive advances in the company's technology at a faster pace.
   E) All of these.

   Answer: E   Difficulty: Easy

7. When there is vigorous competition among alternative technologies for building various components of the Internet infrastructure, technology rivals can try to achieve market supremacy for their favored technological approach by
   A) running ads to tout the advantages of their technology.
   B) forming strategic alliances to block the adoption of standardized technological approaches.
   C) hedging the company's technological bets by investing resources in two or more of the competing technologies so as to be better able to shift to another technological approach should it win out.
   D) touting the stability and simplicity of their own technological approaches and avoiding rapid introduction of next-generation technologies that would cause users to repeatedly spend monies to staying on the cutting edge.
   E) lobbying Congress and regulators to establish rules that favor the adoption of their favored technological approach and that, simultaneously, put the technological approaches of rivals at a disadvantage.

   Answer: C   Difficulty: Medium

8. Which of the following represent attractive strategic options for rivals with competing Internet technologies?
   A) Forming strategic alliances with suppliers and other companies with complementary technologies
   B) Hedging the company's bets by investing in more than one technological alternative
   C) Acquiring other companies with complementary technological expertise
   D) Investing aggressively in R&D
   E) All of these

   Answer: A   Difficulty: Easy

9. Which of the following strategic initiatives is the least appealing when a company finds itself in vigorous competition with rivals as to which of several alternative technological approaches will be favored and ultimately win out in building various components of the Internet infrastructure?
   A) Forming strategic alliances with potential customers, suppliers, and those with complementary technologies to try to win consensus for its own favored technological approach and industry standard
   B) Advertising heavily to convince users and the general public that the firm's own technological approach is really superior and should become the industry standard
   C) Hedging the company's technological bets by investing resources in two or more of the competing technologies so as to be better able to shift to another technological approach should it win out
   D) Acquiring other companies with complementary technological expertise so as to broaden and deepen the company's technological capabilities and thereby drive advances in the company's technology at a faster pace
   E) Investing aggressively in R&D to win the technological race against rivals

   Answer: B   Difficulty: Medium

The Impact of Internet Technology on Company and Industry Value Chains

10. Internet technology
    A) opens up opportunities for improving value chain efficiency but does little to enhance the effectiveness with which particular value chain activities can be performed.
    B) is more suited to improving supply chain management than to improving internal operations.
    C) typically offers more opportunities to improve distribution channel efficiency than to improve supply chain efficiency.
    D) presents a host of opportunities for better configuring both company and industry value chains.
    E) is more suited to improving internal operations to improving either supply chain management or distribution efficiency.

    Answer: D   Difficulty: Medium

11. In evaluating the impact of Internet technology on company and industry value chains, it is fair to say that
   A) there are strong reasons for companies to utilize e-procurement techniques but not strong reasons for companies to use Internet technology to collaborate more closely with their suppliers.
   B) company value chains are much more strongly impacted than industry value chains.
   C) use of Internet technology offers important opportunities for improving supply chain efficiency, internal operating efficiency, and distribution channel efficiency.
   D) use of Internet technology makes it more cumbersome to implement build-to-order manufacturing approaches but does help promote e-procurement and real-time data-sharing all along the supply chain.
   E) the amount of paperwork associated with coordinating value chain activities is significantly reduced but the time it takes to perform all the various value chain activities, given all the new Internet applications being incorporated into company and industry value chains, is now somewhat longer.

   Answer: C   Difficulty: Medium

12. Which of the following is not one of the valid impacts that the Internet and Internet technologies are having on industry and company value chains?
   A) Enhancing the capabilities for just-in-time deliveries and otherwise enhancing supply chain efficiency
   B) Lengthening the time it takes to do accurate demand forecasting and also making the task of demand forecasting more complex
   C) Speeding internal communications, allowing real-time data-sharing, breaking down internal corporate bureaucracies, and reducing overhead costs
   D) Allowing producers to bypass traditional distribution channels and sell direct to end-users
   E) Facilitating reduced production times and lower labor costs

   Answer: B   Difficulty: Medium

How the Internet Reshapes the Competitive Environment

13. Growing use of the Internet and Internet-related technologies tends to
   A) reduce the rivalry among industry participants because of the greater emphasis put on product quality.
   B) make buyers more informed and give them somewhat greater bargaining power.
   C) raise entry barriers into most industries.
   D) substantially increase the strength of competitive pressures from substitute products.
   E) greatly increase the bargaining power of suppliers to industry members.

   Answer: B   Difficulty: Medium

14. Growing use of the Internet and Internet-related technologies tends to
   A) increase the rivalry among industry participants.
   B) reduce buyer bargaining power and increase supplier bargaining power.
   C) raise entry barriers into most industries and reduce the strength of competitive pressures from substitute products.
   D) lower entry barriers into most industries and also substantially increase the strength of competitive pressures from substitute products.
   E) greatly increase the bargaining power of both buyers and sellers.

   Answer: A   Difficulty: Hard

15. Growing use of the Internet and Internet-related technologies tends to
    A) increase the rivalry among industry participants, reduce seller-buyer collaboration, and reduce the strength of competitive pressures from substitute products.
    B) increase buyer bargaining power, increase seller-supplier collaboration, and increase the intensity of rivalry among competing sellers.
    C) raise entry barriers into most industries, weaken the degree of rivalry among competing sellers, and decrease the strength of competitive pressures from substitute products.
    D) lower entry barriers, reduce the rivalry among competing sellers, and give buyers somewhat more bargaining leverage.
    E) greatly increase the bargaining power of both buyers and sellers and also increase the strength of competitive pressures from substitute products.

    Answer: B Difficulty: Hard

16. Growing use of the Internet and Internet-related technologies tends to alter the shape of competition in an industry by
    A) raising entry barriers into most industries, weakening the degree of rivalry among competing sellers, and increasing the strength of competitive pressures from substitute products.
    B) reducing buyer bargaining power, reducing seller-supplier collaboration, and increasing the intensity of rivalry among competing sellers.
    C) increasing both the rivalry among industry participants and the degree of seller-supplier collaboration.
    D) lowering entry barriers, strengthening the rivalry among competing sellers, and giving buyers somewhat less bargaining leverage.
    E) greatly increasing the motivation of sellers to work collaboratively with both their suppliers and their distribution channel allies, increasing the strength of competitive pressures from substitute products, and raising entry barriers into many industries.

    Answer: C Difficulty: Hard

17. The Internet tends to make buyers more informed and perhaps give them somewhat greater bargaining power because
    A) rival dot-com vendors are anxious to make a sale, take sales away from old-fashioned brick-and-mortar vendors, and build a larger customer base.
    B) most user requirements are the same.
    C) online shoppers have unprecedented ability to compare the prices, products, and shipping times of rival vendors and find the best value.
    D) it is primarily price sensitive buyers that use the Internet to shop for bargains.
    E) None of the above; the Internet actually shifts bargaining power away from buyers and toward sellers.

    Answer: C Difficulty: Medium

18. Use of the Internet and Internet technologies tends to shift bargaining power away from sellers and toward buyers because
    A) buyers of all types (manufacturers, wholesalers, retailers, and individuals) can readily join a buying group to pool their purchasing and approach vendors for better terms than could be gotten individually.
    B) the Internet eliminates the geographic protection of distance that has traditionally given small-town businesses the advantage of being the only source within reasonable driving distance.
    C) the Internet gives buyers unprecedented ability to compare the prices, products, and shipping times of rival vendors and find the best value.
    D) a multinational company's geographically scattered units can use online communications to pool their purchase orders with the same suppliers and bargain for volume discounts.
    E) All of the above.

    Answer: E Difficulty: Easy

19. Use of the Internet and Internet technologies tends to shift bargaining power away from sellers and toward buyers because
    A) buyers of all types (manufacturers, wholesalers, retailers, and individuals) have much less motivation to join a buying group for the purpose of pooling their purchasing and approaching vendors for better terms than could be gotten individually.
    B) there are strong motivations for sellers to collaborate closely with their distribution channel allies (wholesalers and retailers) for the purpose of convincing end-use consumers to make more of their purchases online.
    C) the Internet gives buyers unprecedented ability to compare the prices, products, and shipping times of rival vendors and find the best value.
    D) online buyers are typically very quality and service sensitive and not particularly price sensitive.
    E) the incentives of sellers to enter into collaborative arrangements with their wholesale/retail partners makes them less able to haggle with their partners over price and other terms and conditions of sale.

    Answer: C Difficulty: Medium

20. Which one of the following is not a factor that accounts for why the Internet shifts bargaining power away from sellers and toward buyers?
    A) A multinational company's geographically scattered units can use online communications to pool their purchase orders with the same suppliers and bargain for volume discounts
    B) Buyers of all types (manufacturers, wholesalers, retailers, and individuals) can readily join a buying group to pool their purchasing and approach vendors for better terms than could be gotten individually
    C) Use of the Internet gives buyers unprecedented ability to compare the prices, products, and shipping times of rival vendors and find the best value
    D) Most online sellers allow buyers to put up bids for what they are willing to pay for the items they are offering for sale and stand ready to negotiate on price
    E) The Internet eliminates the geographic protection of distance that has traditionally given small-town businesses the advantage of being the only source within reasonable driving distance

    Answer: D Difficulty: Medium

21. The Internet and Internet-related technologies make it more feasible for companies to
   A) collaborate closely with geographically-distant suppliers to streamline ordering and shipping, improve just-in-time deliveries, and work in parallel on the designs for new products.
   B) use online systems to research the products and prices of competing vendors and "shop the world" for the best values.
   C) join a buying group to pool their purchases and bargain with vendors for better terms than could be gotten individually.
   D) sell their products to buyers in distant geographic markets, thus expanding their market reach.
   E) All of the above.

   Answer: E   Difficulty: Easy

22. The Internet and Internet-related technologies make it more feasible for companies to
   A) shift from use of a differentiation strategy to use of a low-cost provider strategy.
   B) use online systems to research the products and prices of competing vendors and "shop the world" for the best values and also to collaborate closely with geographically-distant suppliers to streamline ordering and shipping, improve just-in-time deliveries, and work in parallel on the designs for new products.
   C) combat competitive pressures from substitute products.
   D) compete on the basis of superior product quality and avoid the need to be price competitive.
   E) achieve above-average profitability by selling at rock-bottom prices.

   Answer: B   Difficulty: Medium

23. On balance, Internet-related technologies tend to
   A) increase seller use of low-cost and best-cost provider strategies and to make focused and differentiation strategies less attractive from a profitability perspective.
   B) increase the profit prospects of most companies in most industries.
   C) weaken the strength of competitive pressures that companies face because of the strong incentives for all kinds of seller-supplier and seller-distributor collaboration.
   D) reduce price competition among rival sellers and to increase their overall prospects for better profitability.
   E) increase the strength of competitive pressures that companies face and to weaken industry attractiveness from a profit perspective.

   Answer: E   Difficulty: Medium

Other Strategy-Shaping Features of Internet Technology

24. Aside from the impacts on company/industry value chains and on the five competitive forces, Internet technology has the effect of
    A) globalizing competition and expanding the geographic arena in which firms have a market presence.
    B) increasing worker wages and salaries faster than the overall inflation rate.
    C) encouraging companies to try to outcompete rivals by outspending them on R&D.
    D) giving companies a stronger incentive to race to improve existing products and beat rivals to market with next-generation products having better performance features.
    E) making it more advantageous for companies to be fast followers rather than first movers because of the high costs of being a technological pioneer.

    Answer: A   Difficulty: Medium

25. Which of the following is a strategically-relevant feature of Internet technology?
    A) Internet technology is advancing in a steady and predictable fashion.
    B) Companies are becoming increasingly hesitant to invest in new Internet technology because so many Internet and dot-com companies had flawed strategies and business models and went out of business during 2000-2001.
    C) Internet technologies tend to increase variable costs and reduce fixed costs.
    D) Internet technologies tend to reduce procurement and inventory costs but tend to increase administrative and distribution costs.
    E) The Internet can be an economical means of delivering customer service.

    Answer: E   Difficulty: Medium

26. The strategically-relevant features of Internet technology include
    A) making it less economical to deliver customer service via online means.
    B) much faster diffusion of new technology and new ideas across the world along with a tendency to reduce variable costs and to tilt cost structures more towards fixed costs.
    C) strong incentives for dot-com companies to spend heavily on advertising to build name recognition and attract new users in substantial numbers.
    D) making it easier for online companies to earn attractive profits at a low volume of sales.
    E) causing all companies in all industries to operate in a globally competitive market.

    Answer: B   Difficulty: Medium

27. Which of the following is not a strategically-relevant feature of the Internet and Internet technology?
    A) Internet technology tends to advance at uncertain speeds and in uncertain directions.
    B) The capital for funding new e-commerce business tends to be readily available for ventures with solidly attractive business models and strategies and has dried up for ventures with dubious prospects.
    C) Internet technologies tend to increase variable costs and reduce fixed costs.
    D) The Internet results in much faster diffusion of new technology and new ideas across the world
    E) The Internet can be an economical means of delivering customer service.

    Answer: C   Difficulty: Medium

The Difficulty of Relying on Internet Technology to gain Sustainable Competitive Advantage

28. Experience indicates that companies which move early to deploy cutting-edge Internet technology
    A) are gaining a strong and sustainable competitive advantage over slower-moving rivals.
    B) are gaining a slight but nonetheless sustainable competitive advantage over slower-moving rivals.
    C) have a stronger brand name recognition and more loyalty among buyers than do firms which have been slow to incorporate the use of the Internet and Internet technologies.
    D) are gaining, at most, a fleeting competitive edge over slower-moving rivals because the vast majority of competitors gravitate to use of many of the same Internet applications and achieve comparable benefits.
    E) Both C and D are correct.

    Answer: D Difficulty: Medium

29. In the world of e-commerce enterprises, the advantages accruing to first-movers have proved to be
    A) both sizable and durable.
    B) small but durable because of moderately strong switching costs and network effects.
    C) competitively powerful because of relatively high switching costs and stronger than expected network effects.
    D) elusive because of higher than anticipated switching costs and stronger than expected network effects.
    E) fleeting because of lower than anticipated switching costs and weaker than expected network effects.

    Answer: E Difficulty: Hard

30. For the most part, e-commerce enterprises have found that so-called first-mover advantages have been
    A) fairly sizable for a few months but then have eroded quickly and disappeared.
    B) the key to sustaining above-average profitability.
    C) fleeting and elusive because of lower than anticipated switching costs and weaker than expected network effects.
    D) both fairly sizable and fairly durable because of moderately strong buyer loyalty to particular web sites.
    E) competitively powerful because of relatively low switching costs and weaker than expected network effects.

    Answer: C Difficulty: Hard

31. Many dot-com startups and e-commerce firms have had trouble gaining durable operating advantages by doing a world-class job of incorporating Internet technologies across their value chains systems because
    A) the vast majority of companies are scouring the market for best-of-breed Internet technologies and are "e-commercing" their value chains to squeeze out cost-savings and realize improvements in operating effectiveness.
    B) the concept of first-mover advantages has been discredited and does not apply to high-technology situations.
    C) of stronger than expected network effects and lower than expected switching costs.
    D) the misguided advertising campaigns on the part of many dot-com start-ups failed to produce strong buyer loyalty.
    E) many traditional businesses initiated brick-and-click strategies powerful enough to overwhelm and defeat pure dot-com strategies.

    Answer: A Difficulty: Medium

Strategic Mistakes Made by Early Internet Entrepreneurs

32. During the 1990s many dot-com startups made such strategic mistakes as
    A) ignoring the competitive pressures from substitute products.
    B) ignoring low barriers to entry.
    C) discounting the importance of strategic alliances and close seller-supplier collaboration.
    D) putting too little emphasis on price competition.
    E) underemphasizing customer service and product quality.

    Answer: B Difficulty: Medium

33. During the 1990s many dot-com startups made such strategic mistakes as
    A) not capitalizing on high entry barriers, underemphasizing the importance of developing ancillary revenue sources, and failing to utilize brick-and-click strategies.
    B) making too little use of strategic alliances, trying to sell direct to end-users as opposed to relying on established distribution channels, and trying to charge too big a price premium.
    C) ignoring low barriers to entry, trying to compete solely on the basis of low price, and relying too heavily on ancillary revenues to cover their losses on "core" products.
    D) overemphasizing price competition, discounting the competitive pressures from substitute products, and not building strong wholesaler/retailer distribution networks.
    E) overemphasizing online customer service, ignoring low barriers to entry, and spending too much on advertising.

    Answer: C Difficulty: Hard

34. Dot-com business models that are highly dependent on generating advertising revenues at their website to cover costs and earn a profit
    A) are among the lowest risk strategic approaches that a dot-com enterprise can employ.
    B) are highly attractive because of the relatively low bargaining power of Internet advertisers.
    C) are highly risky at best and highly suspect at worst (partly because of the strong bargaining power of Internet advertisers and the danger of becoming reliant on an ever-rising stream of advertising revenues).
    D) are likely to be less profitable than utilizing a business model/strategy that calls for attracting customers via ultra-low prices.
    E) work fairly well when a company is selling products to other businesses but doesn't work well when a company is mainly selling products to individuals and households.

    Answer: C Difficulty: Hard

35. In the future, successful dot-com strategies will likely need to incorporate such features as
    A) delivering unique value to buyers and making buying online very appealing.
    B) having ways to generate ancillary revenues (from website advertising and other sources) equal to at least 50 percent of total revenues.
    C) concentrating only on website operations and marketing, maintaining no inventories, purchasing goods from manufacturers and distributors only after an order has been received, and contracting with shippers to pick up the ordered merchandise from manufacturer/distributors and deliver it to customers.
    D) doing one's own manufacture of the items being sold, stocking these goods at regional warehouses, and delivering the items directly using a fleet of company-owned vehicles.
    E) relying on massive ad campaigns to attract website traffic and build a name brand image, matching or beating the prices of brick-and-mortar retailers, mailing out discount coupons to frequent site visitors who have not yet made a purchase, offering a wide smorgasbord of products (one stop shopping), and outsourcing warehousing, shipping, and customer service functions to third parties.

    Answer: A   Difficulty: Medium

36. In the years to come, successful dot-com strategies will likely need to incorporate such features as
    A) doing one's own manufacture of the items being sold, stocking these goods at regional warehouses, and delivering the items directly using a fleet of company-owned vehicles.
    B) having ways to generate ancillary revenues (from website advertising and other sources) equal to at least 50 percent of total revenues, making sparing use of strategic alliances, being judicious about the amount spent on advertising, and relying heavily on low price to attract buyers and retain their loyalty.
    C) concentrating only on website operations and marketing, maintaining no inventories, purchasing goods from manufacturers and distributors only after an order has been received, strong brand name awareness created by extensive advertising in the media, prices that are lower than traditional brick-and-mortar retailers, and quick delivery via FedEx or UPS or similar carriers.
    D) delivering unique value to buyers and making buying online very appealing; a value chain that enables differentiation or lower costs or more value for the money; minimal dependence on ancillary revenues; and strong capabilities in cutting-edge Internet technology.
    E) lower prices than brick-and-mortar retailers, large ad campaigns to attract website traffic, special discounts for new site visitors who have not yet made a purchase, extensive product selection (one stop shopping), and outsourcing warehousing, shipping, and customer service functions to third parties.

    Answer: D   Difficulty: Hard

37. In the years to come, which of the following is least likely to be a key element of a successful dot-com strategy?
    A) Delivering unique value to buyers, making buying online very appealing, and also keeping the web site innovative, fresh, and entertaining.
    B) Focusing on a limited number of competencies and performing a specialized number of value chain activities where proprietary Internet applications and capabilities can be developed.
    C) Having ways to generate ancillary revenues (from website advertising and other sources) equal to at least 50 percent of total revenues, making sparing use of strategic alliances, being judicious about the amount spent on advertising, having a broad product offering, outsourcing the order fulfillment function, and relying heavily on low price to attract buyers and retain their loyalty.
    D) Using innovative marketing techniques that are efficient in reaching the targeted audience and effective in stimulating purchases (or perhaps boosting ancillary revenues from such sources as advertising), being minimally dependent on ancillary revenues; and having strong capabilities in cutting-edge Internet technology.
    E) Engineering a value chain that enables differentiation or lower costs or more value for the money.

    Answer: C   Difficulty: Medium

38. The advantages of a brick-and-click strategy (as opposed to a pure dot.com strategy or a pure brick-and-mortar strategy) include
    A) lower advertising costs, lower customer service costs, and greater capability to employ a low-cost provider strategy.
    B) being able to offer a much wider product line than is stocked at brick-and-mortar stores and being able to attract bargain-hunting shoppers by selling the company's merchandise online at lower prices than in traditional company-owned retail outlets.
    C) low incremental investments to establish a website, the ability to access a wider customer base, the ability to leverage a well-known brand name, and the ability to use existing company store locations as warehouse and distribution points for nearby customers who buy online.
    D) lower personnel costs for customer service, being able to maintain lower inventories, and less risk of merchandise theft.
    E) the ability to rely less heavily on strategic alliances, being able to eliminate the cost of creating order fulfillment systems, and lower online advertising costs.

    Answer: C   Difficulty: Medium

39. The two big appeals of a brick-and-click strategy are
    A) lower advertising costs and lower costs for filling and delivering customer orders.
    B) economically expanding a company's geographic reach and giving existing and potential customers another choice of how to communicate with the company, shop for company products, make purchases, or resolve customer service problems.
    C) low incremental investments to establish a website and the ability of customers to use existing company store locations to view and inspect items prior to purchase.
    D) the ability to leverage a well-known brand name and lower personnel costs for customer service.
    E) the ability to rely less heavily on strategic alliances and being able to eliminate the cost of creating order fulfillment systems.

    Answer: B   Difficulty: Medium

Internet Strategies for Traditional Businesses

40. Traditional businesses can use which of the following strategic approaches to try to capitalize on new opportunities afforded by the Internet and e-commerce technologies?
    A) Using the Internet to communicate and collaborate with suppliers and distribution channel allies
    B) Making greater use of build-to-order manufacturing and assembly
    C) Building systems to pick and pack products that are shipped individually
    D) Using the Internet to give both existing and potential customers another way to interact with the company
    E) All of these.

    Answer: E   Difficulty: Easy

41. One of the biggest Internet-related strategic issues facing traditional businesses is
    A) whether to have a company website.
    B) whether and how to incorporate use of Internet technology applications in performing various internal value chain activities.
    C) how best to try to offset the company's competitive disadvantage vis-à-vis its rivals employing a pure dot-com strategy.
    D) whether to form a strategic alliance with a pure dot-com enterprise or else a company already employing a combination brick-and-click strategy.
    E) how to use the Internet in positioning the company in the marketplace (i.e., how much emphasis to place on the Internet as a distribution channel for accessing buyers).

    Answer: E   Difficulty: Medium

42. Which of the following is not one of the options that traditional businesses have for using the Internet to position themselves in the marketplace?
    A) Simply establishing a company website
    B) Operating a website that provides existing and potential customers with extensive product information but that relies on click-throughs to distribution channel partners to handle orders and transactions
    C) Using online lines as a relatively minor distribution channel
    D) Employing a brick-and-click strategy to sell direct to consumers and to compete directly with traditional wholesalers and retailers
    E) Making greater use of build-to-order manufacturing and assembly as a basis for bypassing traditional distribution channels entirely

    Answer: A   Difficulty: Easy

Short Answer Questions

43. Identify and briefly discuss at least three strategic initiatives that a company can employ when it confronts vigorous competition from alternative technologies for building various components of the Internet infrastructure and creating a globally-wired economy and desires to win the battle for technology supremacy on behalf of the technological approach that it is pursuing.

    Difficulty: Hard

44. Discuss and explain how Internet technology impacts company and industry value chains.

Difficulty: Hard

45. What impact is growing use of the Internet having on the bargaining power of buyers? Discuss and explain.

Difficulty: Medium

46. What impact is the Internet and Internet technology applications having on the relationship a company has with its suppliers? Discuss and explain.

Difficulty: Medium

47. What impacts are the Internet and Internet technologies having on the rivalry among firms competing against each other in a given industry? Discuss and explain.

Difficulty: Medium

48. What impacts are the Internet and Internet technologies having on industry entry barriers?

Difficulty: Medium

49. Briefly identify and discuss any two of the flaws and mistakes made by the early Internet entrepreneurs?

Difficulty: Medium

50. Who is in the best position to win out in the end-dot-com e-tailers or brick-and-click retailers or traditional brick-and-mortar retailers? Who is in the weakest position and stands the best chance of losing out? Explain and defend your answer using what you have learned about strategy in the chapters you have been assigned so far.

Difficulty: Hard

51. Identify four different ways that traditional businesses can incorporate use of the Internet in their basic competitive strategy and to position themselves in the marketplace.

Difficulty: Medium

52. Explain why it is currently hard for companies to gain competitive advantage over rivals by implementing cutting-edge Internet technologies.

Difficulty: Medium

53. Why have dot-com start-ups that moved early and aggressively to employ cutting-edge Internet technologies and create online businesses generally failed to capture any first-mover advantages of much significance?

Difficulty: Hard

Chapter 8: Tailoring Strategy to Fit Specific Industry and Company Situations

Multiple Choice Questions

Matching Strategy to the Situation

1. The most important drivers shaping a company's most appealing strategic options fall into two broad categories:
   A) a company's core competencies and the make-up of its value chain.
   B) the company's financial condition and its current reputation/image with buyers.
   C) the nature of industry and competitive conditions and the firm's own resource strengths and weaknesses, competitive capabilities, opportunities and threats, and market position.
   D) a company's internal strengths and weaknesses and its external opportunities and threats.
   E) the company's competitive strength vis-à-vis rivals and which strategic group it is in.

   Answer: C   Difficulty: Medium

Strategies for Competing in Emerging Industries of the Future

2. Which of the following is <u>not</u> usually a characteristic of a young, emerging industry?
   A) There are no established "rules" for how the market works or how firms compete; there's much uncertainty about how the industry will function, how fast it will grow, how big it will get; and the little historical information that is available contributes little to the task of making sales and profit projections.
   B) Technological know-how is freely shared and exchanged among the early participants, with no competitive advantage attached to patents and proprietary technology.
   C) There is uncertainty regarding which of several competing technologies will prove to be the most efficient.
   D) Many potential buyers expect first-generation products to be rapidly improved and delay their purchase until technology and product design mature.
   E) Entry barriers tend to be relatively low.

   Answer: B   Difficulty: Medium

3. Competing in emerging industries presents managers with such strategic challenges as
   A) how to finance the start-up phase, fund necessary R&D and product development, work out product design issues, and get through several lean years until the product catches on.
   B) how to successfully implement a best-cost producer strategy.
   C) whether to use a differentiation strategy or a focus/market niche strategy.
   D) how many core competencies to try to build and nurture.
   E) how steep the industry's experience curve will be and whether to expect cost reductions to come quickly or slowly.

   Answer: A   Difficulty: Medium

4. Which of the following is not a typical challenge that companies in emerging industries have to contend with and try to overcome?
   A) Mounting global competition and increasing vertical integration
   B) Many potential buyers expect first-generation products to be rapidly improved and delay their purchase until technology and product design mature
   C) How to induce first-time purchase and overcome customer concerns about product features, performance reliability, and conflicting claims of rival firms
   D) Low barriers to the entry of new firms
   E) A situation where there is no consensus about which of several competing technologies will win out and/or which product features will gain the most buyer favor

   Answer: A Difficulty: Medium

5. To be successful in emerging industries, companies usually have to pursue such strategic avenues as
   A) avoiding the "first mover disadvantages" associated with making early commitments to alternative technologies, wider product selection, different styling, and staking out a position in new distribution channels.
   B) building internal competencies and capabilities rapidly so as to avoid forming strategic alliances and partnerships and having to share the firm's potential long-term profitability with outsiders.
   C) pushing hard to perfect the technology, improve product quality, and develop attractive performance features.
   D) being a technological follower, so as to conserve scarce financial resources.
   E) striving to build a distinctive competence in product innovation and being a first-mover in introducing new products.

   Answer: C Difficulty: Medium

6. Success in emerging industries usually requires that companies pursue such strategic avenues as
   A) capturing first mover advantages associated with making early commitments to promising technologies, product line expansion, improving product styling, and entering new distribution channels.
   B) forming strategic alliances and partnerships with key suppliers and/or other companies having complementary technology or expertise.
   C) pushing hard to perfect the technology, improve product quality, and develop attractive performance features.
   D) moving quickly to as technological uncertainty clears and a dominant technology appears.
   E) All of these.

   Answer: E Difficulty: Easy

7. Young companies in fast-growing markets face such hurdles as
   A) learning to exercise bold entrepreneurship, sustaining a willingness to pioneer.
   B) managing rapid expansion, defending against competitors trying to horn in on their success, and building a strong competitive position for the long term.
   C) acquiring an intuitive feel for what buyers will like and how they will use the product.
   D) how to conduct reliable market research, how to build scale economies, how to ride the learning and experience curves more rapidly than rivals, and how to craft a winning strategy.
   E) which of the five basic generic strategies to adopt, whether to rely more on guerilla tactics or on end-run offensives, and how much resources to invest in defensive strategies.

   Answer: B Difficulty: Medium

Competing in Turbulent High Velocity Industries

8. A high-velocity industry environment is characterized by
   A) rapid entry and exit of participating firms (there's an unusually high competitor turnover rate compared to other industries).
   B) the need for industry members to change to radically different strategies several times a year (company strategies have a very short life).
   C) the rapid appearance and disappearance of industry driving forces, such that the industry is in constant turmoil.
   D) rapid-fire technological change, short product life-cycles, frequent launches of fresh competitive moves by industry members, and quickly evolving customer requirements and expectations.
   E) rapid and sizable shifts in the industry's experience curve that make it difficult for industry members to accurately predict future costs.

   Answer: D Difficulty: Easy

9. The central strategy-making challenge in a turbulent market environment is
   A) how to remain the industry's first-mover.
   B) how to build the strongest supply chain alliances.
   C) managing change.
   D) deciding when to cut prices versus when to improve product features and performance.
   E) how often to change the company's business model without impairing profitability.

   Answer: C Difficulty: Easy

10. In turbulent high-velocity markets, a company's approach to coping with rapid change should, ideally, incorporate
    A) a bigger emphasis on competing on the basis of low-cost/low-price than on the basis of strong product differentiation or best-cost.
    B) efforts to react to change, to anticipate change, and to lead change—though not in the same proportion.
    C) consistent efforts to be a first-mover or a fast follower or a slow-mover—whichever best fits management's temperaments and shareholder expectations.
    D) a far bigger effort to employ offensive strategies than to employ defensive strategies.
    E) an strong emphasis on building and strengthening the company's long-term market position rather than worrying excessively about profitability and ROE.

    Answer: B Difficulty: Medium

11. In trying to deal with high-velocity change, a company's three strategic postures or options are
    A) to pursue low-cost, differentiation, or best-cost strategies.
    B) to react to change, to anticipate change, and to try to lead change.
    C) to be a first-mover, a fast follower, or a slow-mover—as may be most expedient.
    D) play offense, play defense, or utilize end-run offensives to compete in those market segments where change occurs at a more leisurely pace.
    E) to pursue short-term profitability, intermediate-term profitability, or long-term profitability.

    Answer: B Difficulty: Medium

12. In trying to deal with high-velocity change, a company
    A) can either pursue profitability or market share, but not both.
    B) can react to change, anticipate change, and/or try to lead change.
    C) should be a first-mover, a fast follower, or a slow-mover—as may be most expedient.
    D) can play offense, play defense, or utilize end-run offensives to compete in those market segments where change occurs at a more leisurely pace.
    E) should be a technological leader, a product quality leader, or a customer service leader—whichever is most appealing to buyers.

    Answer: B   Difficulty: Medium

13. Competitive success in fast-changing or high velocity markets tends to hinge on a company's ability to
    A) be the first-mover in reacting and responding to change.
    B) be at worst a fast follower if it is not the first-mover in leading change.
    C) to do a better job than rivals of anticipating change and being well-prepared for what happens next.
    D) stay on the cutting-edge of technological change.
    E) improvise, experiment, adapt, reinvent, and regenerate as market and competitive conditions shift rapidly and sometimes unpredictably.

    Answer: E   Difficulty: Medium

14. Those strategic moves and initiatives that seem to offer the best payoff in turbulent, high velocity markets include
    A) developing and maintaining the organizational capability to respond quickly to the moves of rivals and surprising new developments.
    B) relying on strategic partnerships with outside suppliers and with companies making tie-in products to perform value chain activities where they have specialized expertise and capabilities.
    C) investing aggressively to stay on the leading edge of technological know-how.
    D) initiating fresh actions every few months, not just when a competitive response is needed, and keeping the company's products fresh and exciting enough to stand out in the midst of all the change that is taking place.
    E) All of these.

    Answer: E   Difficulty: Easy

15. The types of strategic moves and initiatives that seem to offer the best payoff in turbulent, high velocity markets include
    A) being clever at being a fast follower, doing a better job than rivals in anticipating and planning for change, and striving for a low-cost edge over rivals.
    B) having a wider product line than rivals, making sure the company's products are strongly differentiated, and have a shorter value chain than rivals so that the company has fewer activities to revamp as the market changes.
    C) investing aggressively to stay on the leading edge of technological know-how; launching fresh actions every few months, not just when a competitive response is needed; and keeping the company's products fresh and exciting enough to stand out in the midst of all the change that is taking place.
    D) doing a better job than rivals of leading industry change and being a successful first mover; having sufficient internal resources and competencies that the company does not need to have many strategic partners; and outspending rivals on new product R&D.
    E) doing a better job than rival of reacting and responding to rapid change, concentrating on a few crucial value chain activities and farming the rest out to strategic partners, and being a fast follower as opposed to a first-mover/leader in technology.

    Answer: C Difficulty: Hard

Strategies for Competing in Maturing Industries

16. The transition to a slower-growth, maturing industry environment tends to result in
    A) a greater emphasis on cost and service among rival sellers.
    B) more sophistication and greater bargaining power on the part of buyers.
    C) rising industry profitability as rivalry tapers off and there's less head-to-head competition for market share among rival firms.
    D) reduced risks associated with capacity additions and significantly faster rates of product innovation as sellers endeavor to rekindle buyer interest.
    E) Both A and B.

    Answer: E Difficulty: Medium

17. In a maturing industry, slackening growth rates tend to alter the competitive environment in such ways as
    A) weakening competitive rivalry and dampening the forces of multinational or global competition.
    B) boosting rates of product innovation, accelerating the search for additional end-use applications, improving product quality, raising the frequency with which new performance features are added, and causing product differentiation to be stronger.
    C) increasing the number of competitors and reducing the number of mergers and acquisitions among competing firms.
    D) lowering the emphasis on cost control and reducing price competition among rivals.
    E) increasing buyer bargaining power, as savvy and experienced buyers shop hard for the best deal on repeat purchases.

    Answer: E Difficulty: Hard

18. Which one of the following statements does not represent one of the typical fundamental changes in an industry as it reaches maturity?
   A) Industry profitability decreases, sometimes permanently.
   B) Competition on an international or global scale begins to intensify.
   C) New scale economies develop, the industry experience curve drops sharply, and overall costs per unit produced and sold drop significantly.
   D) Increased competitive emphasis is placed on lowering costs and improving service.
   E) Firms encounter growing difficulty in coming up with new product innovations and developing new uses and applications for the product.

   Answer: C Difficulty: Medium

19. One of the major mistakes a firm can make during the transition to industry maturity is to
   A) steer a middle course between low cost, differentiation, and focusing because such strategic compromises typically result in a firm ending up "stuck in the middle" with a fuzzy strategy and no competitive advantage.
   B) expand into foreign markets.
   C) attack weaker firms and try to capture some of their market share.
   D) purchase rival companies at bargain prices—this simply makes the company a bigger slow-growth company.
   E) dissolve its strategic alliances and partnerships.

   Answer: A Difficulty: Medium

20. In a maturing market where the rates of growth are on the decline, rival firms can often improve their competitive position in the marketplace by
   A) pursuing backward and/or forward vertical integration to capture greater control over the industry value chain, shifting to standardized product offerings, and competing aggressively on the basis of superior customer service.
   B) concentrating on adding new models and performance features, boosting product quality, and striving hard to achieve much stronger product differentiation vis-à-vis rivals.
   C) shifting to focus or market niche strategies and concentrating exclusively on those buyers and models/styles where demand is continuing to grow at above average rates.
   D) pruning marginal products and models, putting more emphasis on value chain innovation, emphasizing cost reduction, acquiring rival firms at bargain prices, building new or more flexible capabilities, and expanding internationally.
   E) increasing advertising and promotional efforts to gain a brand image advantage over rivals and increase sales to present customers, pursuing new distribution channels, and outsourcing less critical value chain activities.

   Answer: D Difficulty: Medium

21. The typical strategic mistakes companies can make during the transition from fairly rapid growth to industry maturity include
    A) pursuing a low-cost strategy instead of a differentiation strategy; not capitalizing on economies of scale; and failing to go all out to achieve strong product differentiation so as to set the company's product offering well apart from those of rivals.
    B) steering a middle course between low-cost, differentiation, and focusing; being slow to adapt existing competencies and capabilities to changing customer expectations; getting caught with too much capacity as growth slows; and waiting too long to respond to price cutting by rivals.
    C) pursuing a low-cost leadership strategy; overspending on marketing and advertising efforts to boost sales growth; and putting too much emphasis on new product R&D and product innovation.
    D) sacrificing long-term competitive position for short-term profit; outsourcing too many value chain activities to allies and partners; inaccurately predicting the next moves of close rivals; and pursuing aggressive acquisition of weaker rival firms.
    E) merging with another firm; failing to pursue cost reduction soon enough and aggressively enough; and abandoning strategic alliances with outsiders.

    Answer: B   Difficulty: Hard

Strategies for Firms in Stagnant or Declining Industries

22. Businesses competing in stagnant or declining industries must
    A) resign themselves to performance targets consistent with the available market opportunities, emphasize profit and cash flow and return-on-investment criteria as opposed to sales growth and market share growth, concentrate on drawing sales and market share away from weaker rivals (if they want to expand their market share), and strive to drive costs down (perhaps by acquiring weaker rivals and consolidating operations).
    B) pursue vertical integration and gain greater operating control over more stages of the industry's value chain.
    C) initiate deep price cuts to rejuvenate long-term demand and expand into the markets of foreign countries, especially emerging country markets.
    D) consider selling out or else exiting the industry.
    E) steer a middle course between low-cost, differentiation and focusing and adopt a best-cost producer strategy aimed at the middle of the market spectrum.

    Answer: D   Difficulty: Medium

23. Potentially promising strategies for firms in stagnant or declining industries include
    A) deemphasizing superior quality and customer service and shifting to a more standardized product offering.
    B) concentrating on vertical integration to gain operating control over more stages of the industry's value chain.
    C) initiating deep price cuts to rekindle demand for the product.
    D) pursuing a focused strategy aimed at identifying, creating, and exploiting the growth segments within the overall market and/or stressing differentiation based on quality improvement and product innovation.
    E) steering a middle course between low-cost, differentiation and focusing and adopting a best-cost producer strategy aimed at the middle of the market spectrum.

    Answer: D   Difficulty: Medium

24. Competitive advantage in industries with stagnant or declining market demand usually involves
    A) acquiring rival firms at bargain prices so as to grow the company's overall market share.
    B) expanding into the markets of more and more foreign countries using a global differentiation strategy.
    C) focusing on growth segments within the overall market, stressing differentiation based on quality improvement and product innovation, or becoming a lower cost producer.
    D) achieving a higher degree of vertical integration than rivals and then pursuing value chain revamping and reconfiguration to gain a cost advantage.
    E) initiating price cuts, boosting advertising, adding new features and more models, and stressing improved customer service, so as to achieve strong product differentiation.

    Answer: C Difficulty: Medium

Strategies for Competing in Fragmented Industries

25. An industry is said to be fragmented when
    A) it consists of many different market segments and buyer groups.
    B) demand for the product is scattered over many different country markets.
    C) the industry value chain is divided into 15 or more distinctly different stages.
    D) the supply side of the market is populated by hundreds, perhaps thousands of sellers, no one of which has a substantial share of total industry sales.
    E) the annual number of buyer-seller transactions is in the millions (or higher).

    Answer: D Difficulty: Medium

26. Which of the following does not generally account for why the supply side of an industry may be fragmented and contain hundreds or even thousands of companies?
    A) The market for the industry's product is becoming more global and/or the market is young and crowded with aspiring contenders, no one of which has the resource and competitive strength to command a significant market share.
    B) There's an absence of scale economies and low entry barriers allow small firms to enter cheaply and quickly.
    C) Buyers require relatively small quantities of customized products.
    D) Market demand is so extensive and diverse that very large numbers of firms can easily co-exist trying to accommodate buyer requirements and to cover all the needed geographic locations.
    E) Most all of the competitors have chosen to pursue focus and market niche strategies.

    Answer: E Difficulty: Medium

27. Which of the following is not usually a promising option for competing in a fragmented industry?
    A) Specializing by product type or by customer type
    B) Becoming a low-cost operator
    C) Employing a best-cost provider strategy aimed at giving buyers more value for their money and trying to appeal to a broader customer base
    D) Focusing on a limited geographic area
    E) Constructing and operating "formula" facilities at many different locations

    Answer: C Difficulty: Hard

Strategies for Sustaining Rapid Growth

28. For a company to sustain rapid revenue and earnings growth, it needs to
    A) regularly launch fresh offensives to take market share from its rivals.
    B) pursue a global or multicountry strategy aimed at becoming the global market share leader.
    C) have a portfolio of strategic initiatives that range from strengthening its existing businesses to entering businesses with promising growth opportunities to planting the seeds for entirely new ventures.
    D) be a first-mover in R&D and new product innovation, strive for global market dominance, and aggressively pursue value chain reconfiguration.
    E) leverage use of the Internet and e-commerce technologies, acquire growth-oriented firms in other businesses, invest in its own venture capital subsidiary, and strive for global low-cost leadership.

    Answer: C   Difficulty: Medium

29. Companies that simultaneously pursue multiple strategy horizons in an effort to sustain rapid growth
    A) have to avoid placing bets on every opportunity that appears on their radar screens, be willing to absorb losses on new ventures that don't pan out, and be wary of straying far from their resource strengths and competencies lest they end up in businesses for which they are ill-suited.
    B) have to be willing to stray from their core competencies and resource strengths in order to locate enough growth opportunities.
    C) generally have to compete globally, be willing to diversify outside their areas of resource strength, and make a variety of acquisitions in several altogether new industry arenas.
    D) need to be well-established industry leaders, avoid getting into fragmented industries, and put most of their new investments in emerging industries where rapid growth potential is the greatest.
    E) should use a defensive strategy to protect their present market position, use offensive strategies to pursue their best opportunities in other new businesses, and avoid squandering their financial resources on making new acquisitions.

    Answer: A   Difficulty: Medium

Strategies for Industry Leaders

30. What is the key strategic issue or strategic concern that faces an industry leader?
    A) Whether to pursue a large market share globally as well as domestically
    B) Whether to acquire weaker rivals
    C) How to defend and strengthen its overall leadership position in the industry, perhaps even becoming the dominant leader
    D) Whether to lower prices faster than competitors
    E) How fast to pursue experience curve effects and scale economies

    Answer: C   Difficulty: Medium

31. The basic strategic options for an industry leader include
    A) global strategies of all types, a multicountry country strategy keyed to broad differentiation, and technology leadership.
    B) staying on the offensive, fortifying the defending the company's present position, and playing competitive hardball when smaller rivals rock the boat and try to mount a challenge.
    C) introducing more varieties and brands of the product to match the product attributes of challengers' brands or fill vacant niches, any initiatives to raise buyer switching costs to other brands, and muscle-flexing strategies.
    D) an export strategy, global low-cost or differentiation strategies, first-mover offensives, product innovation leadership, and end-run offensives.
    E) preemptive strikes, simultaneous offensives on many fronts, offensives to attack competitors' strengths, and muscle-flexing strategies.

    Answer: B Difficulty: Hard

32. Which of the following strategies is not likely to be attractive to a firm that is the acknowledged market share leader in its industry?
    A) Stay-on-the-offensive and muscle-flexing strategies
    B) Vacant niche and harvesting strategies
    C) Fortify-and-defend strategy
    D) A global differentiation strategy
    E) Low-cost leadership

    Answer: B Difficulty: Easy

33. Which of the following is not consistent with a fortify-and-defend strategy?
    A) Pursuing methods to increase how much it costs customers to switch over to rivals
    B) Expanding the product line and lowering prices to broaden the company's appeal to buyers
    C) Building new capacity ahead of market demand
    D) Negotiating exclusive purchase agreements with the best suppliers and/or dealer distributors
    E) Introducing more varieties and brands of the product to match the product attributes of challengers' brands or fill vacant niches

    Answer: B Difficulty: Hard

Strategies for Runner-up Firms

34. Runner-up and second-tier firms
    A) can range from up-and-coming market challengers to perennial followers with little chance of improving their lot.
    B) are well advised to avoid head-on competition with the market leaders and either pursue market niche strategies or be content followers.
    C) seldom have a realistic chance of closing the gap with the present market leaders and eventually joining their ranks.
    D) need to be very proficient in crafting defensive strategies aimed at protecting the present positions from encroachment by aggressive market-leading rivals.
    E) can sometimes make occasional market gains by employing clever guerilla warfare tactics, but for the most part have to succeed by outwitting the market leaders in reacting to change, anticipating change, and leading change.

    Answer: A   Difficulty: Medium

35. Runner-up firms or second-tier firms often have to overcome such obstacles as
    A) a deficiency of entrepreneurial skills and management acumen.
    B) weaker ability to use mass media advertising, difficulty in gaining customer recognition, less access to scale economies, and difficulty in funding capital requirements.
    C) an inability to be competitive in foreign markets and pursue global strategies.
    D) having more resource deficiencies and weaknesses than resource strengths.
    E) All of these.

    Answer: B   Difficulty: Medium

36. Which of the following strategy options is generally <u>not</u> very suitable for a runner-up firm trying to build a stronger competitive market position?
    A) A muscle-flexing offensive strategy extending over many market segments and that attacks the leaders head-on
    B) A distinctive image strategy and a superior product strategy
    C) Acquisition of or merger with other firms in the industry
    D) A content follower strategy
    E) A vacant niche strategy or specialist strategy

    Answer: A   Difficulty: Easy

37. Runner-up or second-tier firms can deal with the handicaps of small size by
    A) competing only in carefully chosen market segments and avoiding head-on, across-the-board competition with the market leaders.
    B) building core competencies in new product development, technical assistance to customers, or low-cost production (if economies of scale are not an obstacle).
    C) being content to remain small and not being lured into a full-line, serve-every-type-of-customer and every-customer-need kind of approach.
    D) using market niche or specialization type strategies.
    E) All of the above.

    Answer: E   Difficulty: Medium

38. Strategy options for firms handicapped by small size and market share include
   A) focusing on a few market segments where the firm's resource strengths offer prospects of a competitive edge.
   B) pioneering a technological breakthrough or developing technical expertise that will be highly valued by customers.
   C) being more agile and innovative in adapting to evolving market conditions and customer expectations than slower-to-change market leaders.
   D) getting new or better products to market ahead of rivals and gaining a reputation for product leadership.
   E) All of these.

   Answer: E   Difficulty: Easy

39. A runner-up firm anxious to become a market challenger needs a strategy aimed at
   A) imitating the strategies of the market leaders.
   B) low-cost rather than differentiation.
   C) building a competitive advantage of its own—perhaps by pioneering a leapfrog technological breakthrough, beating larger rivals to market with next-generation products, being quicker than larger rivals in adapting to significant market changes, or revamping the industry value chain in ways that dramatically drive down costs.
   D) attacking the leaders head-on with a series of offensive initiatives across many geographic regions.
   E) gaining buyer attention by cutting its price significantly below those of the leaders or else, if the financial resources are available, being bold in acquiring one of the market leaders.

   Answer: C   Difficulty: Medium

Strategies for Weak and Crisis-Ridden Businesses

40. Potentially attractive strategy options for a company in an also-ran or declining competitive position include
   A) a strategy to merge with or acquire other firms in an attempt to join forces and create a stronger enterprise, a guerilla warfare strategy, a harvesting strategy aimed at turning the firm into a cash cow instead of a cash hog by selling off some of the company's assets, or a preemptive strike strategy.
   B) buying market share with deep price cuts and trying to gain significantly greater buyer recognition and attention.
   C) shifting to a strategy that is largely a carbon copy of the market leader's strategy.
   D) an offensive turnaround strategy, a fortify-and-defend strategy, an immediate abandonment strategy, or an end-game strategy.
   E) broadening the company's product line to incorporate models and styles not offered by rival firms, boosting advertising, cutting prices, and/or aggressive internal efforts to correct the company's resource deficiencies.

   Answer: D   Difficulty: Medium

41. Potentially attractive turnaround strategy options for a struggling business include
   A) a harvesting strategy, a guerilla warfare strategy, some type of focus strategy, or a preemptive strike strategy.
   B) selling off assets, shifting to a different strategy, and/or bold efforts to reduce costs.
   C) shifting to a strategy that combines the most attractive strategy elements of one or more of the market leaders.
   D) aggressive cost reduction and value chain revamping to try to become the industry's low-cost leader.
   E) concentrating on the same kinds of product features emphasized by the market leaders and matching or beating the leaders' prices.

   Answer: B   Difficulty: Hard

42. An end-game or harvesting strategy is ill-suited for which one of the following situations?
    A) When the industry's long-term prospects are unattractive
    B) When the firm has a weak competitive position, its profit prospects are not good, and rejuvenation would be costly
    C) When the business is a crucial or core component of a diversified firm's overall lineup of businesses
    D) When the firm's market share is becoming increasingly costly to maintain or defend
    E) When reduced levels of competitive effort will not immediately trigger sharp declines in sales or a falloff in market position

    Answer: C   Difficulty: Medium

43. End-game strategies involve
    A) retreating to a market niche which the firm can defend for a few years.
    B) the various strategic options which a firm has to prepare for closing down operations and liquidating the business.
    C) steering a middle course between preserving the status quo and exiting as soon as possible, trying in the meantime to reap the greatest possible harvest of cash.
    D) the various strategic options which a firm has for selling the business and exiting the industry.
    E) Both B and D

    Answer: C   Difficulty: Medium

44. Which of the following approaches is not a logical component of a strategy to turn around a struggling single-business company?
    A) Replacement of top management and other key personnel and giving the new management team rein to make whatever changes they deem appropriate
    B) Revenue-increasing actions
    C) Actions to reduce costs
    D) Guerrilla warfare tactics aimed at creating a market niche on the leaders' flanks
    E) Actions to sell some of firm's assets and to retrench to a narrower base of operations

    Answer: D   Difficulty: Medium

45. Which of the following is not a reasonable option for turning around or salvaging a distressed business?
    A) Revamping the firm's competitive approach
    B) Strategies aimed at imitating what the market leaders are doing
    C) Strategies to boost revenues
    D) Actions to cut costs
    E) Selling off assets to raise cash to save the remaining part of the business

    Answer: B   Difficulty: Easy

46. Rejuvenating a distressed business can include such action approaches as
    A) shifting to a new competitive strategy and trying to reposition the business in the marketplace.
    B) merger with another firm.
    C) retrenching to a core of products and a customer base more closely matched to the firm's resource strengths and capabilities.
    D) overhauling internal operations and functional area strategies to produce better support of the same basic overall business strategy.
    E) All of the above.

    Answer: E   Difficulty: Easy

Ten Commandments for Crafting Successful Business Strategies

47. Which of the following is not among the ten commandments for crafting a successful business strategy?
    A) Avoid strategies capable of succeeding in only the most optimistic circumstances.
    B) Consider that attacking competitive weakness is usually more profitable and less risky than attacking competitive strength.
    C) Be judicious in cutting prices without an established cost advantage.
    D) Always pursue full vertical integration so as to have full command of the industry value chain.
    E) Place top priority on crafting and executing strategic moves that enhance the company's long-term competitive position.

    Answer: D   Difficulty: Medium

Short Answer Questions

48. What are the characteristics of competing in an emerging industry of the future? Describe at least three strategic approaches or initiatives that are well-suited for this type of market-environment?

    Difficulty: Hard

49. What kinds of changes in the competitive environment occur when an industry begins to mature? What strategic approaches are well-suited for this type of industry environment?

    Difficulty: Hard

50. Briefly discuss the strategic approaches that are well-suited for competing in a turbulent, high velocity market environment.

    Difficulty: Hard

51. What are the dominant business and economic characteristics of a fragmented industry? Describe three strategy options that are suitable for competing in a fragmented industry?

    Difficulty: Hard

52. Explain why a company wanting to sustain rapid sales and earning growth needs a portfolio of strategies?

Difficulty: Medium

53. Discuss briefly each of the primary competitive strategy options for companies that are industry leaders.

Difficulty: Medium

54. Identify and briefly discuss any three of the strategic approaches that are well-suited for runner-up companies.

Difficulty: Medium

55. Runner-up companies tend to be weakly positioned and less profitable than industry leaders. True or false. Explain.

Difficulty: Medium

56. When and why is liquidation a last-resort strategic option?

Difficulty: Medium

57. Identify and describe four circumstances under which an end-game strategy (or harvesting strategy) makes good strategic sense.

Difficulty: Medium

Chapter 9: Strategy and Competitive Advantage in Diversified Companies

Multiple Choice Questions

The Elements of Corporate Strategy

1. The task of crafting corporate strategy for a diversified company encompasses
    A) picking the new industries to enter and deciding on the means of entry.
    B) initiating actions to boost the combined performance of the businesses the firm has diversified into.
    C) pursuing opportunities to leverage cross-business value chain relationships and strategic fits into competitive advantage.
    D) establishing investment priorities and steering corporate resources into the most attractive business units.
    E) All of these.

    Answer: E   Difficulty: Easy

2. Which one of the following is <u>not</u> one of the elements of crafting corporate strategy for a diversified company?
    A) Picking the new industries to enter and deciding on the means of entry
    B) Choosing the appropriate value chain for each business the company has diversified into
    C) Pursuing opportunities to leverage cross-business value chain relationships and strategic fits into competitive advantage
    D) Establishing investment priorities and steering corporate resources into the most attractive business units
    E) Initiating actions to boost the combined performance of the businesses the firm has diversified into

    Answer: B   Difficulty: Medium

When To Diversify

3. Diversification generally doesn't need to become a strategic priority until a company
    A) has integrated backward and forward as far as it can.
    B) begins to run out of growth opportunities in its present business and has opportunities to utilize its resources and capabilities in other market arenas.
    C) has achieved industry leadership in its main line of business.
    D) has expanded globally in its mainstay business and runs out of additional foreign markets to enter.
    E) starts considering entry into foreign markets.

    Answer: B   Difficulty: Medium

4. When to diversify
    A) is based more on management preferences than any other factor.
    B) is a function of how soon a company can identify businesses that can pass the attractiveness test, the competitive advantage test, and the profit test.
    C) depends partly on the firm's remaining growth opportunities in its present industry and partly on the available opportunities to utilize its resources, expertise, and capabilities in other industries.
    D) varies from firm to firm according to whether the company is financially strong enough to fund a diversification effort.
    E) is a function of whether a firm has attractive opportunities to expand its present value chain or whether it needs altogether new value chain opportunities in different industries.

    Answer: C   Difficulty: Medium

5. Diversification ought to be considered when
    A) a company's profits are being squeezed and it needs to increase its net profit margins and return on investment.
    B) a company lacks sustainable competitive advantage in its present business.
    C) a company begins to encounter diminishing growth prospects in its mainstay business.
    D) a company needs to enhance the likelihood of its achieving a distinctive competence.
    E) a company is under the gun to create a more attractive value chain.

    Answer: C   Difficulty: Medium

6. Important reasons for a company to consider diversification include
    A) a need to soak up excess resources and avoid the temptation to allocate unneeded resources to the company's various internal functional area activities.
    B) the benefits of giving company managers the opportunity to develop first-hand knowledge of other businesses, customers, technologies, and industry environments.
    C) giving the company a broader base to pursue product innovation.
    D) a desire to avoid putting all of its "eggs" in one industry basket, dimming growth opportunities in its present business, and opportunities to transfer its resources, expertise, and capabilities to other industries.
    E) reducing the need to use price cuts to grow the company's profits and return on investment in its main line of business.

    Answer: D   Difficulty: Medium

The Advantages and Disadvantages of Concentrating on a Single Business

7. Concentrating on a single line-of-business has such advantages as
    A) creating a distinctive competence as concerns one or more industry key success factors.
    B) promoting a high degree of strategic fit among functional and operating strategies.
    C) focusing the full force of organizational resources on becoming better at what it does and expanding into geographic markets it doesn't serve.
    D) reducing shareholder risk that the enterprise will fail.
    E) not spreading the company's resources and managerial expertise over too many diverse industries and value chain activities.

    Answer: C   Difficulty: Easy

8. The big risk of single-business concentration is
   A) putting all of the firm's eggs in one industry basket.
   B) not building a distinctive competence.
   C) failing to capture strategic fit opportunities.
   D) not winning a sustainable competitive advantage.
   E) being outgunned and outmanaged by competitors.

   Answer: A   Difficulty: Easy

9. Factors that signal it may be time for a company to consider diversifying include
   A) having the financial and organizational resources to support a diversification effort, opportunities to capture cross-business strategic fits by entering related businesses, and opportunities to add value for its customers or gain competitive advantage by getting into businesses having complementary technologies or products.
   B) not being able to build a distinctive competence in its present business.
   C) failing to earn attractive profits in its present business.
   D) being outgunned and out-managed by competitors in its present business, thus making it desirable to reposition the company and shift its investment to other market arenas.
   E) All of these

   Answer: A   Difficulty: Easy

Building Shareholder Value: The Ultimate Reason For Diversifying

10. Diversifying into new businesses is a justifiable investment if it
    A) results in increased profit margins and bigger total profits.
    B) builds shareholder value.
    C) helps the company escape the rigors of competition in its present business.
    D) leads to the development of a greater variety of distinctive competencies and competitive capabilities.
    E) helps the company overcome the barriers to entering additional foreign markets.

    Answer: B   Difficulty: Easy

11. To create value for shareholders via diversification, a company must
    A) get into businesses that are profitable.
    B) diversify into industries that are growing rapidly.
    C) only acquire firms that are strong competitors.
    D) get into businesses that can perform better under common management than they could perform operating as independent or stand-alone enterprises.
    E) diversify into businesses that have the same key success factors as its present businesses.

    Answer: D   Difficulty: Medium

12. Businesses may be able to perform better under common management than they can as stand-alone enterprises when
    A) there are opportunities to transfer competitively valuable skills or technology from one business to another.
    B) there are opportunities to share use of a common brand name.
    C) there are opportunities to leverage existing competencies or capabilities or to create valuable new competencies or capabilities.
    D) there are opportunities to share technology or facilities or functional activities across businesses and thereby reduce costs.
    E) All of these.

    Answer: E Difficulty: Medium

Tests for Judging Whether Diversification Is Likely to Build Shareholder Value

13. The three tests for judging the merits of a particular diversification move are
    A) the attractiveness test, the profitability test, and the shareholder value test.
    B) the strategic fit test, the competitive advantage test, and the return on investment test.
    C) the resource fit test, the profitability test, and the shareholder value test.
    D) the attractiveness test, the cost-of-entry test, and the better-off test.
    E) the shareholder value test, the cost-of-entry test, and the return on investment test.

    Answer: D Difficulty: Hard

14. To test the probable impact of a particular diversification move on shareholder value, corporate strategists should use
    A) the profit test, the competitive strength test, the industry attractiveness test, and the capital gains test.
    B) the better-off test, the competitive advantage test, the expectations test, and the shareholder value test.
    C) the barrier to entry test, the competitive advantage test, the growth test, and the stock price effect test.
    D) the strategic fit test, the industry attractiveness test, the growth test, the dividend effect test, and the capital gains test.
    E) the attractiveness test, the cost of entry test, and the better-off test.

    Answer: E Difficulty: Hard

15. The better-off test for evaluating whether a particular diversification move has promise involves
    A) determining whether the proposed diversification into another industry promotes strategic fit and strengthens competitive advantage opportunities.
    B) determining whether the proposed diversification affords a firm needed ways to build the entrepreneurial skills of its senior managers.
    C) determining whether the proposed diversification spreads stockholders' risks across a greater number of lines of business.
    D) examining potential new businesses to determine if they have competitively valuable value chain match-ups with the company's present businesses such that the businesses can perform better together than apart.
    E) determining whether the proposed diversification has good potential for increasing a firm's overall profitability and rate of return on invested capital.

    Answer: D Difficulty: Medium

16. The attractiveness test for evaluating whether diversification into a particular industry is likely to build shareholder value involves
    A) determining whether it is likely that the firm's earnings per share will rise after the acquisition has been made.
    B) determining whether the corporation can bring some competitive advantage to the new business it enters or whether the new business offers added competitive advantage potential to the corporation's other businesses.
    C) guestimating whether the company's stock price will go up or down when the diversification move is announced.
    D) determining whether conditions in the target industry are sufficiently attractive to permit earning consistently good profits and returns on investment.
    E) evaluating the value of strategic fits between the value chains of the company's present businesses and the value chain of the target industry.

    Answer: D   Difficulty: Medium

Related Diversification

17. Different businesses are said to be "related" when
    A) there are competitively valuable relationships among the activities comprising their respective value chains.
    B) the products of the different businesses are bought by much the same types of buyers.
    C) the products of the different businesses are sold in the same types of retail stores.
    D) the businesses have several key suppliers in common.
    E) the businesses have similar scale economies and experience curve effects, are produced with similar assembly line methods, and use some common elements of technology.

    Answer: A   Difficulty: Medium

18. Which of the following is the best example of related diversification?
    A) An airline firm acquiring a rent-a-car company
    B) A greeting card manufacturer deciding to open a chain of stores to retail its lines of greeting cards
    C) A manufacturer of ready-to-eat cereals acquiring a producer of cake mixes and frozen cakes
    D) A manufacturer of snack foods diversifying into fast-food restaurants
    E) A manufacturer of ski equipment acquiring a chain of retail shops specializing in Christmas ornaments and decorations

    Answer: C   Difficulty: Medium

19. Which of the following is the best example of related diversification?
    A) A beer brewer acquiring a maker of aluminum cans
    B) A manufacturer of canoes diversifying into the production of tennis rackets
    C) A PC producer acquiring a developer of e-commerce software for e-tailers
    D) A producer of golf clubs and golf bags acquiring a maker of golfing apparel and golf shoes
    E) A supermarket chain acquiring a chain of frozen yogurt shops

    Answer: B   Difficulty: Medium

20. An advantage of related diversification is that
    A) it offers ways for a firm to realize $1 + 1 = 3$ benefits because of competitively valuable value chain matchups.
    B) it is less capital intensive and usually more profitable than unrelated diversification.
    C) it involves diversifying into industries having the same kinds of key success factors.
    D) it is less risky than either vertical integration or unrelated diversification because of the lower capital requirements.
    E) it offers the best route to passing the industry attractiveness test, avoiding strategic fit mismatches, and focusing on the same types of buyer groups and buyer needs.

    Answer: A   Difficulty: Easy

21. Related diversification has appeal from such strategic angles as
    A) being able to capture opportunities for skills or technology transfer or for cost reduction.
    B) being able to spread investor risks over a broader business base.
    C) providing sharper focus for managing diversification and gaining a useful degree of strategic unity across a company's various business activities.
    D) being able to leverage use of a competitively powerful brand name and to create valuable new competencies and capabilities.
    E) All of these.

    Answer: E   Difficulty: Easy

22. Related diversification
    A) involves diversifying into businesses whose value chains are related in ways that satisfy the industry attractiveness test and the financial fit test.
    B) offers opportunities to turn cross-business strategic fits into competitive advantage.
    C) comes closer to satisfying the attractiveness test and the cost of entry test than does unrelated diversification.
    D) involves diversifying into businesses whose value chains are related in ways that satisfy the cost-of-entry test and the capital gains test.
    E) involves diversifying into businesses whose value chains are related in ways that satisfy the competitive strength and resource adequacy tests.

    Answer: B   Difficulty: Medium

23. A company pursuing a related diversification strategy would likely address the issue of what additional industries/businesses to diversify into by
    A) locating businesses that offer attractive financial returns and having large relative market shares.
    B) identifying industries with the greatest long-term attractiveness.
    C) locating an attractive industry whose value chain has good strategic fit with one or more of the firm's present businesses.
    D) identifying businesses with the potential to diversify the number and types of different activities in the firm's value chain make-up.
    E) locating new businesses with the most potential to satisfy the industry attractiveness test.

    Answer: C   Difficulty: Medium

Cross-Business Strategic Fits

24. Strategic fit between two or more businesses exists when one or more activities comprising their respective value chains present opportunities
    A) to transfer expertise or technology or capabilities from one business to another.
    B) to leverage use of a common brand name.
    C) to combine the related activities of different businesses into a single operation and reduce costs.
    D) for combining resources to create valuable new resource strengths and competitive capabilities.
    E) All of these.

    Answer: E Difficulty: Easy

25. One strategic fit-based approach to related diversification would be to
    A) diversify into new industries that present opportunities to transfer a company's technological expertise in its mainstay business to the new businesses (or to transfer the expertise from the new business back to the present business).
    B) diversify into those industries where the same kinds of driving forces and competitive forces prevail, thus allowing use of much the same competitive strategy in all of the business a company is in.
    C) acquire rival firms that have broader product lines so as to give the company access to a wider range of buyer groups.
    D) acquire companies in forward distribution channels (wholesalers and/or retailers).
    E) expand into foreign markets where the firm currently does no business.

    Answer: A Difficulty: Medium

26. Cross-business strategic fits can exist in
    A) R&D and technology activities.
    B) supply chain activities.
    C) sales and marketing activities and managerial and administrative support activities.
    D) distribution activities.
    E) All of these.

    Answer: E Difficulty: Easy

27. Cross-business strategic fits can be found
    A) in unrelated as well as related businesses.
    B) principally in businesses whose products aim at satisfying the same general types of buyer needs.
    C) anywhere along the value chains of two or more related businesses.
    D) in the markets of foreign countries as well as in domestic markets.
    E) mainly in either technology related activities or sales and marketing activities.

    Answer: C Difficulty: Medium

28. What makes related diversification an attractive strategy is
    A) the ability to spread investor risk over a broader range of businesses and industries.
    B) the opportunity to convert cross-business strategic fits into competitive advantages over rivals that have not diversified or that have diversified in ways that do not give them comparable strategic fit benefits.
    C) the potential for increasing the company's financial performance over the course of the business cycle.
    D) the ability to serve the needs of a broader number of buyer groups and buyer needs.
    E) the added capability it provides in overcoming the barriers to entering foreign markets.

    Answer: B Difficulty: Medium

29. Which of the following statements is not accurate as concerns strategic fit in a diversified enterprise?
    A) Strategic fit between two businesses exists where the management know-how accumulated in one business is transferable to another.
    B) Strategic fit exists when two businesses present opportunities to economize on marketing, selling, and distribution costs.
    C) Competitively valuable cross-business strategic fits are what enable related diversification to produce a 1 + 1 = 3 performance outcome.
    D) Strategic fit is primarily a byproduct of unrelated diversification and exists when the value chain activities of unrelated businesses possess economies of scope and good financial fit.
    E) Strategic fit exists when a company can transfer its brand name to the products of a newly acquired business and gain added competitive power for the new business because of its brand name recognition and reputation.

    Answer: D Difficulty: Medium

Economies of Scope

30. Economies of scope
    A) exist whenever it is less costly for two or more businesses to be operated under centralized management than to function independently.
    B) can arise from strategic fit relationships anywhere along businesses' value chains.
    C) are more associated with unrelated diversification than related diversification.
    D) are present whenever diversification satisfies the attractiveness test and the cost-of-entry test.
    E) Both A and B are correct.

    Answer: E Difficulty: Medium

31. Economies of scope
    A) stem from the cost-saving efficiencies of operating over a wider geographic area.
    B) have to do with the cost-saving efficiencies of distributing a firm's product through many different distribution channels simultaneously.
    C) exist whenever it is less costly for two or more businesses to perform certain value chain activities jointly under centralized management than it is for these activities to be performed independently.
    D) refer to the cost-savings that flow from operating across all or most of an industry's value chain activities.
    E) arise from the cost-saving efficiencies of having a wide product line and offering customers a big selection of models and styles to choose from.

    Answer: C Difficulty: Hard

32. Which of the following best illustrates an economy of scope?
    A) Being able to eliminate or reduce costs by combining related value-chain activities of different businesses into a single operation
    B) Being able to eliminate or reduce costs by performing related value chain activities at the same location rather than having them spread out over different locations
    C) Being able to eliminate or reduce costs by extending the firm's scope of operations over a wider geographic area
    D) Being able to eliminate or reduce costs by expanding the size of a company's manufacturing plants
    E) Being able to eliminate or reduce costs by having more value chain activities performed in-house rather than outsourcing them

    Answer: A   Difficulty: Medium

Capturing Strategic Fit Benefits

33. Companies that become quite adept at capturing cross business strategic fit benefits can often gain added competitive advantage by using this know-how to
    A) build a distinctive competence in each key success factor in each industry where they operate.
    B) integrate forward or backward more inexpensively than rivals lacking such strategic fits and know-how.
    C) expand their pool of resources and strategic assets and to create new ones faster and more cheaply than rivals who are not diversified across related businesses.
    D) diversify into a wider and more profitable range of businesses than rivals lacking such strategic fits and know-how.
    E) enter a bigger number of country markets faster and more inexpensively than rivals lacking such strategic fits and know-how.

    Answer: D   Difficulty: Hard

Unrelated Diversification

34. Different businesses are said to be "unrelated" when
    A) the businesses are in different industries.
    B) the products of the different businesses are not bought by the same types of buyers or sold in the same types of retail stores.
    C) the products of the different businesses satisfy different buyer needs.
    D) the businesses have different supply chains and different suppliers.
    E) the activities comprising their respective value chains are very dissimilar.

    Answer: E   Difficulty: Medium

35. Which of the following is the best example of unrelated diversification?
   A) A newsprint manufacturer acquiring a chain of newspapers.
   B) An electrical equipment manufacturer acquiring a potato chip company.
   C) A producer of canned soups acquiring a maker of breakfast cereals.
   D) A pizza chain acquiring a chain of hamburger outlets.
   E) A network TV company buying a professional baseball team and a professional basketball team so it can televise more live sporting events.

   Answer: B   Difficulty: Medium

36. The basic premise of unrelated diversification is that
   A) the least risky way to diversify is to seek out businesses that are leaders in their respective industry.
   B) the best companies to acquire are those that can pass the capital gains test as opposed to those which can pass the better-off test.
   C) the best way to build shareholder value is to acquire businesses with strong cross-business financial fit.
   D) any company that can be acquired on good financial terms and that has good profit prospects represents a good business to diversify into.
   E) the task of building shareholder value is better served by seeking to stabilize earnings across the entire business cycle than by seeking to capture cross-business strategic fits.

   Answer: D   Difficulty: Hard

37. In companies with an unrelated multi-business portfolio
   A) the main basis for competitive advantage and improved shareholder value is the ability to achieve economies of scope.
   B) each business is on its own in trying to build a competitive edge and the consolidated performance of the businesses is likely to be no better than the sum of what the individual businesses could achieve if they were independent.
   C) there is a good chance that the consolidated performance of the various businesses will produce a 1 + 1 = 3 outcome as opposed to just a 1 + 1 = 2 outcome.
   D) the main basis for competitive advantage and improved shareholder value is strong cross-business financial fits.
   E) the main basis for competitive advantage and improved shareholder value is strong cross-business financial fits.

   Answer: B   Difficulty: Hard

38. Which of the following is not among the risks and disadvantages of unrelated diversification?
   A) Failing to develop or acquire the skills to manage a business in which one has no prior experience
   B) Spreading corporate resources too thinly over too many different lines of business
   C) The strain it places on corporate-level management in trying to cope with the variety of problems encountered in managing a widely diversified portfolio of businesses
   D) A bigger risk of sizable ups and downs in sales and profits over the course of the business cycle.
   E) A bigger chance that corporate managers will drift into letting corporate strategy be little more than a composite of each line of business strategy

   Answer: D   Difficulty: Medium

39. The two biggest drawbacks or disadvantages of unrelated diversification are
   A) the difficulties of passing the cost-of-entry test and of earning a larger total profit than can be achieved with related diversification.
   B) spreading corporate resources too thinly over too many different lines of business and the difficulties of capturing financial fit.
   C) the strain it places on corporate-level management in competently managing many different businesses and being without the added source of competitive advantage that cross-business strategic fit provides.
   D) a bigger risk of sizable ups and downs in sales and profits over the course of the business cycle and a lack of strong strategic focus.
   E) the difficulties of achieving economies of scope and an inability to employ cross-market subsidization tactics.

   Answer: C   Difficulty: Hard

40. A fundamental weakness of unrelated diversification is that
   A) it places too much emphasis on financial measures of performance.
   B) it reduces a company's access to economies of scale.
   C) it is much easier for line of business strategy to conflict with corporate strategy, thus increasing business risk.
   D) there is far greater risk of entering unattractive industries and getting trapped in tough struggles with strong competitors.
   E) the more wide-ranging is the scope of diversification and the greater the number of diversified business units that corporate management has to oversee, then the more complex are the problems of checking out what is really going on out in the divisions and the greater the chances that corporate management will not know much about how to fix the problems of poorly performing divisions.

   Answer: E   Difficulty: Medium

41. One of the chief advantages of unrelated diversification is that it
   A) expands a firm's competitive advantage opportunities to include a wider array of businesses.
   B) spreads the stockholders' risks across a group of diverse businesses.
   C) increases strategic fit opportunities and the potential for a 1 + 1 =3 outcome.
   D) helps achieve greater economies of scope.
   E) helps boost a company's profit margins and permit more efficient deployment of capital resources.

   Answer: B   Difficulty: Medium

42. With an unrelated diversification strategy, the types of companies that make particularly attractive acquisition targets are
   A) financially distressed companies with good turnaround potential or companies whose assets are undervalued or companies that have bright growth prospects but are short on investment capital.
   B) companies offering the biggest potential to achieve economies of scope.
   C) businesses with excellent cross-business financial fit.
   D) companies that have bright growth prospects, plenty of cash, and interrelated value chains.
   E) companies capable of readily passing the cost-of-entry test, the profit test, the dividend growth test and the capital gains test.

   Answer: A   Difficulty: Hard

43. Unrelated diversification has appeal when
    A) a company has ample capital to invest and sees good acquisition opportunities in industries with above-average profit prospects.
    B) corporate management is exceptionally astute at picking appropriate companies to acquire, such that shareholder value can be enhanced.
    C) shareholders are strongly inclined to spread business risk over a variety of different industries.
    D) company profitability can be made somewhat more stable across the business cycle (because hard times in one industry can be balanced by good times in another industry).
    E) All of these.

    Answer: E Difficulty: Medium

44. Unrelated diversification
    A) is primarily a financial approach to diversification where shareholder value accrues from spreading investment risks across a number of different businesses and from astute financial management of the collection of businesses the company has diversified into.
    B) seeks to achieve competitive advantage by acquiring businesses that can capitalize on use of a common brand name.
    C) is more likely to result in increasing shareholder value than is related diversification.
    D) is more attractive to multinational companies than to domestic-only companies.
    E) seeks to achieve competitive advantage by building a business portfolio with a highly diverse set of internally-performed value chain activities.

    Answer: A Difficulty: Medium

Strategies for Entering New Businesses

45. A company that wants to diversify into new industries can achieve diversification by
    A) forming a strategic alliance with a company already in the target industry.
    B) collaborating with one or more companies in the target industry.
    C) acquiring a company already operating in the target industry, creating a new subsidiary internally to compete in the target industry, or forming a joint venture with another company to enter the target industry.
    D) forming a strategic partnership with a company in the target industry to perform some of that companies value chain activities.
    E) All of these.

    Answer: C Difficulty: Medium

46. A joint venture is an attractive way for a company to enter a new industry when
    A) it is uneconomical for the firm to expand the length of its value chain on its own initiative.
    B) it needs access to economies of scope and good financial fits in order to be cost-competitive.
    C) a firm is missing some essential skills or capabilities or resources and needs a partner to supply the missing expertise and competencies or fill the resource gaps.
    D) the firm has no prior experience with diversification.
    E) All of the above represent situations where a joint venture may be attractive.

    Answer: C Difficulty: Medium

47. Entering a new industry by creating a new subsidiary to compete in the target industry is an attractive way to diversify when
    A) all of the potential acquisition candidates in the target industry are highly profitable.
    B) the target industry is comprised of several relatively large and well-established firms.
    C) there is ample time to launch the new business from the ground up.
    D) the company has been pursuing a single-business concentration strategy and has built up a hoard of cash with which to finance a diversification effort.
    E) All of these.

    Answer: C Difficulty: Easy

48. Generally, internal entry into a new business is more attractive than acquiring an existing firm in the targeted industry when
    A) the costs associated with internal startup are less than the costs of buying an existing company and there is ample time to launch the new business from the ground up.
    B) there will be positive effects on the entrant's other existing businesses.
    C) the target industry is young, fragmented, and growing rapidly.
    D) all of the potential acquisition candidates are losing money.
    E) the target industry is comprised of several relatively large and well-established firms.

    Answer: A Difficulty: Medium

49. The most popular strategy for entering new businesses and accomplishing diversification is
    A) forming a joint venture with another company to enter the target industry.
    B) internal startup.
    C) acquisition of an existing business already in the chosen industry.
    D) forming a strategic alliance with another company to enter the target industry.
    E) strategic alliance and joint ventures are equally popular and rank well ahead of acquisition and internal start-up in frequency of use.

    Answer: C Difficulty: Easy

Strategy Options for Companies That Are Already Diversified

50. The strategic options for a company that is already diversified include
    A) retrenching to a narrower business base by divesting some of its present businesses.
    B) multinational diversification.
    C) corporate restructuring and turnaround strategies.
    D) broadening the firm's business base by diversifying into additional businesses.
    E) All of the above.

    Answer: E Difficulty: Easy

51. The strategic options for a diversified company include
    A) making new acquisitions to broaden the firm's business base.
    B) becoming a multinational multi-industry enterprise.
    C) restructuring the company's portfolio of businesses.
    D) divesting some of its present businesses.
    E) All of the above.

    Answer: E Difficulty: Easy

52. Once a firm has built a diversified business portfolio, then its post-diversification strategic move alternatives include
    A) making additional acquisitions to build positions in new industries.
    B) divesting weak-performing businesses.
    C) retrenchment to a narrower diversification base.
    D) restructuring the make-up of the whole portfolio (especially if the future performance outlook for many of its businesses looks poor).
    E) All of these.

    Answer: E Difficulty: Easy

Broadening a Diversified Company's Business Base

53. A company that is already diversified may choose to broaden its business base by building positions in new related or unrelated businesses because
    A) it has resources or capabilities that are eminently transferable to other related or complementary businesses or it runs across an opportunity to acquire an attractive company.
    B) the company's growth is sluggish and it needs the sales and profit boost that a new business can provide.
    C) management wants to broaden the firm's competitive scope and/or expand the company's technological expertise into new areas.
    D) it wants to make new acquisitions to strengthen or complement some of its present businesses.
    E) All of these.

    Answer: E Difficulty: Easy

Retrenchment and Divestiture Strategies

54. Retrenching to a narrower diversification base
    A) is usually the most attractive long-run strategy for a broadly diversified company confronted with recession, high interest rates, mounting competitive pressures in several of its businesses, and sluggish growth.
    B) has the advantage of focusing a diversified firm's energies on building strong position in a few core businesses rather the stretching its resources and managerial attention too thinly across many businesses.
    C) is an attractive strategy option for revamping a diverse business lineup that lacks strong cross-business financial fit.
    D) is sometimes an attractive option for deepening a diversified company's technological expertise and supporting a faster rate of product innovation.
    E) may make good sense if a company is in poor financial shape, but otherwise there is more merit in building a competitive position in a growing number of industries (rather than retreating to occupy a smaller business base).

    Answer: B Difficulty: Hard

55. Retrenching to a narrower diversification base can be attractive or advisable when
    A) a diversified company has struggled to make certain businesses attractively profitable.
    B) a diversified company has businesses that have little or no strategic fits with the "core" businesses that management wishes to concentrate on.
    C) divesting businesses frees resources that can be used to pay down debt.
    D) some of a diversified company's businesses are too small to make a meaningful contribution to sales and earnings.
    E) All of these.

    Answer: E Difficulty: Medium

56. Retrenchment strategies in diversified companies typically entail
    A) shortening and streamlining the firm's value chains in each business it has diversified into so as to boost efficiency.
    B) divesting weak businesses and using the proceeds to finance new acquisitions and expansion into attractive, new industries.
    C) pruning the number of businesses in the corporate portfolio and narrowing the scope of the firm's diversification.
    D) cutting back on the number of geographic areas in which the firm does business.
    E) cutting back on the number of different models and styles of products offered in each of a diversified firm's businesses.

    Answer: C Difficulty: Medium

57. Divestiture is an attractive corporate strategy option
    A) for abandoning businesses which do not "fit".
    B) for getting out of businesses which are no longer attractive (even though they may still be profitable).
    C) for unloading poorly performing businesses.
    D) for freeing up resources tied up in low priority business units.
    E) All of the above.

    Answer: E Difficulty: Easy

58. Divesting a business that is no longer attractive or that doesn't fit in with management's strategic vision for the company
    A) should rarely be considered unless the business is losing money or else has negative cash flows.
    B) can be accomplished either by selling the unit outright or by spinning the business off as a financially and managerially independent company (in which the parent may or may not retain an ownership interest).
    C) is usually difficult to pull off successfully because it requires finding a "sucker" onto whom a poorly performing business can be unloaded.
    D) doesn't make good financial sense as long as the business is able to maintain a positive cash flow.
    E) All of the above.

    Answer: B Difficulty: Medium

Corporate Restructuring and Turnaround Strategies

59. Which of the following is normally not an alternative for improving the performance of a diversified company's business portfolio?
    A) Liquidating the company's core businesses
    B) Reducing the scope of diversification to a smaller number of businesses
    C) Revamping the composition of the corporate portfolio by divesting marginal businesses or businesses that don't fit and reinvesting the proceeds in new and existing businesses where the profit prospects are more attractive
    D) Shifting resources out of weak performing units and allocating more resources to business units with better prospects
    E) Launching turnaround efforts to restore the profitability of money-losing business units

    Answer: A Difficulty: Medium

60. The difference between corporate restructuring strategies and corporate turnaround strategies is that
    A) restructuring entails a revamping of the value chains of each of a diversified company's businesses whereas turnaround strategies aim at restoring the profitability of particular businesses.
    B) restructuring entails reducing the scope of diversification to a smaller number of businesses whereas turnaround strategies aim at restoring a diversified company's overall profitability.
    C) restructuring strategies entail revamping the strategies of a diversified company's different businesses whereas turnaround strategies aim at revamping the strategies of a diversified company's poorly performing businesses.
    D) restructuring strategies involve divesting some businesses and acquiring new ones so as to put a new face on a diversified company's business makeup whereas corporate turnaround strategies focus on restoring a diversified company's money-losing businesses to profitability.
    E) restructuring entails broadening the scope of diversification to include a larger number of businesses whereas turnaround strategies aim at restoring a diversified company's overall profitability.

    Answer: D Difficulty: Hard

61. Corporate restructuring strategies
    A) involve making radical changes in diversified company's business portfolio, divesting some businesses and acquiring new ones.
    B) entails reducing the scope of diversification to a smaller number of businesses and restoring a diversified company's overall profitability.
    C) entail revamping the strategies of a diversified company's different businesses.
    D) focus on restoring a diversified company's money-losing businesses to profitability.
    E) entails broadening the scope of diversification to include a larger number of businesses and boost the company's growth and profitability.

    Answer: A   Difficulty: Medium

62. Conditions that may make corporate restructuring strategies appealing include
    A) diminishing growth and profitability prospects in several of a diversified company's major businesses.
    B) a business portfolio that consists of too many slow-growth, declining, or competitively weak businesses.
    C) the appointment of a new CEO with a new or different strategic vision for the company that doesn't include many of the company's present businesses.
    D) the emergence of "wave-of-the-future" technologies or products that mandate a major shakeup of the companies businesses in order to capitalize on the new developments.
    E) All of these.

    Answer: E   Difficulty: Medium

Multinational Diversification Strategies

63. What sets a multinational diversification strategy apart from other diversification strategies is
    A) the presence of extra degrees of strategic fit and more economies of scope.
    B) the potential to have a higher degree of technological expertise.
    C) a diversity of businesses and a diversity of national markets.
    D) the potential for faster growth, higher rates of profitability, and more profit sanctuaries.
    E) greater diversity in the types of value chain activities in its different businesses.

    Answer: C   Difficulty: Medium

64. A multinational diversification strategy allows a firm to build competitive advantage by
    A) fully capturing economies of scale and experience curve effects and also pursuing economy of scope opportunities.
    B) exploiting opportunities for both cross-business and cross-country collaboration.
    C) leveraging use of a well-known and competitively powerful brand name.
    D) transferring competitively valuable resources from one business to another and one country to another.
    E) All of these.

    Answer: E   Difficulty: Easy

65. The sources of a competitive advantage for a diversified multinational corporation include
   A) transferring competitively valuable resources from one business to another and one country to another.
   B) the ability to coordinate strategic activities and strategic initiatives across businesses and countries.
   C) the ability to leverage use of a well-known and competitively powerful brand name.
   D) an ability to cross subsidize across country markets and across businesses to help build long-term competitive position in one or more of its businesses.
   E) All of these.

   Answer: E Difficulty: Medium

66. Which one of the following is <u>not</u> a way for a company to build competitive advantage by pursuing a multinational diversification strategy?
   A) Fully capturing economies of scale and experience curve effects
   B) Exploiting opportunities for both cross-business and cross-country collaboration and also pursuing cross-business economy of scope opportunities
   C) Fully capturing both cross-business financial fits and cross-country financial fits
   D) Transferring competitively valuable resources from one business to another and one country to another
   E) Leveraging use of a well-known and competitively powerful brand name across two or more of its businesses

   Answer: C Difficulty: Medium

67. A diversified company may wish to expand the operations of several of its businesses into the markets of additional foreign countries in order to
   A) fully capture economies of scale and experience curve effects in these businesses.
   B) exploit opportunities for both cross-business and cross-country coordination of value chain activities and strategic initiatives.
   C) gain the benefits of using cross-country market subsidization techniques.
   D) transfer competitively valuable resources in these businesses from one country to another.
   E) All of these.

   Answer: E Difficulty: Medium

68. When a multinational company has expertise in a core technology and has diversified into a family of businesses using this technology, then it is in position to build competitive advantage
   A) by pursuing a global focus strategy to serve all customers who can take advantage of the firm's technological expertise.
   B) by using common distribution channels to gain access to every country market where there are customers for the technology.
   C) by shifting from a multi-country strategy to a global strategy in each of the businesses using the technology.
   D) through a collaborative and strategically coordinated company-wide R & D/technology effort on behalf of all these businesses as a group.
   E) by using its technological expertise in virtually every possible value chain activity in these businesses.

   Answer: D Difficulty: Hard

69. One of the primary reasons why a diversified multinational corporation is in strategic position to outmuscle either a one-business competitor or a one-country competitor is that
    A) the DMNC is almost certainly going to have a better market image than a one-business or one-country competitor because of its multi-business, multi-country operations.
    B) the DMNC is almost certainly going to have more economies of scope because of its multi-country operations.
    C) the DMNC has more strategic fit across its value chain activities than does a one-business competitor or a one-country competitor.
    D) the DMNC has the financial resources to out-advertise a one-business competitor or a one-country competitor.
    E) the DMNC can resort to both cross-business and cross-country subsidization to support a long-term price-cutting, market-share-building offensive that gradually whittles away a one-business or one-country competitor's market share and profitability.

    Answer: E   Difficulty: Hard

Short Answer Questions

70. Discuss why a strategy of concentrating in a single business can be attractive.

    Difficulty: Medium

71. Identify and briefly discuss when it makes good strategic sense for a company to consider diversification. Under what circumstances is diversification, either related or unrelated, probably unwise for a company?

    Difficulty: Medium

72. Identify and briefly discuss each of the three options for entering new businesses.

    Difficulty: Medium

73. What is meant by the term strategic fit? What are the advantages of pursuing strategic fit in choosing which industries to diversify into?

    Difficulty: Medium

74. Carefully explain the difference between related and unrelated diversification.

    Difficulty: Easy

75. Identify and explain the meaning and strategic significance of each of the following terms:
    a.) related diversification
    b.) strategic fit
    c.) economies of scope
    d.) unrelated diversification
    e.) the attractiveness test (as it relates to a potential diversification move)
    f.) divestiture
    g.) corporate restructuring
    h.) the better-off test

    Difficulty: Medium

76. Which is the better approach to diversification—related diversification or unrelated diversification? Explain and support your answer.

    Difficulty: Hard

77. Discuss the disadvantages of a strategy of unrelated diversification.

    Difficulty: Medium

78. Unrelated diversification is principally a financial approach to diversification whereas related diversification is principally a strategic approach. True or False. Explain.

    Difficulty: Easy

79. Under what circumstances might a diversified firm choose to divest one of its businesses?

    Difficulty: Medium

80. Briefly explain the difference in the strategic focus of a corporate retrenchment strategy, a corporate restructuring strategy, and a corporate turnaround strategy.

    Difficulty: Medium

81. Under what circumstances might an already diversified company chose to enter additional businesses and broaden its diversification base?

    Difficulty: Hard

82. Explain the relevance of the following as they relate to building shareholder value via diversification:
    a.) the attractiveness test.
    b.) the cost-of-entry test.
    c.) the better-off test.

    Difficulty: Medium

83. Why might a diversified multinational enterprise deliberately refrain from employing cross-business or cross-country subsidization tactics to try to out-compete its rivals in particular businesses or in particular country markets?

    Difficulty: Hard

84. Identify and briefly describe at least four types of competitive advantages that can accrue to a multinational corporation pursuing related diversification.

    Difficulty: Medium

85. Once a company achieves diversification, what are the post-diversification strategic moves that it can employ to improve the performance of its business portfolio?

    Difficulty: Medium

Chapter 10: Evaluating the Strategies of Diversified Companies

Multiple Choice Questions

Evaluating a Diversified Company's Strategy: The Analytical Steps

1. The procedural steps in evaluating and critiquing a diversified company's strategy include
   A) applying the industry attractiveness test.
   B) determining the competitive strength of each business in the portfolio to see which ones are the strongest/weakest contenders in their respective industries.
   C) ranking business unit profitability and determining the priorities for resource allocation.
   D) evaluating the strategic and resource fits among sister businesses in the company's portfolio.
   E) All of the above.

   Answer: E   Difficulty: Easy

2. A comprehensive evaluation of the group of businesses a company has diversified into involves
   A) evaluating the attractiveness of each industry in which the firm does business and the competitive strength of each business unit.
   B) evaluating the strategic fits and resource fits among the various sister businesses.
   C) ranking the business units from highest to lowest on the basis of both historical performance and future prospects and also ranking the different businesses in terms of their priority for resource allocation and new capital investment.
   D) using the results of the prior analytical steps as a basis for crafting new strategic moves to improve the performance of the total business portfolio via acquisitions, divestiture, or shifts in internal priorities and resource allocation.
   E) All of the above.

   Answer: E   Difficulty: Easy

3. Evaluating a diversified company's corporate strategy and critiquing its business portfolio involves
   A) a SWOT analysis of each industry in which the firm has a business interest.
   B) applying the cost-of-entry test, the better-off test, the profitability test, and the shareholder value test to each business and industry represented in the company's business portfolio.
   C) evaluating the strategic fits and resource fits among the various sister businesses and deciding what priority to give each of the company's business units in allocating resources and making new capital investment.
   D) looking at each industry/business to determine where competitive forces and driving forces are strongest/weakest and how many profitable strategic groups that each industry has.
   E) determining how many of the business units are industry leaders and "stars", how many are cash cows, and how many are cash hogs, how many are following focus strategies, how many are using differentiation strategies, and how many are pursuing cost leadership strategies.

   Answer: C   Difficulty: Medium

4. Which one of the following is not a standard part of analyzing the strategy of a diversified company?
    A) Assessing the competitive strength of each business the company has diversified into.
    B) Determining which business units have the most potential for employing low-cost producer strategies, differentiation strategies, focus strategies, and best-cost producer strategies and also determining how soon the company's cash hogs can be transformed into cash cows.
    C) evaluating the strategic fits and resource fits among the various sister businesses.
    D) Identifying the company's current corporate strategy and applying the industry attractiveness test to each of the industries the company has diversified into.
    E) Rating each business unit on the basis of its historical performance and future prospects and deciding what priority to give each of the company's business units in allocating resources and making new capital investments.

    Answer: B   Difficulty: Medium

5. Evaluating a diversified company's strategy and collection of businesses does not involve
    A) appraising the attractiveness of each industry the company has invested in.
    B) comparing the actual historical performance and future performance prospects of each business unit.
    C) applying the strategic fit and resource fit tests.
    D) evaluating the competitive strength of each business the company is in.
    E) determining how soon the company's cash hogs can be transformed into cash cows.

    Answer: E   Difficulty: Easy

Identifying a Diversified Company's Strategy

6. To identify a multi-business firm's corporate strategy, one should consider such factors as
    A) the extent to which the firm is diversified (as measured by the proportion of sales and profit contributed by each business and by whether its diversification base is broad or narrow).
    B) whether the company is focusing on "milking its cash cows" or "feeding its cash hogs."
    C) the technological proficiencies, labor skill requirements, and functional area strategies characterizing each of the firm's businesses.
    D) each business's competitive approach—whether it is pursuing low-cost leadership, differentiation, best-cost, or focus strategy.
    E) how many core competencies each business in the portfolio has.

    Answer: A   Difficulty: Medium

7. When identifying a diversified company's present corporate strategy, which of the following would not be something to look for?
    A) Recent actions to add new businesses to the portfolio and build positions in new industries.
    B) The percentages of total capital expenditures allocated to each business unit in prior years.
    C) The nature of recent management actions to improve performance of key businesses in the portfolio and/or to strengthen existing business positions.
    D) Actions to divest weak or unattractive business units.
    E) Actions to substitute global strategies for multi-country strategies in one or more business units over the past few years.

    Answer: E   Difficulty: Easy

Evaluating Industry Attractiveness

8. In judging the group of businesses a multi-business company has diversified into, it is important to consider
   A) the attractiveness of each industry represented in the company's collection of business units.
   B) each industry's attractiveness relative to the others.
   C) the attractiveness of all the industries as a group.
   D) whether there are strategic fit and resource fit relationships among the sister businesses comprising the company's business portfolio.
   E) All of the above.

   Answer: E Difficulty: Medium

9. As a rule, all the industries represented in a diversified company's business portfolio should be judged on such attractiveness factors as
   A) market size and projected growth rate.
   B) emerging opportunities and threats, the intensity of competition, and industry uncertainty and business risk.
   C) resource requirements and the presence of cross-industry strategic fits and resource fits.
   D) seasonal and cyclical factors, industry profitability, and whether an industry has significant social, political, regulatory, and environmental problems.
   E) All of these.

   Answer: E Difficulty: Easy

10. Which of the following is <u>not</u> generally something that ought to be considered in evaluating the attractiveness of the industries represented in a diversified company's business portfolio?
   A) Market size and projected growth rate, industry profitability, and the intensity of competition
   B) Industry uncertainty and business risk
   C) The use of strategic alliances and collaborative partnerships in each industry, the extent to which firms in the industry utilize outsourcing, and how many of what kinds of key success factors each industry has
   D) Seasonal and cyclical factors, resource requirements, and whether an industry has significant social, political, regulatory, and environmental problems
   E) The presence of cross-industry strategic fits and resource fits

   Answer: C Difficulty: Medium

11. Assessments of the long-term attractiveness of each industry represented in a diversified company's portfolio should be based on
   A) a complete value-chain analysis of each industry.
   B) whether the industries have the same kinds of driving forces.
   C) how many companies in each industry are making money and how many are losing money.
   D) formal, quantitative, attractiveness scores derived from ratings of each relevant attractiveness measure (weighted by its relative importance).
   E) the competitive advantage potential offered by each industry's key success factors.

   Answer: D Difficulty: Medium

12. The chief purpose of quantitatively evaluating each industry's attractiveness relative to the others is to
   A) determine which industry is the biggest and fastest growing.
   B) rank the industries from most competitive to least competitive.
   C) provide an indication of which industries offer the best and worst long-term profit opportunities.
   D) evaluate how each industry ranks relative to the others on the important key success factors.
   E) determine which industry has the most attractive value chain.

   Answer: C   Difficulty: Medium

13. When industry attractiveness ratings are calculated for a multi-business company, the results help indicate
   A) which industries are most attractive and which are least attractive from the standpoint of overall long-term profitability.
   B) which industries have the most attractive key success factors and which industries have relatively unattractive key success factors.
   C) which industries are most competitive and which are least competitive.
   D) the relative attractiveness of the value chains of the different industries.
   E) which industries have the most attractive key success factors and which are most attractive from the standpoint of industry driving forces.

   Answer: A   Difficulty: Hard

14. A weighted industry attractiveness assessment is generally analytically superior to an unweighted assessment because
   A) a weighted ranking identifies which industry opportunities are likely to offer the greatest long-term profit prospects.
   B) an unweighted ranking doesn't discriminate between strong and weak industry driving forces and industry competitive forces.
   C) it does a more accurate job of singling out which industry key success factors are the most important.
   D) an unweighted ranking doesn't help identify which industries have the easiest and hardest value chains to execute.
   E) the various measures are not likely to be equally important in determining industry attractiveness or in contributing to achievement of the company's strategic vision and objectives or in matching up well with the company's circumstances.

   Answer: E   Difficulty: Medium

15. Calculating quantitative attractiveness ratings for the industries represented in a diversified company's business portfolio
   A) is a way of determining which industry offers a diversified company the greatest overall competitive advantage and which industry offers the greatest overall competitive disadvantage.
   B) is a technique for benchmarking each industry's barriers to entry, driving forces, competitive forces and key success factors.
   C) is a way of gauging which industry has the best value chain and overall approach to creating customer value.
   D) helps provide a basis for deciding whether and why some of the industries a company has diversified into are more attractive than others and, if a particular industry's attractiveness ratings are low, whether the company should consider getting out of that particular business.
   E) is a reliable way of determining which industry the company is most likely to be successful in.

   Answer: D   Difficulty: Medium

16. Calculating quantitative attractiveness ratings for the industries represented in a diversified company's business portfolio involves
    A) determining each industry's key success factors, calculating the ability of the company to be successful on each industry KSF, and obtaining overall measures of the firm's ability to compete successfully in each of its industries based on the combined KSF ratings.
    B) determining each industry's competitive advantage factors, calculating the ability of the company to be successful on each competitive advantage factor, and obtaining overall measures of the firm's ability to achieve sustainable competitive advantage in each of its industries based on the combined competitive advantage factor ratings.
    C) selecting a set of industry attractiveness measures, weighting the importance of each measure, rating each industry on each attractiveness measure, multiplying the industry ratings by the assigned weight to obtain a weighted rating, adding the weighted ratings for each industry to obtain an overall industry attractiveness score, and comparing the overall attractiveness scores for each of the industries represented in a diversified company's portfolio.
    D) determining which industries possess good strategic fit and resource fit and which do not.
    E) identifying each industry's barriers to entry, rating the difficulty of overcoming each barrier, and deciding whether overall entry barriers into each industry are high or low.

    Answer: C Difficulty: Hard

Comparing the Competitive Strength of a Diversified Company's Business Units

17. Assessments of how a diversified company's subsidiaries compare in competitive strength should be based on such factors as
    A) relative market share, ability to match or beat rivals on key product attributes, and brand name recognition and reputation.
    B) vulnerability to seasonal and cyclical downturns, vulnerability to driving forces, and vulnerability to fluctuating interest rates and exchange rates.
    C) costs relative to competitors, technology and innovation capabilities, and how well the business unit's competitive assets and competencies match industry key success factors.
    D) the ability to hurdle barriers to entry, the number of strategic alliances and collaborative partnerships, value chain attractiveness, and business risk.
    E) Both A and C.

    Answer: E Difficulty: Medium

18. Calculating quantitative competitive strength ratings for the business units in a diversified company's portfolio involves
   A) determining each industry's key success factors, rating the ability of each business to be successful on each industry KSF, and adding the individual ratings to obtain overall measures of each business's ability to compete successfully.
   B) identifying the competitive forces facing each business, rating the difficulty of overcoming each competitive force, and deciding whether the overall competitive intensity in each industry is sufficiently low to be overcome in a profitable manner.
   C) selecting a set of competitive strength measures, weighting the importance of each measure, rating each business on each strength measure, multiplying the strength ratings by the assigned weight to obtain a weighted rating, adding the weighted ratings for each business unit to obtain an overall competitive strength score, and comparing the overall strength scores for each of the businesses.
   D) determining which businesses possess good strategic fit with other businesses, identifying the portion of the value chain where this fit occurs, and evaluating the strength of the competitive advantage attached to each of the strategic fits to get an overall measure of competitive advantage potential.
   E) evaluating which business units possess good resource fit with each other and which do not, so as to determine whether the company has adequate resources to be a strong market contender in each of the industries where it competes.

   Answer: C Difficulty: Hard

19. Relative market share is
   A) calculated by dividing a business's percentage share of total industry sales volume by the percentage share held by its largest rival.
   B) best measured on the basis of dollar volume (sales revenues) rather than unit volume so as to be useful in indicating whether a business has the ability to compete on the basis of quality, service, and product performance.
   C) a better indicator of a business's competitive strength than is a simple percentage measure of market share.
   D) particularly useful in identifying cash cows and cash hogs—cash cow businesses have big relative market shares (above 1.0) and cash hog businesses have low relative market shares (below 0.5).
   E) Both A and C.

   Answer: E Difficulty: Hard

20. Using relative market share to assess a business's competitive strength is analytically superior to simple percentage measures of market share because relative market share
   A) is a better measure of a business's potential for increased sales.
   B) is a better indicator of comparative market strength and competitive position and because it is also likely to reflect a business's relative cost position based on experience curve effects and economies of large-scale production.
   C) is a better overall measure of a business's ability to compete on the basis of quality, service, and product performance as well as on price.
   D) is more closely related to whether a business is a cash cow or a cash hog.
   E) provides a more accurate indication of the business's brand image and reputation with buyers.

   Answer: B Difficulty: Hard

21. The basic purpose of assessing the relative competitive strength of a diversified company's business units is to determine
   A) which one has the most competitive prices, the lowest costs, and best overall profit margins.
   B) how well positioned each business unit is in its industry and the extent to which it already is or can become a strong market contender.
   C) which business unit has the greatest number of resource strengths, competencies, and competitive capabilities and which one has the least.
   D) which one has the biggest market share and is growing the fastest.
   E) which one has the best value chain.

   Answer: B Difficulty: Medium

22. A weighted competitive strength analysis of a diversified company's business units is conceptually stronger than an unweighted analysis because
   A) it provides a more accurate assessment of the strength of industry competitive forces.
   B) it provides better indication of which industry driving forces will have the greatest impact.
   C) the different measures of competitive strength are unlikely to be equally important.
   D) the different business units in a company's portfolio are unlikely to be equally important.
   E) an unweighted ranking provides no insight into which business has the strongest arsenal of competitive assets and which has the weakest.

   Answer: C Difficulty: Medium

23. The value of using relative market share in assessing a business's competitive strength is
   A) increased ability to identify which businesses have competitive advantages and which do not.
   B) the ability to compare financial performance against market share changes.
   C) more accurate identification of competitive strengths and weaknesses, business by business.
   D) that relative market share more clearly indicates (1)competitive position and comparative strength in the market place than do percentage market shares and (2)whether a business is likely to be in a strong relative cost position based on scale economies and experience in producing the product.
   E) None of the above.

   Answer: D Difficulty: Medium

24. The value of determining the relative competitive strength of each business in a diversified company's portfolio is
   A) to identify which businesses have what kinds of competitive advantages.
   B) to learn which business have the best/worst financial performance and whether their market shares are rising or falling.
   C) to compare resource strengths and weaknesses, business by business.
   D) to probe each business's arsenal of competitive assets and liabilities and rate them from strongest to weakest in contending for market leadership in their respective industries.
   E) to learn which businesses in the portfolio have the most competitive strengths and which have the most competitive weaknesses.

   Answer: D Difficulty: Medium

Industry Attractiveness/Business Strength Matrix

25. The nine-cell industry attractiveness-competitive strength matrix
    A) graphically portrays the relative strategic positions of the various businesses a diversified company is in and is useful for helping decide which businesses should have high, average, and low investment priorities.
    B) indicates which businesses are cash hogs and which are cash cows.
    C) pinpoints what strategies are most appropriate for businesses positioned in the middle of the matrix but is less clear about the best strategies for businesses positioned in the four corners of the matrix.
    D) identifies which businesses have the greatest strategic fit.
    E) identifies which businesses have the greatest resource fit.

    Answer: A   Difficulty: Medium

26. The most important strategic implication resulting from drawing a 9-cell industry attractiveness-competitive strength matrix is
    A) which businesses in the portfolio have the most potential for cost sharing or skills transfer.
    B) why cash cow businesses are more valuable than cash hog businesses.
    C) that corporate resources should be concentrated on those businesses enjoying both a higher degree of industry attractiveness and competitive strength and that businesses having low competitive strength in relatively unattractive industries should be looked at for possible divestiture.
    D) which businesses have the biggest competitive advantages and which ones confront serious competitive disadvantages.
    E) which businesses are in industries with strong experience curve effects and which are in industries with weak experience curve effects.

    Answer: C   Difficulty: Medium

27. The most significant contributions to strategy-making in diversified companies provided by the 9-cell industry attractiveness/competitive strength matrix include
    A) why it is important to use weights to evaluate each key determinant of resource fit.
    B) providing a basis for rating a company's business units in terms of investment priority and for pinpointing which businesses should be considered for possible divestiture.
    C) its ability to identify cash cow and cash hog businesses.
    D) its ability to pinpoint what kind of competitive advantage or disadvantage each business has.
    E) the ability to identify the strategic fits and resource fits that exist among the different businesses.

    Answer: B   Difficulty: Medium

28. The industry attractiveness/business strength matrix can be used to
    A) plot how well each business unit's resource strengths match up against its respective industry's key success factors.
    B) plot and compare the strategic positions of different businesses in a diversified company's portfolio.
    C) compare the profitability of each business in a diversified company's portfolio.
    D) rank the degree of strategic fit among the businesses a company has diversified into.
    E) rank the growth potential of a diversified company's business units from highest to lowest.

    Answer: B   Difficulty: Medium

29. The industry attractiveness/business strength matrix is two-dimensional grid
    A) depicting which businesses in a diversified company's portfolio are most profitable and least profitable and why (based on the business's position in the matrix).
    B) comparing the attractiveness and strength of the strategies employed by each of a diversified company's businesses and the likely success of each strategy based on that business's position in the matrix.
    C) comparing the strategic positions of various business units of a diversified company and their respective ability to contend for market leadership in their industry.
    D) showing the extent of strategic fit among a diversified company's different businesses.
    E) depicting which businesses in a diversified company's portfolio have the greatest potential for competitive advantage based on strong resource fit.

    Answer: C   Difficulty: Medium

Strategic Fit Analysis and the Potential for Cross-Business Competitive Advantage

30. In a diversified company, a business subsidiary is more valuable strategically when
    A) it has potential to become a cash cow.
    B) it has value chain relationships with other business subsidiaries that present competitively valuable opportunities to transfer skills or technology or intellectual capital from one business to another, combine the performance of related activities and reduce costs, leverage use of a well-respected brand name, or collaborate to create new competitive capabilities.
    C) it is the company's biggest profit producer or is capable of becoming the biggest.
    D) it is in a fast-growing industry.
    E) All of these.

    Answer: B   Difficulty: Medium

31. Determining the extent to which there are competitively valuable value chain match-ups among a diversified company's business subsidiaries is an integral part of
    A) the strategic fit test.
    B) the industry attractiveness test.
    C) the resource fit test.
    D) the competitive strength test.
    E) the profitability and competitive advantage test.

    Answer: A   Difficulty: Medium

32. Evaluating a diversified company's business portfolio for strategic fits involves ascertaining
   A) which business units have value chain match-ups that offer opportunities to combine the performance of related value chain activities and reduce costs.
   B) which business units have value chain match-ups that offer opportunities to transfer skills or technology or intellectual capital from one business to another.
   C) which business units have opportunities to exploit common use of a well-respected brand name.
   D) which business units have value chain match-ups that offer opportunities to create new competitive capabilities or to leverage existing resources.
   E) All of these.

   Answer: E   Difficulty: Easy

33. Applying the strategic fit test to a diversified firm's business portfolio entails checking for
   A) the effectiveness of cross-business transfers of cash and investment capital.
   B) whether the firm's strategy is focused on technology-based diversification rather than customer-based diversification.
   C) whether the company is concentrating corporate resources on those cash cow businesses with a high relative market share.
   D) the presence of competitively valuable relationships between the value chains of sister business units.
   E) the extent of similarities among the competitive strategies and competitive positioning of the various businesses.

   Answer: D   Difficulty: Medium

34. Checking a diversified company's business portfolio for cross-business competitive advantage potential does not involve which one of the following?
   A) Ascertaining which business units have value chain match-ups that offer opportunities to combine the performance of related value chain activities and reduce costs
   B) Ascertaining which business units have value chain match-ups that offer opportunities to transfer skills or technology or intellectual capital from one business to another
   C) Ascertaining which business units have similar industry key success factors
   D) Ascertaining which business units have value chain match-ups that offer opportunities to create new competitive capabilities or to leverage existing resources
   E) Ascertaining which business units present opportunities to exploit common use of a well-respected brand name

   Answer: C   Difficulty: Medium

35. Strategic fit analysis of a diversified company's business portfolio involves determining
    A) whether each business unit meshes well with the firm's long-term key success factors.
    B) whether the company has the resources to support the requirements of all its different business units.
    C) whether there are competitively valuable match-ups in the value chains of the company's different businesses and whether there are any businesses in the portfolio that do not fit in well with the company's long term direction and strategic vision.
    D) if sister business units in the corporate portfolio confront similar industry rivals and are in similar strategic groups and thus can utilize essentially the same type of competitive strategy.
    E) if the strategic alliances and collaborative partnerships in one business match up well with the strategic alliances and collaborative partnerships in another business.

    Answer: C Difficulty: Medium

36. In a diversified company, business subsidiaries that lack strategic fit
    A) should always be divested.
    B) should be considered for divestiture unless they are unusually good financial performers or else offer superior growth opportunities.
    C) should be harvested, then divested.
    D) should be milked for maximum cash flow, then sold.
    E) should be kept if they require only minimal levels of corporate resource support to maintain profitability.

    Answer: B Difficulty: Medium

Resource Fit Analysis

37. A diversified company's business units exhibit good resource fit when
    A) individual businesses add to a company's resource strengths, either strategically or financially.
    B) a company has the resources to adequately support the requirements of its businesses as a group without spreading itself too thinly.
    C) each business is profitable and generates a solid return on invested capital.
    D) each business unit produces large internal cash flows over and above what is needed to build and maintain the business.
    E) Both A and B are correct.

    Answer: E Difficulty: Medium

38. The businesses in a diversified company's portfolio exhibit good resource fit when
    A) the company has more cash cows than cash hogs.
    B) individual businesses add to a company's resource strengths, either strategically or financially and when a company has the resources to adequately support the requirements of its businesses as a group without spreading itself too thinly.
    C) each business is profitable and generates a solid return on invested capital.
    D) each business unit produces large internal cash flows over and above what is needed to build and maintain the business.
    E) there are enough cash cow businesses to support the capital requirements of the cash hog businesses.

    Answer: B Difficulty: Medium

39. The difference between a "cash-cow" business and a "cash hog" business is that
   A) a cash cow business is making money whereas a cash hog business is losing money.
   B) a cash cow business generates enough profits to pay off long-term debt whereas a cash hog business does not.
   C) a cash cow business generates positive retained earnings whereas a cash hog business produces negative retained earnings.
   D) a cash cow business produces large internal cash flows over and above what is needed to build and maintain the business whereas the internal cash flows of a cash hog business are inadequate to fully fund its needs for working capital and new investment.
   E) a cash cow business generates very large increases in sales revenues whereas a cash hog business has declining sales revenues and chronic deficiencies of working capital.

   Answer: D Difficulty: Medium

40. A star business (one with a leading market share, a widely respected reputation, a solid track record of profitability, and excellent future growth and profit opportunities)
   A) is nearly always a cash cow.
   B) has to have a market share above 50 percent to qualify as a star.
   C) may well require regular infusions of capital to support rapid growth and continued high performance.
   D) usually turns into a cash hog as it matures.
   E) is usually a cash hog and thus is not as valuable a business as a cash cow.

   Answer: C Difficulty: Medium

41. A "cash cow" type of business
   A) generates unusually high profits and returns on equity investment.
   B) is one which is so profitable that it has no long-term debt.
   C) generates positive cash flows over and above what is needed to build and maintain the business thus providing monies that can be used for financing new acquisitions, funding the capital requirements of cash hog businesses, and paying dividends.
   D) is a business with such a strong competitive advantage that it generates big profits, big returns on investment, and big cash surpluses after dividends are paid.
   E) represents good strategic fit with a cash hog business.

   Answer: C Difficulty: Medium

42. The businesses in a diversified company's line-up exhibit good resource fit when
   A) there is a good mix of cash cow and cash hog businesses and when each business contributes to the achievement of corporate performance objectives (profit growth, return on investment, recognition as an industry leader, and so on).
   B) one or more businesses can benefit from the transfer of resources/capabilities form one business to another.
   C) the company's resource strengths are well-matched to the key success factors of the businesses/industries it has diversified into.
   D) the company has ample resource depth to support all of its businesses—especially the managerial depth and expertise to cope with the assortment of managerial and operating problems posed by its different businesses.
   E) All of these.

   Answer: E Difficulty: Easy

43. Checking a diversified company's business line-up for competitive and managerial resource fits involves determining
   A) whether the company's resource strengths are well-matched to the key success factors of the industries it has diversified into.
   B) whether competitive capabilities in one business can be leveraged by transferring them to another business.
   C) whether the company has (or can readily develop) ample resource depth to support all of its businesses.
   D) whether the company needs to invest in upgrading its resource base in order to stay ahead of (or abreast of) the efforts of rivals to upgrade their resource base.
   E) All of these.

   Answer: E   Difficulty: Easy

44. Checking a diversified company's business line-up for competitive and managerial resource fits does not involve which one of the following?
   A) Determining whether the company's resource strengths are well-matched to the key success factors of the industries it has diversified into
   B) Determining whether the value chains of different businesses are similar in a number of competitively important respects
   C) Determining whether the company has or can readily develop the managerial depth and expertise to cope with the assortment of managerial and operating problems posed by its different businesses
   D) Determining whether the company needs to invest in upgrading its resource base in order to stay ahead of (or abreast of) the efforts of rivals to upgrade their resource base
   E) Determining whether competitive capabilities in one business can be leveraged by transferring them to another business

   Answer: B   Difficulty: Medium

45. Diversifying into businesses with seemingly good resource fit is, by itself, not sufficient to produce success because
   A) the rivals that a company will have to face in the new business may have potent resource strengths and capabilities of their own.
   B) it is not a simple matter to successfully transfer a company's resource strengths to a new business.
   C) the new business may be a cash hog.
   D) the new industry's competitive forces, driving forces, and key success factors may be different.
   E) Both A and B are correct.

   Answer: E   Difficulty: Medium

Comparing Business Unit Performance

46. Important considerations in judging which of a diversified company's businesses have been the strongest and weakest performers in recent years include
   A) sales and profit growth.
   B) the return on capital invested in the business.
   C) the percentage contribution each business makes to the company's total earnings.
   D) the amount of annual cash flow a business generates—whether a business is currently a cash cow or a cash hog.
   E) All of these.

   Answer: E   Difficulty: Easy

47. The most important considerations in judging which of a diversified company's businesses have the best future growth and profit prospects include
   A) the industry attractiveness and competitive strength evaluations (as summarized in the attractiveness-strength matrix)—normally strong businesses in attractive industries have better profit prospects than weak businesses in unattractive industries.
   B) which businesses have the strongest strategic fits and which have the weakest.
   C) the competitive intensity found in each of the industries where the company competes.
   D) which businesses have the strongest and weakest resource fits.
   E) the amount of annual cash flow a business is expected to generate down the road—whether a business is projected to be a cash cow or a cash hog.

   Answer: A   Difficulty: Easy

Deciding on Resource Allocation Priorities

48. Conclusions about what the priorities should be for allocating resources to the various businesses of a diversified company need to be based on such considerations as
   A) whether and how corporate resources and capabilities can be used to enhance the competitiveness and profitability of particular business units.
   B) industry attractiveness and competitive strength of the various businesses—normally strong businesses in attractive industries should carry a higher priority than weak businesses in unattractive industries.
   C) strategic fit with other business units.
   D) compatibility with the corporation's long-term direction and strategic vision.
   E) All of these.

   Answer: E   Difficulty: Easy

49. Which one of the following is not a particularly relevant consideration in deciding what the priorities should be for allocating resources to the various businesses of a diversified company?
   A) Whether and how corporate resources and capabilities can be used to enhance the competitiveness and profitability of particular business units
   B) What competitive strategy the business is presently using
   C) Whether a business exhibits good strategic fit and resource fit
   D) Compatibility with the corporation's long-term direction and strategic vision
   E) Industry attractiveness and competitive strength of the various businesses—normally strong businesses in attractive industries should be given higher priority than weak businesses in unattractive industries

   Answer: B   Difficulty: Medium

50. As a general rule, a diversified company should give top priority in allocating corporate resources to those businesses which
    A) can realize significant profit gains from resource investments aimed at improving the business in some area crucial to long-term competitive success.
    B) have strong industry attractiveness and also have the competitive strength to maintain or contend for market leadership.
    C) exhibit strong strategic fit with other business units.
    D) are compatible with the corporation's long-term direction and strategic vision.
    E) All of these.

    Answer: E   Difficulty: Easy

51. The options for allocating a diversified company's financial resources include
    A) adding new businesses to the corporate portfolio and establishing positions in new industries.
    B) investing in ways to strengthen or expand existing businesses.
    C) funding long-range R&D ventures.
    D) paying off existing debt, increasing dividends, or repurchasing shares of the company's stock.
    E) All of these.

    Answer: E   Difficulty: Easy

52. Which one of the following is not a reasonable option for deploying a diversified company's financial resources?
    A) Spending to add new businesses to the corporate portfolio and establish positions in new industries
    B) Concentrating most of a company's financial resources in cash cow businesses and allocating little or no additional resources to cash hog businesses until they show enough strength to generate positive cash flows
    C) Funding long-range R&D ventures
    D) Paying down existing debt, increasing dividends, or repurchasing shares of the company's stock
    E) Investing in ways to strengthen or expand existing businesses

    Answer: B   Difficulty: Medium

Crafting a Corporate Strategy to Improve Performance

53. When the aggregate performance of the businesses in a diversified company's portfolio is not expected to be good enough to achieve corporate performance targets, then top management can take such actions as
    A) adding new businesses to the corporate portfolio.
    B) divesting weak-performing businesses.
    C) altering the strategies of business units to try to squeeze out a higher level of performance.
    D) reducing corporate performance objectives to levels more in line with what is achievable.
    E) All of these.

    Answer: E   Difficulty: Easy

54. Which of the following should be a last resort option for a diversified company that is experiencing a decline in performance?
   A) Divest weak performing business units and acquire attractive new business units
   B) Reduce corporate performance objectives
   C) Alter strategic plans of some of its business units in ways that should boost performance
   D) Upgrade the company's resource base
   E) Form strategic alliances and/or collaborative partnerships to try to alter conditions responsible for subpar performance

   Answer: B Difficulty: Medium

55. In which of the following cases does it make the most sense for a diversified company to consider divesting some business units?
   A) A multi-business firm that has more cash cows than it needs to finance the requirements of its cash hogs
   B) A diversified firm that has several businesses with little or no strategic fit with other business units in its portfolio
   C) A diversified firm whose businesses are above and to the left of the diagonal in the attractiveness-strength matrix
   D) A broadly diversified company that has many businesses with a relative market share between 0.8 and 1.25
   E) A diversified multinational company that has more businesses employing multi-country strategies than it has employing global strategies

   Answer: B Difficulty: Medium

56. Decisions to divest a business unit should be based on
   A) whether the company has negative cash flows and is a cash hog.
   B) resource fit and strategic fit considerations, industry attractiveness and competitive strength considerations, and compatibility with corporate direction, objectives, and long-term corporate strategy.
   C) whether the business is above and to the left of the diagonal in the attractiveness-strength matrix.
   D) whether it produces less than 5% of the company's total profits—companies that don't account for more than 5% of total profit are too unimportant to carry a high priority for corporate resource allocation and don't deserve much top management attention.
   E) All of the above.

   Answer: E Difficulty: Medium

57. In diversified companies, shareholder interests are generally best served by
   A) pursuing narrow rather than broad diversification.
   B) divesting businesses that are currently not earning an attractive profit.
   C) concentrating corporate resources on businesses that can contend for market leadership in their industry.
   D) trying to maximize overall corporate growth in revenues.
   E) trying to maximize the firm's short-term profits, cash flow, and return on investment.

   Answer: C Difficulty: Hard

58. In companies pursuing an unrelated diversification strategy, decisions to add new businesses to the portfolio are usually based on
    A) whether the timing is right for another acquisition.
    B) whether the firm is in a strong enough financial condition to make another acquisition.
    C) whether new acquisitions are badly needed to boost overall corporate performance.
    D) whether there is a pressing acquisition opportunity that needs to be acted on before other potential acquirers emerge.
    E) All of the above.

    Answer: E   Difficulty: Easy

Short Answer Questions

59. Shareholder interests are generally best served by concentrating corporate resources on businesses that can contend for market leadership. True or false. Explain your answer.

    Difficulty: Medium

60. Draw an industry attractive-business strength matrix and explain its advantages and benefits in analyzing a diversified company's business portfolio.

    Difficulty: Hard

61. Explain the difference between a cash cow business and a cash hog business.

    Difficulty: Easy

62. What does the industry attractiveness test involve in evaluating a diversified company's business portfolio? Why is it relevant?

    Difficulty: Medium

63. Identify and briefly describe the eight steps involved in evaluating a diversified company's business portfolio.

    Difficulty: Hard

64. What is the relevance of the strategic fit test in evaluating a diversified company's business portfolio?

    Difficulty: Medium

65. What is the relevance of the resource fit test in evaluating a diversified company's business portfolio?

Difficulty: Medium

66. What is the relevance of quantitatively measuring the competitive strength of each business in a diversified company's business portfolio and determining which business units are strongest and weakest?

Difficulty: Medium

67. Why is it pertinent in evaluating a diversified company's business portfolio to look at the historical performance and projected future performance of each business?

Difficulty: Medium

68. Briefly explain what is meant by each of the following terms:
    a.) a cash cow business
    b.) a cash hog business
    c.) resource fit
    d.) relative market share

Difficulty: Medium

Chapter 11: Building Resource Strengths and Organizational Capabilities

Multiple Choice Questions

Implementing and Executing Strategy: The Principal Tasks and Characteristics

1. Once company managers have decided on a strategy, the task is to
   A) convert the strategic plan into action and exert the leadership to get on with what needs to be done to achieve the vision and targeted results.
   B) empower employees to revise and reorganize value chain activities to match the strategy and determine which core competencies and competitive capabilities to build into the organization structure.
   C) ensure that strategy is adjusted in ways that avoid conflicts with established policies and procedures.
   D) develop a detailed implementation plan that set forth what every department and every manager needs to do to promote better execution of the company's strategy.
   E) All of these.

   Answer: A   Difficulty: Medium

2. What makes the managerial task of strategy implementation and execution so challenging and demanding is
   A) the wide sweep of managerial activities that have to be attended to and the many ways managers can proceed in tackling each strategy-implementing activity.
   B) the demanding people-management skills required.
   C) the resistance to change that has to be overcome and the number of bedeviling issues that must be worked out.
   D) the perseverance it takes to get a variety of initiatives launched and kept moving along.
   E) All of these.

   Answer: E   Difficulty: Easy

3. Whereas crafting strategy is largely a market-driven entrepreneurial activity, implementing strategy
   A) is primarily an operations-driven activity revolving around the management of people and business processes.
   B) involves building and strengthening organizational resources, competencies and competitive capabilities.
   C) is an action-oriented make-things-happen task.
   D) tests a manager's ability to lead and direct organizational change, achieve continuous improvement in business processes, create a strategy-supportive corporate culture, and meet or beat performance targets.
   E) All of these.

   Answer: E   Difficulty: Easy

4. Getting an organization to implement and execute a new strategy
   A) calls for essentially the same kinds of creative management talent and innovative thinking as does crafting strategy.
   B) presents essentially the same kinds of management challenges from strategy to strategy, organization to organization, and industry to industry.
   C) is a job for a company's whole management team, not just a few select executives at the top.
   D) depends heavily on the caliber of a CEO's business vision, industry and competitive analysis skills, and entrepreneurial creativity.
   E) tends to be a simpler, quicker management task to perform as compared to crafting a winning strategy.

   Answer: C Difficulty: Medium

5. Management's handling of the strategy implementation process can be considered successful
   A) when the internal organization structure ends up being well-matched to the requirements of successful strategy execution.
   B) if and when the company achieves the targeted strategic and financial performance and shows good progress in achieving management's strategic vision for the company.
   C) if the company's policies and procedures are strategy-supportive.
   D) if the budget is made after the strategy is chosen, rather than before, so that resource allocation is fully supportive of strategy execution.
   E) if managers and employees support the company's strategy and long-term direction and are motivated to pursue aggressive implementation.

   Answer: B Difficulty: Medium

6. In developing an action agenda for implementing and executing the chosen strategy, managers at all levels should
   A) begin by putting wise policies and procedures into place and enforcing them rather strictly (so as to avoid losing control over how the organization conducts its business).
   B) think through the answer to "What has to be done in my area to implement our part of the strategic plan and what should I do to get these things accomplished?"
   C) usually make decisions authoritatively rather than on the basis of consensus.
   D) do a survey of all key managers and employees to determine their views on what types of changes need to be made.
   E) start by deciding which competitive capabilities to build first.

   Answer: B Difficulty: Medium

7. Which of the following is not one of the principal managerial components associated with implementing and executing strategy?
   A) Building an organization with the skills, competencies, capabilities, and resources to carry out the strategy successfully and steering ample resources into those value chain activities critical to strategic success
   B) Establishing strategy-supportive policies and procedures
   C) Deciding which value chain activities to revise first and which to leave as is
   D) Instituting best practices and pushing for continuous improvement in how value chain activities are performed
   E) Tying incentives and rewards to the achievement of performance targets and to good strategy execution

   Answer: C Difficulty: Medium

8. In devising an action agenda to implement and execute a new or different strategy, managers should
   A) begin with the task of building a capable organization.
   B) start by choosing which leadership style to employ in trying to carry out the strategy successfully.
   C) start by evaluating whether existing policies and procedures are adequately strategy-supportive.
   D) begin with an evaluation of whether current patterns of resource allocation are fully supportive of strategy execution.
   E) communicate the case for organizational change clearly and persuasively so as to build commitment among managers and employees for the company's strategy and for achieving the targeted levels of performance.

   Answer: E   Difficulty: Medium

Leading the Implementation Process

9. The managerial task of implementing strategy primarily falls upon the shoulders of
   A) a company's chief executive officer and, to a lesser extent, its chief operating officer.
   B) first-line supervisors who have day-to-day responsibility for seeing that key activities are done properly.
   C) the heads of major organizational units, principally vice-presidents and department heads.
   D) all managers, each attending to what needs to be done in their respective areas of authority and responsibility; moreover, all employees are participants in the process.
   E) the CEO and other senior officers.

   Answer: D   Difficulty: Easy

10. While ultimate responsibility for implementing and executing strategy falls upon the shoulders of senior executives,
    A) top-level managers still have to rely on the active support and cooperation of middle and lower-level managers in pushing needed changes in major departments and operating activities and in getting employees to continuously improve on how strategy-critical value chain activities are performed.
    B) the pivotal strategy-implementing actions are principally carried out by front-line supervisors who have day-to-day responsibility for seeing that key activities are done properly.
    C) it is a company's employees who most determine whether the implementation process will succeed or fail.
    D) the really pivotal leadership issue concerns how best to empower employees to make day-to-day operating decisions.
    E) the success or failure of the implementation/execution effort hinges chiefly on a company's reward system and whether its policies and procedures are strategy-supportive.

    Answer: A   Difficulty: Easy

11. Responsibility for implementing strategy
    A) is primarily the job of the chief executive officer.
    B) is a task for every manager and the whole management team.
    C) is primarily a senior management responsibility.
    D) should be delegated to a chief strategy implementer appointed by the chief executive officer.
    E) is primarily a task for middle and lower-level managers because it is they who have responsibility for pushing the needed changes all the way down to the lowest levels of the organization.

    Answer: B   Difficulty: Easy

12. The most important leadership skill in implementing and executing strategy successfully is
    A) for managers to know what the "right" organizational structure is.
    B) having the courage to insist on steering resources out of non-critical activities into strategy-critical activities.
    C) having the courage to push hard and fast for needed changes in the internal organization.
    D) a savvy understanding of the business and the organization's circumstances coupled with a strong sense of what needs to be done to achieve the desired results.
    E) having the charisma to personally orchestrate the creation of a strategy-supportive corporate culture and work environment.

    Answer: D   Difficulty: Medium

Building a Capable Organization

13. The three components of building a capable organization are
    A) making periodic changes in the firm's internal organization to keep people from getting into a comfortable rut, instituting a decentralized approach to decision-making, and developing the appropriate competencies and capabilities.
    B) allocating resources in a manner most conducive to efficient performance of key value chain activities, empowering employees, and hiring a capable top management team.
    C) putting a centralized decision-making structure in place, determining who should have responsibility for each value chain activity, and aligning the organization structure with key policies, procedures, and operating practices.
    D) staffing the organization, building core competencies and competitive capabilities, and structuring the organization and work effort.
    E) flattening the organization structure, making sure that all managers and employees are empowered, and establishing effective compensation incentives.

    Answer: D   Difficulty: Medium

14. Building an organization capable of competent strategy implementation and execution entails
    A) staffing the organization, building core competencies and competitive capabilities, and structuring the organization and work effort.
    B) centralizing authority for performing strategy-critical value chain activities.
    C) periodically shifting to a new type of organization design and organization structure in order to keep people from getting complacent.
    D) centralizing authority in the hands of a chief strategy implementer so as to create the leadership authority for driving implementation forward at a rapid pace.
    E) empowering employees, flattening the organization structure, and instituting a results-oriented reward system.

    Answer: A   Difficulty: Medium

15. Putting together a strong and capable top management team
    A) is often a first-step in the strategy implementation process (or at least an early one) and a cornerstone for organization-building.
    B) is particularly important when the firm is pursuing unrelated diversification or making a number of new acquisitions in related businesses.
    C) is important, but nonetheless secondary to the task of training and retraining employees.
    D) entails selecting people with the right personal chemistry and mix of skills.
    E) Both A and D

    Answer: E   Difficulty: Medium

16. The overriding consideration in assembling a capable top management team is to
    A) select people who are knowledgeable about industry and competitive conditions so as to keep the organization market-driven and customer-driven.
    B) put together a compatible group of managers who possess the full set of skills to get things done.
    C) choose managers experienced in building the very kinds of core competencies the company needs for good strategy execution.
    D) select people who have similar management styles, leadership approaches, business philosophies, and personalities.
    E) choose managers who believe in decentralization and empowerment of employees.

    Answer: B   Difficulty: Medium

17. Recruiting and retaining talented employees
    A) is usually one of the last steps in the organization-building task.
    B) is a particularly important organization-building task in enterprises where superior intellectual capital is not only a key resource but also a basis for competitive advantage.
    C) is more important during periods of rapid growth than during periods of crisis and attempted turnarounds.
    D) is an important organization-building element, but usually secondary compared to the importance of assembling a capable top management team.
    E) should be a lower priority organization-building task than training employees and equipping them with cutting-edge skills.

    Answer: B   Difficulty: Medium

18. Which of the following is generally not among the practices that companies use to develop their knowledge base and build intellectual capital?
    A) Careful screening and evaluation of job applicants
    B) Continuous training and retraining of employees
    C) Weeding out the 20% lowest performing employees each year
    D) Giving people skills-stretching assignments and rotating them through jobs that span functional and geographic boundaries
    E) Encouraging employees to be creative and innovative and fostering a stimulating and engaging work environment

    Answer: C   Difficulty: Medium

Building Core Competencies and Competitive Capabilities

19. The strategic importance of deliberately trying to develop organizational competencies and capabilities is
    A) the added decision-making speed which results in responding to market change.
    B) the extra cross-functional coordination and cooperation that results.
    C) the contribution which they can make to winning a competitive edge based on superior strategy execution.
    D) the added ease with which strategic fit and resource fit benefits can be captured.
    E) the contributions they make to empowering employees, boosting morale, and building a strategy-supportive culture.

    Answer: C Difficulty: Easy

20. When it is difficult or impossible to out-strategize rivals (beat them with a superior strategy), the other main avenue to competitive advantage is to
    A) do a better job of empowering employees.
    B) outcompete them with superior internal operating systems and wiser policies and procedures.
    C) beat them on the basis of superior strategy execution (superior talent, stronger or better capabilities, more attention to detail) such that strategy-critical activities are performed in more superior fashion.
    D) outexecute them with a more dynamic and modern corporate culture driven by cutting-edge use of e-commerce practices.
    E) institute a more motivating and cost-efficient compensation and reward system.

    Answer: C Difficulty: Medium

21. Core competencies and competitive capabilities
    A) usually are lodged in the narrow skills and specialized work efforts of a single department, as opposed to the combined expertise and capabilities of specialists scattered across several departments.
    B) typically emerge incrementally as a company acts to respond to customer problems, new technological or market opportunities, and the competitive maneuvers of rivals or else tries to capitalize on the skills, abilities, and know-how that contributed to its earlier successes.
    C) are most often composites of skills and activities performed at different locations in a firm's value chain that, when linked and coordinated, create unique organizational capability.
    D) tend to result in competitive advantage when they are highly specific, grounded in deep technical expertise, and involve know-how that can be kept proprietary.
    E) Both B and C are correct.

    Answer: E Difficulty: Hard

22. Which of the following is not one of the traits of core competencies?
    A) The key to leveraging core competencies into competitive advantage is concentrating sufficient effort and talent on deepening and strengthening them that the firm achieves dominating depth and gains the capability to outperform rivals by a meaningful margin.
    B) Core competencies should be broad enough and flexible enough to respond to changing customer needs and other market conditions.
    C) Core competencies typically are lodged in the combined efforts of different work groups and departments, making it hard for individual supervisors or department heads to be responsible for building such competencies.
    D) Core competencies generally grow out of company efforts to master a strategy-critical technology, to develop in-depth expertise in some functional specialty, to invent and patent a valuable technology, or to learn an unusual skill in performing a key value-chain activity.
    E) Core competencies tend to emerge gradually rather than blossoming quickly from a series of recent organization-building.

    Answer: D   Difficulty: Medium

23. A key to leveraging a company's core competencies into competitively valuable capabilities with potential for long-term competitive advantage hinges on
    A) outspending rivals on core competence-related activities.
    B) having more intellectual capital than rivals.
    C) having more employees with the skills and expertise underlying the core competencies than rivals have.
    D) concentrating enough resources and management attention on deepening and strengthening the competencies and capabilities to achieve the dominating depth needed for competitive advantage.
    E) pushing hard to perform the functional specialties underlying the core competencies better than rivals.

    Answer: D   Difficulty: Medium

24. Building and strengthening a firm's core competencies involves
    A) spending more money on competence-related activities than present or potential competitors.
    B) delegating authority for deepening and strengthening a competence to those supervisors and department heads in whose areas the skills and expertise are being developed.
    C) networking and coordinating the efforts of different work groups and departments at every place in the value chain that are a part of and that contribute to the competencies.
    D) concentrating a company's resources and energies on performing one key value chain activity with greater proficiency than rivals.
    E) pushing hard to perform one or more functional specialties better than rivals.

    Answer: C   Difficulty: Medium

25. For a core competence to emerge from organization-building actions, a company may well have to
    A) add more people with good technical skills and managerial capabilities in every department where strategy-critical tasks are performed.
    B) concentrate resources and management attention on those organizational areas that are involved in building the core competence.
    C) staff all major functional departments with high-caliber managerial and technical talent.
    D) flatten the organization structure, empower employees, shift to team-based organizational structures, and reengineer core business processes.
    E) shorten its value chain, outsource non-critical value chain activities, and focus the company's energies and resources on the specific department and function where the core competencies is desired.

Answer: B   Difficulty: Hard

26. Core competencies and competitive capabilities are a basis for sustainable competitive advantage because
    A) distinctive core competencies and organizational capabilities are not easily duplicated by rivals.
    B) such capabilities usually reside in a company's proprietary technological know-how and, as a consequence, the needed know-how for imitation is not available to rivals.
    C) they can be easily concealed from rivals.
    D) they usually require high capital investments to copy and the capital requirements hurdle this creates for rivals erects a formidable barrier to overcome.
    E) intellectual capital is in short supply.

Answer: A   Difficulty: Medium

27. Strategy implementers can't afford to become complacent once core competencies are in place and functioning because
    A) most core competencies and organizational capabilities are easily and inexpensively copied by rivals.
    B) it is a constant organization-building challenge to broaden, deepen, or modify them in response to ongoing customer-market changes.
    C) it is easy for rivals to create offsetting competencies and capabilities of their own.
    D) most every competent company has competitively valuable distinctive competencies and resource strengths that it can deploy in retaliation.
    E) All of the above.

Answer: B   Difficulty: Medium

28. Capability-building
    A) requires first developing the ability to do something, translating this ability into a competence and/or capability by learning to do the activity consistently well and at an acceptable cost, and then continuing to refine and deepen its know-how until it is better than rivals at the activity.
    B) entails considerable time and organizing skill if the capability is to be developed internally from scratch.
    C) involves collaborating closely with strategic allies and external partners in those areas where they have something valuable to contribute to the capability.
    D) can sometimes be accomplished by acquiring a company that has the desired competencies and know-how.
    E) All of the above.

Answer: E   Difficulty: Medium

29. Developing new organizational capabilities in-house typically involves such actions as
    A) hiring new personnel with the skills, know-how, and experience relevant to the desired organizational capability.
    B) linking the skills/know-how of individuals to form group capability.
    C) building the desired levels of proficiency through repetition (practice makes perfect).
    D) establishing strong links with related value chain activities.
    E) All of the above.

    Answer: E   Difficulty: Medium

30. Building organizational capabilities
    A) involves forming alliances with outsiders and collaborating closely with them to mesh the skills, expertise, and competencies needed to produce a capability.
    B) is a time-consuming, hard-to-replicate exercise and entails conscious effort and considerable organizing skill.
    C) entails developing dominating depth in a company's knowledge base and stock of intellectual capital.
    D) can be done quickest by creating a new department and assigning it the task of imitating the desired capabilities that rivals have already developed.
    E) entails hiring people the talent and expertise to perform one or more functional specialties better than rivals.

    Answer: B   Difficulty: Medium

31. An organizational competence or capability is transformed into a distinctive competence when
    A) an organization learns how to perform an activity consistently well.
    B) a company develops enough dominating depth in a particular functional area.
    C) an organization continues to polish, refine, deepen, and strengthen a capability to the point where it performs the activity better than rivals.
    D) an organization is successful in imitating a capability that rivals have already developed.
    E) an organization has more intellectual capital than rivals.

    Answer: C   Difficulty: Medium

32. Sometimes a company can short-circuit the task of building an organizational capability in-house by
    A) acquiring the desired capability through collaborative efforts with outsiders having the requisite skills, know-how, and expertise.
    B) launching an extensive training effort to develop the capability quickly with newly hired employees.
    C) acquiring a company that has already developed the capability.
    D) imitating a capability that rivals have already developed.
    E) Both A and C.

    Answer: E   Difficulty: Medium

33. Employee training and retraining is an important vehicle for strategy implementation when
   A) a company shifts to a strategy requiring different skills, capabilities, and operating methods.
   B) the organization is trying to build a skills-based core competence.
   C) technical know-how is changing so rapidly that a company loses its ability to compete unless its skilled people are kept updated and have cutting edge expertise.
   D) All of the above.
   E) Just A and C.

   Answer: D   Difficulty: Easy

Matching Organization Structure to Strategy

34. Structuring the organization to promote successful strategy execution involves
   A) identifying strategy-critical activities.
   B) deciding which value chain activities to perform in-house and which to outsource.
   C) making internally-performed value chain activities the main building blocks in the organization structure.
   D) deciding how much authority to centralize and how much to delegate to down-the-line managers and employees.
   E) All of these.

   Answer: E   Difficulty: Medium

35. Which one of the following is <u>not</u> part of a strategy-implementer's task of matching organization structure to strategy?
   A) Pinpointing strategy-critical activities
   B) Deciding which, if any, value chain activities to outsource from partners
   C) Determining how much authority to centralize and how much to delegate to down-the-line managers and employees
   D) Selecting the right people for key positions and determining how to capture resource fit benefits
   E) Providing for cross-unit cooperation and collaboration to build/strengthen strategy-supportive competencies and capabilities

   Answer: D   Difficulty: Medium

36. To design a strategy-supportive organizational structure, a strategy implementer needs to
   A) make those strategy-critical activities/capabilities that are to be performed internally the main building blocks in the internal organization structure.
   B) determine whether some value chain activities can be outsourced more efficiently or effectively than they can be performed internally.
   C) determine the degree of authority and independence to give to each organizational unit.
   D) provide for coordination and collaboration across the various organizational units and also with outside partners.
   E) All of these.

   Answer: E   Difficulty: Easy

Identifying Strategy-Critical Activities

37. To identify what an organization's strategy-critical value chain activities are, one should seek answers to which of the following questions?
    A) What value chain activities have to be performed extra well and in timely fashion to achieve sustainable competitive advantage?
    B) What alliances and partnerships are needed to enhance organizational resources and capabilities?
    C) Do the related activities of related business units need to be tightly coordinated?
    D) How many core competencies does the organization need to outmatch its rivals?
    E) What reasons are there to outsource some of the company's value chain activities?

    Answer: A   Difficulty: Medium

38. To identify what an organization's strategy-critical value chain activities are, one should seek answers to which of the following questions?
    A) "What value chain activities have to be performed extra well and in timely fashion to achieve sustainable competitive advantage?" and "In what value chain activities would poor execution seriously impair strategic success?"
    B) "What alliances and partnerships are needed to enhance organizational resources and capabilities?"; "What value chain activities are linked most closely together?"; and "How closely do they need to be coordinated?"
    C) "Do the related activities of related functional are activities need to be tightly coordinated?" "What important activities do our outside allies and partners perform?"
    D) "How many core competencies does the organization need to outmatch its rivals and where are they located in the value chain?"
    E) "What reasons are there to outsource some of the company's value chain activities and how closely do these activities need to be coordinated with what is done in-house?"

    Answer: A   Difficulty: Hard

Outsourcing Value Chain Activities

39. Outsourcing non-critical value chain activities offers such advantages as
    A) helping concentrate company resources and energies on those value-chain activities where the company can create unique value for customers and/or develop dominating depth in one or more competencies and capabilities.
    B) helping decrease the size and influence of internal bureaucracies.
    C) promoting a total quality management culture.
    D) eliminating the need to employ complex matrix organizational structures.
    E) Both A and B are correct.

    Answer: E   Difficulty: Easy

40. Outsourcing non-critical value chain activities offers such advantages as
    A) dominating depth in those activities that are outsourced, the competitive advantages that alliances and collaborative partnerships can produce, enhanced product quality, and better customer service.
    B) lower costs, less internal bureaucracy, speedier decision-making, more flexibility, and heightened strategic focus.
    C) facilitating the use of best practices and total quality management.
    D) eliminating the need to empower employees and rely on team-based organizational arrangements.
    E) helping a company capture cross-functional strategic fits and resource fits.

    Answer: B   Difficulty: Medium

41. Outsourcing critics contend that shifting responsibility for performing value-chain activities from internal departments to outside specialists
    A) has the disadvantage of raising fixed costs and reducing variable costs, makes it harder to develop distinctive competencies, lengthens the time it takes to build organization capabilities, and makes it harder to empower employees.
    B) can hollow out a company's knowledge base and capabilities, leaving it at the mercy of outside suppliers and short of the resource strengths to be a master of its own destiny.
    C) results in less organizational flexibility, lower employee morale, greater supervision and collaboration costs, and lower competitive capabilities.
    D) slows down decision-making on key strategic issues because outside suppliers have to be consulted first.
    E) dampens a company's ability to implement best practices and total quality management and results in greater bureaucracy, higher costs, longer cycle time (because of the added time it takes to collaborate with outsiders) and slower decision-making.

    Answer: B   Difficulty: Hard

42. Strategic partnerships, alliances, and close collaboration with suppliers, distributors and the makers of complementary products/services make good strategic sense whenever
    A) the company relies on a team-based organization structure, wants to empower employees, and has a total quality management culture.
    B) the result is to enhance organizational resources and capabilities.
    C) related value chain activities need to be tightly coordinated.
    D) a company is trying to imitate the capabilities of rivals as quickly as possible and does not have an empowered work force.
    E) the company's value chain consists of a wide diversity of skills, know-how, expertise, and competencies.

    Answer: B   Difficulty: Medium

Making Strategy-Critical Activities the Key Building Blocks of the Structure

43. If management is to match structure to strategy in an effective way, then it is essential that
    A) strategic and operating decisions be decentralized to the lowest level of management.
    B) each functional department be given full authority and responsibility for developing the needed core competencies and capabilities in its respective area of operations.
    C) activities and responsibilities be deliberately organized so as to produce maximum strategic fit.
    D) jobs be defined in terms of the functions to be performed rather than in terms of the results to be achieved.
    E) those strategy-critical activities/capabilities that are to be performed internally be made the main building blocks in the internal organization structure.

    Answer: E   Difficulty: Hard

44. In a company that is organized around functional departments,
    A) the critical value chain activities tend to be performed more efficiently and effectively.
    B) pieces of strategically relevant activities and capabilities often end up scattered across many departments.
    C) it is easier to build core competencies and competitive capabilities.
    D) there is less room for the organization structure to evolve to remain in step with the new strategy-executing requirements of an evolving strategy.
    E) internal bureaucracies are likely to be smaller and the decision-making process is likely to be speedy.

    Answer: B   Difficulty: Medium

45. Because functional organization structures often result in pieces of strategically relevant activities and capabilities being scattered across many different functional departments, companies have found that
    A) it is necessary to give these functional departments the freedom to collaborate closely with each other to achieve the desired degree of coordination.
    B) it is necessary to outsource those activities that are fragmented to strategic partners in order to achieve the needed coordination.
    C) it is better to reengineer the work effort and create process departments.
    D) it is necessary to revamp their value chains to achieve less cross-functional fragmentation.
    E) it makes good organizational sense to combine those functional departments where fragmentation is a problem and thereby gain the needed degree of collaboration and coordination.

    Answer: B   Difficulty: Medium

46. As an organization's strategy evolves to stay in touch with changing external circumstances, it is normal for
    A) its organization structure to remain fixed unless the company's value chain make-up undergoes significant revision.
    B) the company's organization structure to remain fixed unless management decides to shift from centralized to decentralized authority for decision-making.
    C) its organization structure also to undergo gradual change as key executives retire or leave the company.
    D) the organization structure to evolve in order to remain in step with the new strategy-executing requirements of the evolving strategy.
    E) its organization structure to remain fixed unless the company enters into new or different strategic alliances with various outside enterprises.

    Answer: D   Difficulty: Easy

Delegation, Empowerment

47. In parceling out authority to various sub-units, managers, and employees it is usually better
    A) for company managers to retain full decision-making authority over most day-to-day operating decisions until the whole organization has mastered the strategy execution process—once mastery has been achieved, it is safe to empower employees and delegate considerably more decision-making power to lower-level organizational units, managers, and employees.
    B) to centralize authority for strategy-making decisions and to decentralize authority for strategy-implementing decisions.
    C) to centralize authority for strategy-critical value chain activities and to decentralize authority for non-critical value chain activities.
    D) to delegate decision-making authority to the lowest organizational level capable of making timely, informed, competent decisions.
    E) to require managers and employees to go up the ladder of authority on all issues that affect bottom-line profitability.

    Answer: D   Difficulty: Medium

48. Delegating greater authority to subordinate managers and employees
    A) creates a more horizontal or flatter organization structure with fewer management layers and usually acts to shorten organizational response times.
    B) usually slows down decision-making because so many more people are involved.
    C) can be a de-motivating factor because it requires people to accept more responsibility.
    D) is very risky because it can result in a loss of control by senior management.
    E) often contributes to greater fragmentation of strategically-relevant activities across departmental lines.

    Answer: A   Difficulty: Hard

49. In deciding how much authority to centralize and how much to delegate to lower level managers and employees, top management needs to keep in mind that
   A) it is generally more advantageous to opt for a high level of centralized decision-making.
   B) centralized decision-making is typically faster and involves less bureaucracy.
   C) the flatter organization structures associated with decentralization of authority tend to create high levels of stress and anxiety among those individuals that are given greater levels of authority and responsibility.
   D) there are serious disadvantages to highly centralized decision-making arrangements where a small number of top level executives personally make or approve most decisions.
   E) centralized decision-making tends to work best in functional organization structures while decentralized decision-making works best in companies structured around process departments.

   Answer: D   Difficulty: Medium

50. Organization designs that incorporate flat, decentralized management structures and employee empowerment
   A) represent the best way of matching structure to strategy.
   B) are more conducive to building and strengthening core competencies and competitive capabilities than other structures.
   C) reflect a belief in the benefits of pushing decision-making authority down to the lowest organizational level capable of making informed, competent, timely decisions.
   D) offer the most dependable way to maximize organization performance.
   E) are more likely to be a resource weakness than a resource strength because decision-making is so spread out and because control over strategy-critical activities ends up being so fragmented.

   Answer: C   Difficulty: Medium

51. The case for empowering employees to make decisions and be accountable for their performance is based on the belief that
   A) it is the fastest way to make organizational decisions.
   B) it is the best way to build valuable core competencies and competitive capabilities.
   C) it minimizes the potential for fragmenting strategically relevant activities.
   D) it promotes process organization and avoids many of the pitfalls of functional specialization.
   E) a company that draws on the combined intellectual capital of all its employees can outperform a company where the approach to people management is one of command-and-control.

   Answer: E   Difficulty: Medium

52. The organizing challenge of a decentralized structure which stresses employee empowerment
   A) how to avoid fragmentation across functional departments.
   B) how to motivate and challenge those senior managers who no longer have a heavy decision-making load.
   C) how to avoid the pitfalls of fragmenting decision-making power over strategically relevant activities.
   D) how to exercise control over the actions and decisions of empowered employees so that the business is not put at risk in an effort to capture the benefits of empowerment.
   E) how to train lower-level managers and employees to make good decisions.

   Answer: D   Difficulty: Medium

53. Which of the following is not a means of flattening organizational hierarchies and removing middle management layers?
   A) Centralizing decision-making
   B) Empowerment of employees
   C) Decentralizing decision-making
   D) Reengineering business processes
   E) Outsourcing non-critical value chain activities

   Answer: A   Difficulty: Medium

Providing for Cross-Unit Coordination

54. The key in weaving support activities into the organization design is to establish reporting relationships and coordinating arrangements that
   A) support and complement initiatives to build and develop functional competencies and that allow the benefits of specialization to be fully exploited.
   B) maximize how support activities contribute to enhanced performance of primary and strategy-critical activities, that contain the cost of support activities, and that minimize the time and energy that internal units have to spend doing business with each other.
   C) result in the heads of support activities reporting to the heads of primary, strategy-critical activities.
   D) work against process fragmentation.
   E) are consistent with decentralized decision-making.

   Answer: B   Difficulty: Medium

55. Centralizing authority for some activities at the corporate level in a diversified enterprise has merit when
   A) the company is pursuing unrelated diversification.
   B) the company is financially distressed and is under the gun to execute turnaround strategies in several of its major business subsidiaries.
   C) the related activities of related business units need to be tightly coordinated to capture strategic fit benefits.
   D) the company is pursuing cross-business subsidization tactics.
   E) the company has a number of strategic alliances and collaborative partnerships in the supply chains of its different businesses.

   Answer: C   Difficulty: Medium

Collaborating with Outsiders

56. The organizational challenge in collaborating closely with outsiders is
    A) to find ways to span the boundaries of independent organizations, build bridges of cooperation, nurture the relationships to fruition, and actually produce the collaborative efforts needed to enhance a company's own capabilities and resource strengths.
    B) coming up with a matrix organization design that each partner will agree to.
    C) preserve full control over collaborative efforts and not allow partners to divert the effort down other paths.
    D) pick the right people to appoint as relationship managers.
    E) All of these.

    Answer: A   Difficulty: Medium

Business Process Reengineering

57. Business process reengineering is a tool for
    A) expediting the redesign of existing products and shortening the design-to-market cycle.
    B) reducing the fragmentation of strategy-critical business processes across traditional functional departments.
    C) instituting total quality management.
    D) revamping and reconfiguring a company's value chain.
    E) rapid redesign of an organization's structure so as to rapidly create organizational competencies and capabilities.

    Answer: B   Difficulty: Medium

58. Reengineering how a firm performs a business process
    A) is a way of attacking the fragmentation of business processes across departmental lines and reducing costs.
    B) is a tool best suited for company with a delayered, decentralized organization structure.
    C) yields the most benefit when a company has many strategic partnerships and alliances with outsiders.
    D) has the disadvantage of requiring a more centralized approach to decision-making.
    E) usually requires outsourcing one or more of the process steps formerly performed internally.

    Answer: A   Difficulty: Medium

Organizational Structures of the Future

59. The organizational structures of the future will have such characteristics as
    A) a capacity for rapid change and learning.
    B) fewer barriers between people at different vertical ranks, between functions and disciplines, and between units in different locations.
    C) extensive use of e-commerce technology and e-commerce business practices.
    D) extensive collaborative efforts among people in different specialties and different geographic locations.
    E) All of these.

    Answer: E   Difficulty: Easy

60. Which of the following is an unlikely characteristic of the organizational structures of the future?
   A) Highly centralized decision-making (made possible by much greater use of business process reengineering)
   B) Fewer barriers between people at different vertical ranks, between functions and disciplines, and between units in different locations
   C) Extensive use of e-commerce technology and e-commerce business practices
   D) Extensive collaborative efforts among people in different specialties and different geographic locations
   E) A capacity for rapid change and learning

   Answer: A   Difficulty: Medium

Short Answer Questions

61. Identify and briefly explain the eight principal managerial components of implementing and executing strategy.

   Difficulty: Medium

62. Identify and briefly discuss the three components of building a capable organization.

   Difficulty: Medium

63. Who are the strategy implementers?

   Difficulty: Easy

64. What are the traits of a core competence? What is involved in building and strengthening a core competence?

   Difficulty: Medium

65. What is involved in building an organization capability? What steps are required? How much time does it take? How hard is it?

   Difficulty: Medium

66. Discuss the managerial approaches and tasks associated with building a core competence.

   Difficulty: Medium

67. When it proves infeasible to outcompete rivals by crafting a superior strategy, the next best avenue to beating them out for industry leadership is to outexecute them--that is, beat them with superior strategy execution. True or false. Explain.

   Difficulty: Medium

68. What is meant by empowerment? How does it differ from delegation of authority?

    Difficulty: Medium

69. Why is a functional organization structure susceptible to fragmentation of strategy-critical business processes across traditional departmental lines? How can business process reengineering help correct the problem?

    Difficulty: Hard

70. Building competitively valuable core competencies, resource strengths, and organizational capabilities can be a fruitful avenue to achieving sustainable competitive advantage. True or false. Explain.

    Difficulty: Medium

71. What are the advantages of outsourcing non-critical and sometimes even critical value chain activities?

    Difficulty: Medium

72. Attempting to carry out a new strategy with the company's old organization structure is usually unwise. True or false. Explain.

    Difficulty: Medium

Chapter 12: Managing the Internal Organization to Promote Better Strategy Execution

Multiple Choice Questions

Linking Budgets to Strategy

1. How a firm's budget allocates resources to its various departments and value chain activities is important to the strategy implementation and execution process because
   A) changes in strategy often require shifting resources from one area to another and because organizational units need the proper funding to carry out their part of the strategic plan effectively and efficiently—too little funding slows progress and impedes the efforts of strategy-critical organizational units to carry execute their roles proficiently.
   B) strong budgets are the key to exercising financial control over what organization units can and cannot do in carrying out management's directives to execute the chosen strategy proficiently.
   C) budgets are management's foremost device for controlling organizational behavior in a strategy-supportive fashion.
   D) lean budgets protect the company's financial condition and eliminate wasteful use of cash.
   E) budgets are management's best and most used means of getting organizational units to exercise the fiscal discipline needed to execute the chosen strategy in a cost-efficient manner.

   Answer: A   Difficulty: Easy

2. Managers charged with implementing and executing strategy need to be deeply involved in the budgeting and resource allocation process because
   A) too little funding deprives organizational units of the resources to carry out their piece of the strategic plan.
   B) changes in strategy often require shifting resources from one area to another.
   C) without major budget reallocations there is no chance for the desired core competencies and organizational capabilities to emerge.
   D) lean budgets protect the company's financial condition and eliminate wasteful use of cash.
   E) Both A and B.

   Answer: E   Difficulty: Easy

3. From a strategy-implementing/strategy-executing perspective, budget allocations should primarily be based on
   A) the number of new strategic initiatives being implemented in each department.
   B) the number of people employed in each of the divisions.
   C) how much each organizational unit needs to carry out its part of the strategic plan efficiently and effectively.
   D) the costs of performing value chain activities as determined by benchmarking against best-in-industry competitors.
   E) how much stretch there is in each department's objectives and what additional resources are needed to help reach these performance targets.

   Answer: C   Difficulty: Medium

4. New strategies often entail budget reallocations because
    A) more money will be needed to fund the new strategy initiatives.
    B) the accompanying policy revisions and compensation incentives tend to require different levels of funding than before.
    C) the value chain activities and organizational units critical to executing the old strategy are not necessarily as critical in executing the new strategy, thus making it cost-effective to shift resources out of areas that now have a lesser strategy-executing role and redirecting them to the value chain activities now having a bigger and more important strategy-executing role.
    D) empowering employees to carry out the new strategy elements and shifting to a total quality management type of culture to build skills in competent strategy execution typically require substantial new funding and budget revisions.
    E) the number of people employed in each department is likely to change.

    Answer: C Difficulty: Medium

5. Forceful actions to reallocate operating funds and move people into different organizational units
    A) signal a strong commitment to implementing strategic change and help give the credibility to the implementation process.
    B) can be dysfunctional in trying to implement a new strategy because of the anxiety and insecurity that they breed in the work force.
    C) have to be made carefully, lest management inadvertently create barriers to building the needed competencies and capabilities.
    D) tend to impede the task of empowering employees and shifting to new, more strategy-supportive culture.
    E) are rarely necessary in implementing a new strategy unless the new strategy entails a radically different set of value chain activities.

    Answer: A Difficulty: Medium

Creating Strategy-Supportive Policies and Procedures

6. Prescribing new policies and operating procedures can aid the task of implementing strategy
    A) because they promote greater use of and commitment to best practices and total quality management.
    B) because really effective internal policies and procedures are not easily duplicated by other firms.
    C) because an astutely conceived policy or procedure can result in competitive advantage.
    D) by helping align actions and behavior with strategy, placing limits on independent action, and channeling group efforts in ways that support better strategy execution.
    E) by assisting in reengineering the firm's value chain.

    Answer: D Difficulty: Hard

7. A useful guideline in designing strategy-facilitating policies and operating procedures is
   A) to prescribe enough policies to give organizational members clear direction in implementing strategy and to place desirable boundaries on their actions, then empower them to act within these boundaries however they think makes sense.
   B) that strictly-enforced policies work better than loosely-enforced policies.
   C) that an environment of few policies and laid-back management is not as supportive of a strong corporate culture as is a system where policies and procedures are tightly enforced to ensure conformity and standardized behavior.
   D) to let individuals act in an empowered and self-directed way, subject only to the constraint that their actions and behavior be ethical and consistent with the corporate culture.
   E) to prescribe enough policies and procedures that nothing is left to chance in performing value chain activities—employees should have no leeway to do things in a manner other than the prescribed strategy-supportive fashion.

   Answer: A   Difficulty: Hard

8. Prescribing policies and operating procedures aids the task of implementing strategy by
   A) helping ensure that worker eligibility for incentive bonuses is measured consistently and awarded fairly.
   B) fostering the use of best practices, TQM, and continuous improvement efforts.
   C) acting as a powerful lever for changing employee attitudes about the need for a different incentive and reward system.
   D) helping build employee commitment to strengthening the company's core competencies and competitive capabilities.
   E) helping enforce needed consistency in how particular value chain activities are performed in geographically scattered organization units.

   Answer: E   Difficulty: Medium

9. Which one of the following is not a benefit of prescribing policies and operating procedures to aid management's task of implementing strategy?
   A) Helping align actions and behavior with strategy, placing limits on independent action, and channeling group efforts in ways that support better strategy execution
   B) Providing top-down guidance to operating managers, supervisory personnel, and employees regarding how things need to be done and what behavior is expected
   C) Acting as a lever for helping change corporate culture in ways that promote a stronger fit with strategy
   D) Helping build employee commitment to using best practices and TQM tools
   E) Helping enforce needed consistency in how particular value chain activities are performed in geographically scattered organization units

   Answer: D   Difficulty: Medium

Instituting Best Practices, TQM, Continuous Improvement

10. Total quality management (TQM)
    A) deals with procedures to achieve defect-free production.
    B) is one of the most attractive alternatives to reengineering business processes.
    C) entails creating a corporate culture bent on continuously improving the performance of every task and every value-chain activity.
    D) is more a technique for "managing better" than a way to promote more effective strategy execution.
    E) is generally considered the best philosophy for undertaking the reengineering of strategy-critical business processes.

    Answer: C   Difficulty: Medium

11. Instituting best practices and continuous improvement programs like TQM
    A) usually result in a strong, healthy corporate culture.
    B) require a high degree of employee empowerment to be successful.
    C) are a strategy-implementer's best means for achieving higher levels of customer satisfaction.
    D) help promote effective strategy execution by stressing continuous improvement in the performance of all value-chain activities.
    E) is necessary if a company is to have a realistic chance of building competitively valuable core competencies and organizational capabilities.

    Answer: D   Difficulty: Medium

12. The term "best practices" refers to
    A) policies and procedures that prescribe how to perform a particular value chain activity in the best-known way.
    B) performing specific tasks and activities in a manner approximating best-in-industry or best-in-world standards.
    C) performing strategy-critical activities in a fashion that results in sustainable competitive advantage.
    D) those particular value chain activities that a firm performs best relative to other value chain activities.
    E) those particular value chain activities that management has given top priority to performing in world-class fashion.

    Answer: B   Difficulty: Medium

13. The big difference between reengineering and continuous improvement programs like TQM is that
    A) reengineering is a tool for installing process organization whereas TQM concerns defect-free production methods and delivering world-class customer service.
    B) reengineering helps create core competencies whereas TQM is a tool for making a core competence stronger and more efficient.
    C) reengineering is a tool for achieving one-time quantum improvements in performing a business process whereas TQM seeks ongoing incremental improvement.
    D) reengineering requires benchmarking whereas TQM doesn't.
    E) reengineering represents an effort to totally revamp a firm's value chain whereas TQM looks at incrementally improving the performance of two or three targeted value-chain activities.

    Answer: C   Difficulty: Medium

14. TQM is an important tool for implementing and executing strategy because
    A) it is a proven way to boost the quality of a company's product or service, thus helping to create a quality-based competitive advantage.
    B) it can yield dramatic efficiency gains in how a process is performed, thus helping to create a low-cost advantage.
    C) it is the most proven means of creating the competencies and capabilities needed for competent strategy execution.
    D) it aims at instilling enthusiasm and commitment in all managers and employees to continuously improve on how every task and every value-chain activity is being performed.
    E) it is the single best way of building a distinctive competence in defect-free manufacture.

    Answer: D   Difficulty: Hard

15. To obtain maximum benefits from benchmarking, best practices, reengineering, TQM, and related tools, managers need to
    A) start by defining exactly what they want the organization to accomplish in terms of better strategy execution—whether it be defect-free manufacture, on-time delivery, faster cycle time, superior customer satisfaction, lower costs, or whatever.
    B) have annual TQM contests similar to Motorola's and train managers and key employees in six-sigma quality techniques as Motorola has done through Motorola University.
    C) consider instituting policies and procedures like those at Great Plains, Amalgamated Sugar, and Granite Rock.
    D) install strategy-critical information and operating systems to support effective daily execution of strategy (like Federal Express has done).
    E) deemphasize functional departments and shift to a process-oriented approach to organization.

    Answer: A   Difficulty: Medium

16. One of the primary attributes of TQM and related kinds of continuous improvement programs is
    A) their strong emphasis on inspection and instituting comprehensive methods to check people's work, catch mistakes, and correct errors.
    B) that the benefits can be 90 percent realized within 6 months.
    C) they are relatively inexpensive to implement, as compared to reengineering and benchmarking.
    D) that they preach that there is no such thing as good enough and that everyone has a responsibility to participate in continuously improving the performance of tasks and value-chain activities.
    E) that the focus must always be on enhancing customer satisfaction.

    Answer: D   Difficulty: Medium

17. To build a total quality culture and instill commitment to achieving the target performance outcomes that competent strategy execution requires, managers can take such action steps as
    A) developing a quality vision; setting specific, measurable quality and continuous improvement goals; screening out job applicants who don't have the aptitudes or attitudes for the right quality-based performance; instituting employee training programs, and using online systems to give employees immediate access to best practice information and experiences.
    B) shifting from a functional organization structure to a process organization structure.
    C) instituting greater centralization of decision-making to help enforce strict compliance with quality control procedures.
    D) narrowing employee empowerment boundaries, insisting on standardized performance of most tasks and stressing individual performance rather than team or group performance.
    E) Both A and C are correct.

    Answer: A   Difficulty: Medium

Installing Support Systems

18. Installing innovative state-of-the-art support systems is an important managerial component of implementing and executing strategy because
    A) they are essential to effective benchmarking and continuous improvement.
    B) they may give an organization capabilities that rivals cannot match and thus contribute to competitive advantage.
    C) they help managers run a tight ship and preserve strong, centralized control over internal activities.
    D) they are the basis for revamping value chains, reducing operating costs, and boosting labor productivity.
    E) decentralized decision-making and employee empowerment cannot work well without having good support systems to accurately benchmark internally-performed value chain activities against best-in-industry and best-in-class performers.

    Answer: B   Difficulty: Hard

19. Well conceived, state-of-the-art support systems
    A) are essential because reengineering efforts, TQM, and benchmarking programs can't be carried out effectively without them.
    B) not only facilitate better strategy execution but also can strengthen organizational capabilities enough to yield competitive advantage.
    C) provide an essential link to the budget, making it easier to spot cost overruns and inefficiencies.
    D) should aim at providing all managers and employees with as much information as possible as quickly as possible.
    E) All of these.

    Answer: B   Difficulty: Hard

20. From a strategy-implementing/strategy-executing perspective, well conceived, state-of-the-art support systems
    A) help mobilize information and use knowledge effectively.
    B) can speed decision-making and shorten organizational response times.
    C) can strengthen organizational capabilities.
    D) can be a basis for competitive advantage.
    E) All of these.

    Answer: E Difficulty: Easy

21. Which of the following is not a good example of a support system capable of assisting better strategy implementation and execution?
    A) An online, real-time inventory control and sales tracking system
    B) A sophisticated cost accounting system that can track profits and losses on each item in a company's product line
    C) A formalized program for screening, testing, hiring, and training new employees to be friendly, courteous, and helpful in their contacts with customers
    D) A corporate training program in ethics and corporate values
    E) An online reservation system for a hotel chain

    Answer: D Difficulty: Medium

22. Which of the following does not really account for why installing adequate information, performance tracking, and control systems are an important part of the strategy-implementing/strategy-executing process?
    A) Communicating data and information at Internet speed is a necessity in today's business world—investment in Internet-related, e-commerce systems is revolutionizing the manner in which company operations are conducted.
    B) Diagnostic control systems to track performance relieve managers of the burden of constantly doing their own monitoring and allow them more time for other issues.
    C) Such systems can be used to help ensure that the actions of empowered employees stay within acceptable bounds and don't expose the organization to excessive risk.
    D) Controls systems encourage employee creativity and help keep the work environment exciting and results-oriented.
    E) Data analysis procedures help flag big or unusual variances from preset performance standards.

    Answer: D Difficulty: Medium

23. Installing adequate information, performance tracking, and control systems is an important part of the strategy-implementing/strategy-executing process because
    A) communicating data and information at Internet speed is a necessity.
    B) accurate, timely information is an essential guide to action.
    C) the indicators of strategic and financial performance have to be measured as often as practical—real time tracking systems are rapidly becoming the norm.
    D) investment in Internet-related, e-commerce systems is revolutionizing the manner in which company operations are conducted.
    E) All of these

    Answer: E Difficulty: Medium

Motivation, Incentives, Reward Systems

24. The strategic role of a company's reward system is to
    A) compensate employees for performing their assigned duties in a diligent fashion.
    B) boost employee morale in ways that create widespread job satisfaction.
    C) gain employees' energetic commitment to the organization's strategy and vision by rewarding them, both monetarily and non-monetarily, for their contributions.
    D) relieve managers of the burden of closely monitoring each employee's performance.
    E) boost labor productivity and help lower the firm's overall labor costs.

    Answer: C   Difficulty: Medium

25. The management task of linking the reward system tightly to the needs of strategy involves
    A) establishing ethical compensation policies and putting together an inspiring statement of why employees are the firm's most valuable competitive asset.
    B) being creative in designing monetary and non-monetary incentives that boost labor productivity and help lower the firm's overall labor costs.
    C) developing incentives and compensation practices that reward people for meeting or beating the performance targets spelled out in the strategic plan.
    D) deciding how big a bonus to pay for each strategic and financial objective that is achieved.
    E) challenging employees to establish stretch objectives and propose rewarding ways to achieve them.

    Answer: C   Difficulty: Medium

26. To prevent undermining and undoing the reward structure, a strategy-implementer
    A) must eliminate stress, anxiety, and job insecurity from the work environment.
    B) has to challenge employees by establishing ambitious performance targets.
    C) must insist that actual performance be judiciously compared against the target objectives and the reasons for any deviations then explored to ascertain whether the causes are "poor" individual/group performance or uncontrollable, unforeseeable, and/or unknowable circumstances.
    D) needs to specify the duties and functions of subordinates in great detail so that they will know exactly what to do and how to do it.
    E) balance positive and negative rewards.

    Answer: C   Difficulty: Hard

27. From the standpoint of promoting successful strategy implementation and execution, it is important that the firm's motivation and reward system
    A) be completely free of such elements as tension, pressure, anxiety, job insecurity, and tight deadlines.
    B) emphasize only positive types of rewards.
    C) stress what to accomplish rather than what to do.
    D) tie rewards to the achievement of financial objectives rather than strategic objectives and be reviewed annually to see that the costs of any incentives and bonuses are not out of line with the budget.
    E) result in higher levels of morale, reduce job insecurity, induce employees to stay busy and work hard, help steer employees to behave in an ethical manner, and help instill corporate values.

    Answer: C   Difficulty: Medium

28. An important aspect of creating a good strategy-supportive system of rewards and incentives is to
   A) provide jobholders with clear job descriptions defining their duties and assigned activities.
   B) organize employees into empowered work teams.
   C) define jobs and assignments in terms of "what to achieve" rather than "what to do."
   D) tie rewards to strategic objectives rather than financial objectives and stress weeding out low-performers.
   E) stress that across-the-board wage and salary increases depend on supervisors' assessments of whether employees are staying busy, working hard, and providing an ample number of suggestions for continuous efficiency improvement.

   Answer: C Difficulty: Medium

29. A well-designed reward system
   A) makes strategically relevant measures of performance the dominant basis for incentive compensation.
   B) should be free of elements that induce stress, anxiety, tension, pressure to perform, and job insecurity.
   C) puts the primary emphasis on denying rewards to those who fail to meet their assigned performance targets.
   D) emphasizes weeding out employees who are consistently low performers.
   E) strives for 50-50 balance between positive and negative rewards and 50-50 balance between monetary and non-monetary rewards.

   Answer: A Difficulty: Medium

30. A well-designed reward system needs to feature
   A) 50-50 balance between positive and negative rewards.
   B) motivational incentives that build wholehearted commitment to proficient strategy execution and winning attitudes among employees.
   C) job descriptions that clearly spell out each activity that each employee has to do to execute the firm's strategy.
   D) extensive training of employees in using best practices, a means for weeding out low-performers, and ethical behavior on the part of employees at all times.
   E) freezing or reducing the compensation of poorly-performing managers and employees.

   Answer: B Difficulty: Medium

31. An important consideration in designing a strategy-supportive reward system is to
   A) link the firm's performance targets to the budgeting and resource allocation process.
   B) employ incentives that will help keeping employees busy, make across-the-board wage and salary increases an integral part of the system, and make greater employee empowerment part of the system.
   C) put about 50% of the emphasis on non-monetary rewards and 50% on monetary rewards.
   D) delegate primary responsibility for leading the strategy implementation effort to whichever senior manager is most skilled at empowering employees and inspiring them to do their best.
   E) make non-monetary rewards an integral part of the reward system.

   Answer: E Difficulty: Medium

32. Positive motivational approaches
    A) work best in strong culture organizations, while negative motivational approaches tend to be most successful when a firm's culture is weak.
    B) generally work better than negative motivational approaches and non-monetary rewards.
    C) are seldom successful unless both senior managers and supervisors spend considerable time inspiring employees to do their very best; the threat of denying rewards to sub-par performers is typically the most effective motivator.
    D) are harder to get to work successfully than negative approaches, unless the firm places heavy emphasis on monetary incentives.
    E) work better for non-monetary rewards than monetary rewards.

    Answer: B Difficulty: Hard

33. The most dependable way to keep employees focused on competently executing their part of the company's strategy is to
    A) provide all employees with monthly updates on how well the company is doing with regard to executing the strategy and how well each individual is doing in term of qualifying for bonuses and incentive pay awards.
    B) create empowered work teams and base rewards on group performance rather than individual performance.
    C) define jobs in terms of what to do and how to do it, then train employees extensively in following the prescribed procedures.
    D) generously reward individuals and groups who achieve their assigned performance targets and deny rewards to those who don't.
    E) communicate target objectives to employees in an inspiring fashion, have close to a 100% emphasis on monetary rewards, and provide opportunities for bonuses and incentives of at least 20% over base pay.

    Answer: D Difficulty: Medium

34. A good way to establish a tight link between strategy and the reward structure is to
    A) replace managers who consistently do not achieve their assigned strategic performance targets on schedule.
    B) treat the achievement of agreed-upon performance outcomes as a "contract", compare actual performance against the contracted-for outcomes, and then reward individuals and groups who achieve their assigned performance targets and deny rewards to those who don't.
    C) hold a series of training sessions to explain to all employees what the performance targets are and how the reward system works.
    D) have many managers and employees participate in designing the reward system and in administering it.
    E) budget ample funds for wage and salary increases so that everyone will know that attractive rewards exist.

    Answer: B Difficulty: Easy

35. To win strong employee commitment to competent strategy execution, management
   A) has to develop policies and procedures that are well-accepted by most employees, have a 50-50 balance between monetary and non-monetary rewards, and base bonuses and incentives more on individual performance than group performance.
   B) must allow employees to participate in setting the setting key performance targets, in designing the nature and types of incentives, and in establishing core values and beliefs.
   C) has to use rewards and incentives in ways that make it in employees' self-interest to do what is needed to achieve the targeted strategic performance.
   D) should generally employ participative management practices, establish an employee-centered corporate culture, and base bonuses and incentives more on group performance than individual performance..
   E) has to create an inspiring strategic vision and effectively communicate it to employees, have close to a 100% emphasis on monetary rewards, and use a decentralized approach to decision-making.

   Answer: C   Difficulty: Hard

36. Management's most powerful strategy-implementing/strategy-executing tool is
   A) the establishment of strategy-supportive policies and procedures.
   B) empowering employees and instituting best practices.
   C) the practice of management by walking around, listening to what employees are saying, and following their suggestions.
   D) a system of rewards and incentives tied tightly to the achievement of the targeted strategic performance.
   E) strong core competencies and competitive capabilities.

   Answer: D   Difficulty: Medium

37. The guidelines for designing a strategy-supportive incentive compensation system include
   A) making the payoff for meeting or beating performance targets a major piece of the total compensation package.
   B) having a bonus and incentive plan that applies to managers only (employees should generally not be included in incentive pay plans but should have attractive wages and salaries).
   C) having an outside wage and salary expert administer the system, so that there is no doubt as to its fairness and impartiality.
   D) basing the incentives on group performance rather than individual performance.
   E) making minimal use of non-monetary incentives and relying chiefly on monetary rewards.

   Answer: A   Difficulty: Medium

38. The most successful motivational and incentive compensation practices (i.e. those that contribute to high levels of employee performance) typically
   A) use only positive motivational approaches and never involve the use of tension, fear, job insecurity, stress, or anxiety.
   B) incorporate a blend of positive and negative features.
   C) focus almost exclusively on monetary rewards and seldom incorporate non-monetary factors.
   D) entail paying the highest wages and salaries in the industry and stressing non-monetary rewards for high-performing employees.
   E) put top priority on making employees happy and secure in their jobs and providing ongoing job training opportunities throughout their careers.

   Answer: B Difficulty: Medium

39. Rewarding people for what they accomplish rather than for dutifully performing assigned functions
   A) is a flawed approach to motivation and incentive compensation.
   B) acts to create a results-oriented work environment.
   C) poses a direct conflict with efforts to train workers in how to perform their jobs properly.
   D) makes it more difficult to create high levels of employee morale because of the sizable pay differences that result from performance-based compensation approaches.
   E) works well so long as the rewards are based on individual rather than group performance, the emphasis is on positive rewards, and most of the rewards are non-monetary.

   Answer: B Difficulty: Medium

40. Which of the following is not a sound guideline for designing a strategy-supportive reward and incentive system?
   A) The reward system must be administered with meticulous care and fairness.
   B) The payoff for meeting or beating performance targets must be a major piece of the total compensation package.
   C) The incentive plan should apply to managers and employees at all levels.
   D) Ways should be found to reward deserving non-performers who, for some reason, do not fare well under the incentive system.
   E) Incentives must be tightly linked to achieving the performance objectives contained in the strategic plan.

   Answer: D Difficulty: Medium

41. Which of the following is not characteristic of a well-designed compensation and reward system?
   A) Linking incentives tightly to performance targets that are critical to successful execution of the company's strategy
   B) Keeping the time between performance reviews and payment of the rewards short
   C) Making sure that the performance targets that each individual is expected to achieve involve outcomes that the individual can affect
   D) Generous rewards for people who turn in outstanding performances
   E) A reward system that involves 50 percent non-monetary rewards and a work environment that avoids placing pressure on managers and employees to achieve high performance levels

   Answer: E Difficulty: Medium

42. Some caution needs to be exercised in using performance-based compensation systems because
    A) in some countries, incentive compensation runs counter to local customs and cultural norms.
    B) some managers and employees are not psychologically and emotionally strong enough to cope with performance-based pay systems.
    C) if the performance-based pay exceeds 5 percent of total compensation, the result can be a serious decline in employee morale.
    D) too much emphasis on pay-for-performance tends to have a negative impact on employee productivity.
    E) it detracts from having employees focus diligently on the duties and functions they are supposed to perform.

    Answer: A   Difficulty: Medium

Short Answer Questions

43. What is the role of budgets and resource allocation in successfully implementing and executing strategy? Why does a company's budget need to be closely linked to the needs of good strategy execution?

    Difficulty: Medium

44. In creating a strategy-supportive reward structure, it is important to define jobs and assignments in terms of the results to be accomplished not just in terms of the duties to be performed. True or false. Explain and justify your answer.

    Difficulty: Medium

45. The use of incentives and rewards is the single most powerful tool at management's disposal to win strong employee commitment to carrying out the strategic plan. True or false. Explain.

    Difficulty: Medium

46. Give three examples of support systems that a company can install to support the execution of its strategy.

    Difficulty: Medium

47. What is the value of total quality management from a strategy-executing standpoint? How does TQM differ from business process reengineering?

    Difficulty: Medium

48. How do policies and procedures aid the task of implementing and executing strategy?

    Difficulty: Medium

49. What action steps can managers take to build a total quality culture and instill a strong commitment to continuously improving how strategy is being executed?

Difficulty: Medium

50. Why does it make sense to create some job anxiety, insecurity, and stress as part of a company's motivational and reward scheme for promoting competent strategy execution?

Difficulty: Medium

Chapter 13: Corporate Culture and Leadership–Keys to Effective Strategy Execution

Multiple Choice Questions

What Is Corporate Culture and Why Is It Important?

1. Which one of the following is <u>not</u> a fundamental part of a company's culture?
   A) The manner in which it deals with employees, unions, stockholders, customers, vendors, and the communities where it operates
   B) The traditions the organization maintains
   C) The values and business principles that management preaches and practices
   D) The company's strategy
   E) The peer pressures that exist and the legends and stories that people repeat about company happenings

   Answer: D   Difficulty: Easy

2. Beliefs and practices that become embedded in a company's corporate culture usually originate with
   A) its business mission and set of financial and strategic objectives.
   B) influential individuals (often a founder or prior CEOs or the current CEO—especially if the current CEO has been in office for some time) and influential work groups, departments, or divisions.
   C) the type of organization structure it employs.
   D) the company's approach to employee motivation and incentive compensation.
   E) the types of core competencies and capabilities it has developed.

   Answer: B   Difficulty: Medium

3. The culture of an organization is defined and identified by such factors as
   A) the organization's set ways of approaching problems and conducting activities and its pattern of "how we do things around here."
   B) the legends and stories that people repeatedly tell about company happenings and company taboos and political do's and don'ts.
   C) the values, ethical standards, and business principles that management preaches and practices.
   D) the intangibles of a firm's work environment and atmosphere and the values and beliefs shared by most of the organization's members.
   E) All of these.

   Answer: E   Difficulty: Easy

4. A company's culture manifests itself in
   A) the values, beliefs, business principles, and ethical standards that senior managers espouse.
   B) in the traditions the organization maintains.
   C) in the manner and style with which things are done internally.
   D) in the stories that are repeatedly told about happenings in the organization.
   E) In all of the above.

   Answer: E   Difficulty: Easy

5. Once established, company cultures can be perpetuated by
   A) systematic indoctrination of new employees in the culture's fundamentals and constant reiteration of core values by senior managers and group members.
   B) avoiding frequent or dramatic reorganizations that could disturb existing relationships and networking among departments and company personnel.
   C) incorporating all or most of the culture's norms, characteristics, and defining features into the company's strategic vision.
   D) rewarding departments that follow cultural norms with above-average budget increases and penalizing those who don't with budget cuts.
   E) imbedding the underlying values and beliefs in the company's strategy.

   Answer: A   Difficulty: Medium

6. A work environment where the culture matches well with the conditions for good strategy execution is a valuable managerial ally because
   A) there is much less risk of embarrassing ethical violations.
   B) there are strong peer pressures and informal rules that have the impact of cultivating strategy-supportive work habits—culturally-approved behavior thrives and culturally-disapproved behavior gets squashed and even penalized.
   C) there is reduced need to incorporate negative motivational practices and punitive-type incentives into the company's approach to people management.
   D) there is reduced need to employ benchmarking, best practice programs, reengineering, and TQM to achieve competitive advantage.
   E) the culture can then be readily incorporated into the company's strategic vision and facilitate the establishment of stretch objectives.

   Answer: B   Difficulty: Easy

7. Companies, especially ones with multinational operations and/or newly acquired businesses, typically have
   A) multiple cultures (or subcultures) rather than a single culture.
   B) strong cultures.
   C) weak and splintered cultures.
   D) adaptive cultures.
   E) low performance cultures.

   Answer: A   Difficulty: Medium

8. Conflict between a company's culture and its strategy
    A) can usually be overcome if management is good at articulating why the conflict is more imagined than real and if they commit to resolving the conflict as soon as possible.
    B) sends mixed signals and forces employees to choose between loyalty to the culture and company traditions or going along with actions to execute the strategy.
    C) results in a weak and splintered culture that can be replaced by a strong culture as strategy proves successful and commitment to the strategy builds.
    D) can be overcome so long as a company has a strong company and the strategy-culture conflict does not run counter to any of the industry's key success factors.
    E) can be overcome most readily when the culture is unhealthy and when many employees are ready for a culture change anyway.

    Answer: B   Difficulty: Medium

9. A culture grounded in values, practices, and behavioral norms that match the requirements for good strategy execution
    A) is referred to as a strong culture.
    B) is a powerful lever for promoting high ethical standards.
    C) helps energize organizational members to do their jobs in a strategy-supportive fashion.
    D) is the best environment in which to institute best practices and a TQM philosophy.
    E) promotes the development of core competencies and broad employee commitment to continuous improvement.

    Answer: C   Difficulty: Medium

Strong versus Weak Corporate Cultures

10. Strong company cultures are preferable to weak company cultures because
    A) there is greater likelihood of a tight culture-strategy fit than in weak-culture companies.
    B) weak cultures take longer to fix if they are out-of-sync with the requirements for good strategy execution.
    C) they are less likely to possess unhealthy cultural characteristics.
    D) values and behavioral norms are deeply-rooted and top-management doesn't have to spend any time on culture-building activities.
    E) None of the above.

    Answer: E   Difficulty: Medium

11. When a company's culture is out of sync with the values, practices, and behavioral norms needed for good strategy execution,
    A) it is generally easier to change the strategy than to change the culture.
    B) the culture is an obstacle to successful strategy execution and has to be changed as rapidly as can be managed.
    C) the mismatch impedes the development of core competencies and makes building a competitive advantage virtually impossible.
    D) one good way to bring about better alignment is to reengineer business processes, institute a best practices program and a TQM program, and stress the need for continuous improvement.
    E) the quickest way to achieve better strategy-culture alignment is to empower employees to do their jobs in a strategy-supportive fashion.

    Answer: B   Difficulty: Easy

12. A strong strategy-supportive culture
    A) nurtures and motivates people to do their jobs in ways conducive to effective strategy execution.
    B) provides structure, standards, and a value system in which to operate.
    C) provides a system of informal rules and peer pressures regarding how to conduct business internally and how employees should go about doing their jobs.
    D) promotes strong employee identification with the company's vision, performance targets, and strategy.
    E) All of these.

    Answer: E Difficulty: Easy

13. In a strong culture company,
    A) values and beliefs are widely shared throughout the company's ranks.
    B) there is wide support for strong ethical behavior among both managers and employees.
    C) a company has more strategy flexibility because it can change its strategy and be confident that the culture will welcome the strategy changes and be an ally in implementing whatever changes are called for.
    D) both managers and employees are typically proactive in adapting to changing customer and market requirements.

    Answer: A Difficulty: Medium

14. Companies with strong cultures
    A) have very distinct values, beliefs, rituals, operating styles, and work atmospheres.
    B) have senior managers who reinforce the culture through both word and deed and who stress using company values and principles as the basis for making decisions and taking actions.
    C) typically have values statements or creeds.
    D) work diligently at causing employees to observe cultural norms.
    E) exhibit all of the above traits.

    Answer: E Difficulty: Easy

15. In companies with strong corporate cultures,
    A) policy manuals and detailed rules and procedures are widely used to enforce discipline and norms.
    B) business is conducted according to a clear and explicit set of principles and values that management consciously reiterates time and again and that it stress ought to be employed in taking actions and making decisions.
    C) the chief strategy-implementer tends to be a strong, authoritarian decision-maker with a well-defined business philosophy.
    D) the emphasis on values and principles usually relates to quantifiable things such as profitability, growth rates, market share, financial measures of performance, and operating efficiency.
    E) the core organizational emphasis is more on strategy than it is on shared values and beliefs.

    Answer: B Difficulty: Medium

16. Strong corporate cultures
    A) are best perpetuated by prescribing a comprehensive set of policies, procedures, and best practices for employees to follow.
    B) help promote innovative behavior among employees and rapid adaptation to market-driven and customer-driven changes.
    C) promote good strategy execution where there's good fit with the strategy and hurt execution where there's poor fit.
    D) are not particularly well-suited to heavy emphasis on decentralized decision-making and employee empowerment.
    E) help promote fast development of new competitively valuable competencies and capabilities.

    Answer: C   Difficulty: Medium

17. Which one of the following is not a typical characteristic of a weak company culture?
    A) Many subcultures
    B) Deep hostility to change and to people who champion new ways of doing things and a low commitment to high ethical standards
    C) Few strong traditions
    D) Few values and behavioral norms are widely shared
    E) No strong sense of company identity among company members

    Answer: B   Difficulty: Easy

Unhealthy Cultures

18. Which one of the following is not a typical characteristic of an unhealthy company culture?
    A) A politicized internal environment
    B) Hostility to change and to people who champion new ways of doing things
    C) An aversion to looking outside the company for superior practices and approaches
    D) Values and behavioral norms that are widely shared, decentralized decision-making, and low levels of employee turnover
    E) Promotion of managers that are adept at administration and internal organization maneuvering but that are short on entrepreneurial skills and leadership ability

    Answer: D   Difficulty: Medium

19. Unhealthy company cultures typically have such characteristics as
    A) a politicized internal environment, hostility to change and to people who champion new ways of doing things, and an aversion to looking outside the company for superior practices and approaches.
    B) an aversion to employee empowerment, a preference for conservative strategies, and excessive emphasis on profitability.
    C) tight budget controls, overemphasis on performance-based incentive compensation, and lack of high ethical standards.
    D) entrenched executive leaders, no coherent business philosophy, excessively bureaucratic policies and procedures, and high levels of employee turnover.
    E) excessive emphasis on innovation (many of which don't pan out), overemphasis on recruiting managers from outside the company, and multi-layered management bureaucracies.

    Answer: A   Difficulty: Medium

Adaptive Cultures

20. The hallmarks of an adaptive corporate culture include
    A) values and ethics statements that are revised and updated as the company's vision, mission, objectives, and strategy changes.
    B) emphasis on recruiting senior managers from companies outside the industry that are noted for having strong cultures.
    C) strong management concern for the well-being of stakeholders; receptiveness to risk-taking, experimentation, and innovation; and a proactive approach to coping with the challenges of changing business conditions.
    D) charismatic managerial leadership, extensive use of employee empowerment, and strong commitment to the use of best practices.
    E) high ethical standards, strong commitment to TQM principles, and a preference for performance-based compensation systems.

    Answer: C Difficulty: Medium

21. In adaptive corporate cultures,
    A) the prevailing view is that the best way of looking out for the interests of employees is to utilize performance-based incentive compensation and tie incentives to growth in the company's profits.
    B) members are amenable to changing policies and operating practices as long as the core elements of the company's strategic vision and strategy remain intact.
    C) members are willing to embrace a proactive approach to trying new ideas, altering operating practices, and changing pieces of the strategy provided it doesn't imperil their job security, entail cuts in compensation, or require different best practices.
    D) there's a spirit of doing what's necessary to ensure long-term organizational success provided that core values and business principles are not compromised and provided top management undertakes the changes in a manner that exhibits genuine concern for the legitimate interests of stakeholders.
    E) there is little need for policies and procedures because group members willingly accept experimentation and innovation.

    Answer: D Difficulty: Medium

Changing Corporate Cultures and Bringing Them into better Alignment with Strategy

22. Changing a problem culture
    A) is one of the toughest managerial tasks because of the heavy anchor of deeply held values and beliefs.
    B) is best done by instituting an aggressive program to train employees in the ways and beliefs of the new culture to be implanted.
    C) is tough, but less so than crafting a winning strategy.
    D) requires writing a new values statement and describing in writing the kind of culture that is needed, having a series of lengthy meetings with employees to explain the new culture and the reasons why cultural change is needed, and then having both employees and shareholders vote to ratify and adopt the new culture.
    E) can be done in less than 12 months provided managers go all out to praise and visibly reward people who exhibit the desired new cultural traits.

    Answer: A Difficulty: Medium

23. When approaching the task of creating a better "fit" between strategy and culture, management's first step should be to
   A) design a plan for cultural change and select a team of key employees to lead the culture change effort.
   B) identify which aspects of the present culture are supportive of good strategy execution and which ones are not.
   C) sit down with other senior managers and draw up a set of action steps to take to modify the culture.
   D) conduct an employee survey to determine the organization's cultural norms, present attitudes, and degree of satisfaction with the status quo.
   E) employ a consultant with expertise in culture change and follow his/her advice on how to proceed.

   Answer: B Difficulty: Medium

24. Which one of the following is not part of changing a company's culture and bringing it into better alignment with strategy?
   A) Shifting to decentralized decision-making, altering the company's code of ethics so as to raise ethical standards, and putting all employees through a culture-change training program
   B) Diagnosing which facets of the present culture are strategy-supportive and which are not
   C) Active leadership by the CEO and other senior executives, including pushing for new behaviors and communicating the reasons for cultural change
   D) Undertaking both substantive and symbolic actions to transform the culture
   E) Establishing a new set of corporate values, reiterating the importance and the contribution of these values, and rewarding people who exhibit the desired new cultural traits

   Answer: A Difficulty: Medium

25. Reshaping a company's culture to create better alignment with strategy generally does not involve
   A) replacing old-culture managers with new-breed managers.
   B) changing certain long-standing policies and operating practices.
   C) altering the company's strategic vision to incorporate the desired changes in cultural values and cultural norms and making major changes in budgets, organization structure, and personnel to signal the importance of these new cultural norms.
   D) using company gatherings and ceremonial occasions to praise individuals and groups that display the desired new cultural traits and behaviors.
   E) altering incentive compensation to incorporate rewards for people who visibly display the desired cultural behaviors and the symbolic actions of executives to serve as role models.

   Answer: C Difficulty: Easy

26. Efforts to bring a company's culture into tighter alignment with strategy generally include
    A) designing tight links between culture and the organization structure.
    B) using company gatherings and ceremonial occasions to praise individuals and groups that display the desired cultural traits and behaviors.
    C) trying to minimize the effects of peer pressure, company politics, and maverick behavior.
    D) a managerial campaign to emphasize to employees that competent execution of the organization's strategic plan is the key to long-term corporate success and the creation of a sustainable competitive advantage.
    E) making employee acceptance of the desired culture one of the criteria for rewarding employees with higher monetary compensation.

    Answer: B Difficulty: Medium

27. Which of the following is not one of the managerial actions typically taken to build a more strategy-supportive corporate culture?
    A) Employing both symbolic and substantive actions
    B) Taking actions that are highly visible and serve as unmistakable signals of the seriousness of management's commitment to a new work climate and corporate culture
    C) Trying to mold the organization into a solid, competent team that is psychologically committed to superior strategy execution
    D) Making employee acceptance of the desired culture one of the criteria for rewarding employees with higher monetary compensation and changing the organization structure in ways which promote decentralization and employee empowerment
    E) Executive appearances at company gatherings and ceremonial event to praise individuals and groups that serve as role models for the desired cultural traits and behavior

    Answer: D Difficulty: Medium

28. Generally, management actions and initiatives to tighten the culture-strategy fit ought to
    A) receive approval from all employees.
    B) involve both symbolic and substantive actions that are highly visible and that serve as unmistakable signals of the seriousness of management's commitment to a new work climate and corporate culture.
    C) be made an explicit part of the company's vision statement.
    D) be shielded from competitors' intelligence gathering systems.
    E) be taken before the values statement is written down and distributed to employees.

    Answer: B Difficulty: Medium

29. Creating a strong fit between strategy and corporate culture usually does <u>not</u> involve
   A) instituting employee recognition programs (such as employee of the month awards and individual achievement awards) to call everyone's attention to behavior that reflect the desired cultural norms.
   B) developing a values statement.
   C) preparing a detailed rules and procedure manual that all managers and employees can refer to in trying to practice the desired cultural norms and behavior.
   D) replacing managers who insist on displaying old-culture behavior with managers who will act and function as new-culture role models.
   E) insisting that top managers lead by example; for instance, if the strategy entails being the low-cost producer, top managers might have only spartan office decor, have few if any executive perks, and push cost-cutting moves within their own areas of responsibility.

   Answer: C Difficulty: Medium

Building Ethics into the Corporate Culture

30. An ethical corporate culture
   A) has a positive impact on a company's long-term strategic success.
   B) doesn't necessarily impact a company's long-term strategic success favorably or unfavorably.
   C) generally hurts a company's chances for strategic success and market leadership.
   D) virtually guarantees that the firm will have a spirit of high performance.
   E) is typically reflected in the company's strategic vision.

   Answer: A Difficulty: Medium

31. A corporate culture founded on ethical business principles and moral values
   A) virtually guarantees that the firm will be the acknowledged industry leader because of the ethical manner in which its business is conducted.
   B) doesn't necessarily impact a company's long-term strategic success favorably or unfavorably.
   C) does more to hurt a company's chances for strategic success and market leadership than to help it.
   D) is a vital driving force underlying a company's long-term success because how a company conducts its business ultimately affects its reputation.
   E) is not something that customers or suppliers or employees or shareholders pay much attention to or care deeply about.

   Answer: D Difficulty: Medium

32. Codes of ethics
   A) are the single most effective means of enforcing ethical behavior.
   B) serve as a cornerstone for developing a corporate conscience whereas values statements are a cornerstone for culture-building.
   C) serve as ethical benchmarks for establishing strategic and financial objectives.
   D) need to be personally written by the CEO in order to be taken seriously by employees.
   E) should typically be the centerpiece in all of the company's employee training programs.

   Answer: B Difficulty: Medium

33. Companies that are truly committed to ethical conduct of their business
    A) make ethical behavior a fundamental part of their corporate culture.
    B) put a stake in the ground, explicitly stating what the company intends and expects—usually in the form of a code of ethics.
    C) use codes of ethical conduct as standards for judging both company policies and individual conduct.
    D) incorporate the code of ethics into employee training and educational programs.
    E) All of these.

    Answer: E Difficulty: Easy

34. Which of the following is not an integral part of the ethics enforcement process?
    A) Developing procedures for handling potential ethic violations
    B) Every employee must receive adequate training and education in what constitutes ethical behavior and compliance with the code and what does not
    C) Line managers at all levels must give serious and continuous attention to the task of explaining how the code of ethics applies in their areas
    D) Insisting on ethical behavior must be looked upon by management as a continuous culture-building, culture-nurturing exercise.
    E) Immediately dismissing any employee caught violating or disagreeing with the company's code of ethics

    Answer: E Difficulty: Medium

Ethics and Values Statements

35. If a company is serious about displaying high ethical standards and enforcing ethical behavior, then a written code of ethics
    A) should be provided to every employee and every employee should be asked to sign a statement annually indicating compliance with the code.
    B) should be personally prepared by the company's CEO in order for the company's ethical expectations to be taken seriously by employees.
    C) is a useful way to define the company's ethical position and standards and to indicate explicitly what the company expects in terms of ethical behavior.
    D) should typically be the centerpiece in all of the company's employee training programs.
    E) All of these.

    Answer: C Difficulty: Medium

36. Implementing a values statement and/or a code of ethics generally does not entail
    A) word-of-mouth indoctrination by fellow employees.
    B) strong endorsements by the CEO.
    C) communicating the values and the ethics code to all employees and explaining compliance procedures.
    D) giving explicit attention to values and ethics in recruiting, hiring, and training people.
    E) immediately dismissing any and all employees who openly express disagreement with any of the values or who are caught violating ethical standards.

    Answer: E Difficulty: Medium

37. Whether a company's effort to instill values and insist on ethical conduct succeeds or fails depends largely on
    A) whether the CEO is an effective leader and communicator.
    B) whether the firm's culture is strong or weak.
    C) how well corporate values and ethical standards are visibly integrated into company policies, managerial practices, and decisions at all levels.
    D) whether employees are provided with a written copy of the values and ethical requirements.
    E) whether employees are required to sign a statement endorsing company values and to sign each year a statement certifying their compliance with the company's ethical standards.

    Answer: C   Difficulty: Medium

38. Enforcing ethical behavior generally does not entail which one of the following?
    A) The CEO and other senior officers being openly and unequivocally committed to ethical conduct
    B) Managers at all levels setting an excellent ethical example in their own behavior
    C) Developing procedures for handling enforcement and specifying the consequences for breaching the company's ethical standards
    D) Immediately dismissing any and all employees who are caught violating ethical standards
    E) Providing training in what kind of ethical conduct is expected

    Answer: D   Difficulty: Medium

39. A well-developed program to ensure compliance with ethical standards typically includes
    A) having a committee of senior managers direct and monitor the ongoing training, implementation, and compliance effort.
    B) periodically requiring people to sign documents certifying compliance with ethical standards.
    C) audits of managerial efforts to uphold ethical standards.
    D) having managers file formal reports on the actions they take to discipline known violators or otherwise remedy deficient ethical conduct.
    E) All of the above.

    Answer: E   Difficulty: Easy

40. Which of the following is not an integral aspect of implementing a code of ethics?
    A) Strong endorsements by the CEO
    B) Convincing a majority of the company's shareholders and employees to vote for adoption of the code
    C) Communicating the ethics code to all employees
    D) Incorporating the code of ethics into employee training and education programs
    E) Word-of-mouth indoctrination of new employees by existing employees

    Answer: B   Difficulty: Medium

41. Which of the following topics would least likely be contained in an organization's values statement and/or code of ethics?
   A) Commitment to quality and innovation
   B) Honesty and observance of the law
   C) Corporate citizenship and duties to stockholders, suppliers, and customers
   D) Job security guarantees to employees and the company's commitment to adequately funding employee retirement programs
   E) Use of company assets, resources, and property

   Answer: D   Difficulty: Medium

Building a Spirit of High Performance into the Corporate Culture

42. Companies that succeed in building a spirit of high performance into their culture
   A) treat employees with respect and dignity and are intensely people-oriented.
   B) utilize the full range of rewards and punishment to enforce high performance standards.
   C) grant employees enough autonomy to stand out, excel, and contribute and make champions out of people who turn in winning performances.
   D) hold managers at every level responsible for developing the people who report to them.
   E) All of the above.

   Answer: E   Difficulty: Medium

43. In assessing whether an organization is instilled with a spirit of high performance, the key test is
   A) whether employees are happy and satisfied.
   B) whether labor costs are low relative to key rivals.
   C) whether employees get along and work well together.
   D) the extent to which the organization is focused on achievement and excellence, has a results-oriented culture, and pursues policies and practices that inspire employees to do their best.
   E) whether employee turnover rates and absenteeism are minimal.

   Answer: D   Difficulty: Medium

Exercising Strategic Leadership

44. Which of the following is most integral to the task of exercising effective strategic leadership?
   A) Being charismatic and well-liked
   B) Measuring and evaluating the performance of lower-level managers
   C) Staying on top of how well things are going (managing by walking around)
   D) Making sure that budgets are reallocated fairly
   E) Being good at designing a strategy-supportive reward structure

   Answer: C   Difficulty: Medium

45. Which of the following is not one of the dominant leadership roles that managers have to play in pushing for good strategy execution?
   A) Pushing corrective actions to improve strategy execution and overall strategic performance
   B) Exercising ethics leadership and insisting that the company conduct its affairs like a model corporate citizen
   C) Keeping the organization responsive to changing conditions, alert for new opportunities, innovative, and ahead of rivals in developing competitively valuable competencies and capabilities
   D) Weeding out managers and employees who are consistently in the ranks of the lowest performers (the bottom 10%) and who disagree with either the strategy or how it is being executed
   E) Staying on top of what is happening, monitoring progress, ferreting out issues, and learning what obstacles lay in the path of good strategy execution

   Answer: D   Difficulty: Medium

46. The strategy manager's leadership task in implementing and executing strategy does not involve which one of the following?
   A) Fostering an overall climate and culture in which the organization becomes "energized" to execute strategy proficiently and perform at a high level
   B) Exercising ethics leadership
   C) Pushing corrective actions to improve strategy execution and overall performance
   D) Making sure that the culture is well-matched to the organization structure and to the company's value chain
   E) Keeping the organization responsive to changing conditions, alert for new opportunities, and innovative

   Answer: D   Difficulty: Medium

47. One test of effective managerial leadership in implementing and executing strategy concerns
   A) how well managers succeed in developing an overall esprit de corps and culture that mobilizes organizational members to execute strategy in competent fashion and perform at a high level.
   B) whether the company managers have instituted a strategy-supportive reward system.
   C) whether managers adopt the "champion" style of leadership.
   D) whether a firm's practices enlightened empowerment of employees and uses a decentralized approach to decision-making.
   E) how hard they push lower-level managers and supervisors to practice MBWA.

   Answer: A   Difficulty: Medium

48. MBWA refers to
   A) managing businesses with aggressiveness.
   B) making budgets without accountants.
   C) the management practice of informally communicating with employees and getting out into the field to see what is happening.
   D) modifying business-behavior with adaptive actions.
   E) managing businesses without anxiety.

   Answer: C   Difficulty: Medium

49. The purpose of managing by walking around is
    A) to learn more about company operations and see how activities are really being done.
    B) to gather information informally about what is happening and what is on people's minds.
    C) to improve employee relations by communicating information about organizational activities as quickly as possible.
    D) to gather information about what strategy to follow and to learn what competitors are doing.
    E) All of these.

    Answer: B Difficulty: Medium

50. Managers who are successful in exercising good strategic leadership
    A) are skilled entrepreneurs who also have a talent for delegating authority and responsibility to subordinates.
    B) serve as role models for the rest of the organization and spend a lot of time coaching others how to be like them.
    C) typically do a lot of managing by walking around and push corrective actions to do a better job of strategy execution.
    D) have charismatic personalities and inspire others to follow their lead.
    E) spend more of their time crafting a winning strategy than in personally directing the strategy implementation and execution process.

    Answer: C Difficulty: Medium

51. The task of implanting a corporate culture that is supportive of strategy
    A) tends to be a short-term managerial exercise (something good managers can accomplish within six months).
    B) requires a sincere, sustained commitment by the chief executive who reinforces the desired cultural norms at every opportunity through both word and deed.
    C) is made easier when one of the big qualifications for being promoted is demonstrating support for and conforming to cultural norms.
    D) is made easier when there are monetary incentives for conforming to cultural norms.
    E) is a task that CEOs can safely delegate to subordinates once the CEO has approved the nature of the corporate culture.

    Answer: B Difficulty: Medium

52. In multinational and global companies where some cross-border diversity in the corporate culture is normal, the leadership requirements of culture-changing efforts
    A) are more complex and demanding than in domestic-only enterprises.
    B) entail being sensitive to the cultures and mores of different countries, discerning when to allow some cross border diversity in the corporate culture and when to insist on cross-border conformity.
    C) are made easier by instituting incentives and compensation systems that reward people for conforming to the corporate culture..
    D) require a toleration for cross-border cultural differences and a willingness to let the managers of each country's operations be the leaders of the local corporate culture.
    E) Both A and C.

    Answer: E Difficulty: Easy

53. In order to promote an organizational climate where champion innovators can blossom and thrive, strategy managers should do all but which one of the following?
   A) Encourage individuals and groups to bring their ideas and proposals forward and to exercise initiative
   B) Personally review all the proposals that "champions" propose, revising them as needed and serving as the champion's mentor in pursuing implementation of the proposal
   C) Not look upon people with creative ideas as disruptive and troublesome
   D) Give large, visible rewards to successful champions
   E) Tolerate the maverick style of the champion and give people with innovative ideas room to operate

   Answer: B Difficulty: Easy

54. One of the keys to successful performance as a strategic leader is
   A) being clever at projecting charisma and coming across as a magnetic personality and visionary.
   B) shaping the values and beliefs which undergird the corporate culture and bringing culture into strong alignment with strategy.
   C) being likable, easy to get along with, friendly, and well thought of by subordinates.
   D) being a good company cheerleader, projecting excitement and enthusiasm, and being positive and optimistic about the company's future prospects.
   E) promoting an organizational climate where employee empowerment can thrive and decision-making is decentralized.

   Answer: B Difficulty: Easy

55. Which one of the following is not something a manager in a leadership role should do to promote an organizational climate where champion innovators can blossom and thrive?
   A) Encourage individuals and groups to be creative, hold brainstorming sessions, let their imaginations fly, and come up with innovative proposals
   B) Give large, visible rewards to successful champions
   C) Be willing to turn down the ideas and suggestions of mavericks who propose out-of-the-ordinary ventures or want to experiment with high-risk ideas
   D) Use ad hoc organizational forms to support ideas and experimentation
   E) Encourage lots of "tries" and be willing to tolerate mistakes and failures

   Answer: C Difficulty: Easy

56. The single most visible factor that distinguishes successful culture-change efforts from failed attempts is
   A) ensuring that the new culture embraces employee empowerment.
   B) competent leadership at the top.
   C) delayering the management hierarchy.
   D) developing a new values statement and a more rigid code of ethics.
   E) convincing employees of the benefits of using best practices and pursuing continuous improvement.

   Answer: B Difficulty: Medium

57. Effective leadership in trying to match culture and strategy typically includes such attributes as
    A) a stakeholders-are-king philosophy that links the need to change to the need to serve the long-term best interests of the firm's key constituencies.
    B) initiating forceful actions to flush out undesirable cultural traits.
    C) challenging the status quo with very basic questions: Are we really giving customers what they want? How can we drive costs out of the business and be more competitive on price? Why aren't we taking more business away from rivals? How can we grow revenues at a faster rate?
    D) creating events where everyone in management is forced to listen to angry customers, alienated employees, and disgruntled stockholders.
    E) All of these.

    Answer: E   Difficulty: Medium

58. Which one of the following is not likely to be an effective management action to match culture and strategy?
    A) Calling upon first-level supervisors and rank-and-file- employees to lead the cultural change effort
    B) Making a compelling case for cultural change, persuading individuals and groups to commit to the new direction and culture, convincing skeptics that all is not well, and motivating people to overcome the obstacles to cultural change
    C) Challenging the status quo with very basic questions--Are we really giving customers what they want? How can we drive costs out of the business and be more competitive on price? Why aren't we taking more business away from rivals? Why aren't we doing more to grow revenues at a faster rate?
    D) Recognizing and generously rewarding those who exhibit new cultural norms and who lead successful change efforts
    E) Espousing a stakeholders-are-king philosophy that links the need to change to the need to serve the best long-term interests of the firm's key constituencies

    Answer: A   Difficulty: Medium

59. The leadership task of creating a flexible, responsive, innovative internal environment involves
    A) managing by walking around.
    B) ensuring that the reward system places strong emphasis on incentive compensation.
    C) promoting a culture that accepts continuous adaptation to changing conditions, generating a dependable supply of fresh ideas from managers and employees, empowering champions, and being a leader in developing new organizational capabilities.
    D) delegating responsibility for building consensus on controversial issues to a blue ribbon panel of outside experts.
    E) Both C and D.

    Answer: C   Difficulty: Medium

60. Top management leadership in creating a flexible, responsive, innovative internal environment is especially important in
    A) fast-moving, high technology businesses.
    B) businesses where product life cycles are short.
    C) widely-diversified corporations where opportunities are varied and scattered.
    D) businesses where successful product differentiation depends on out-innovating rivals.
    E) All of these.

    Answer: E   Difficulty: Medium

61. What separates companies that make a sincere effort to carry their weight in being good corporate citizens from companies that are content to do only what is legally required of them
    A) are shareholders who insist that senior executives practice corporate citizenship and social responsibility.
    B) is public pressure and the potential for unfavorable media exposure and publicity if a company steps out of bounds.
    C) are strategy leaders who believe strongly in good corporate citizenship.
    D) is pressure from customers who want and expect the companies they do business with to be honorable and socially responsible in their actions.
    E) is pressure from employees—employees want to be proud of the company they work for and proud of the way it behaves.

    Answer: C   Difficulty: Easy

Short Answer Questions

62. What is meant by the term corporate culture? Why is corporate culture an important factor in implementing and executing strategy?

    Difficulty: Hard

63. Value statements serve as a cornerstone for culture-building; a code of ethics serves as a cornerstone for developing a corporate conscience. True or false. Explain.

    Difficulty: Easy

64. Identify and briefly describe three actions management can take to successfully implement values and a code of ethics?

    Difficulty: Medium

65. What is different and challenging about leading culture change in multinational and global companies?

    Difficulty: Medium

66. Identify and briefly describe the five leadership roles which dominate the managerial agenda in implementing and executing strategy.

Difficulty: Hard

67. What is the CEO's role in enforcing ethical behavior? in setting ethical standards?

Difficulty: Medium

68. Values and ethical standards not only must be explicitly stated but they also must be deeply ingrained into the corporate culture. True or False. Explain.

Difficulty: Medium

69. The main purpose of ethics enforcement is to encourage compliance rather than administer punishment. True or False. Explain and justify your answer.

Difficulty: Medium

70. The core of the corporate culture is a shared commitment to achieve the firm's strategic and financial objectives. True or False. Justify your answer.

Difficulty: Medium

71. What are the characteristics of unhealthy cultures?

Difficulty: Medium

72. What are the hallmarks of adaptive corporate cultures?

Difficulty: Medium

73. The single most visible factor that distinguishes successful culture-change efforts from failed attempts is competent leadership at the top. True or false. Explain and justify your answer.

Difficulty: Medium

74. What is MBWA and why is it important?

Difficulty: Medium